Members, Methods, and Measures

Stepping into an IT leadership role for the first time? Feeling overwhelmed by the transition from technical expert to people manager? You're not alone.

In *Members, Methods, and Measures*, Thomas E. Armstrong delivers the guide he wishes he had when he was thrust into management—without a roadmap, training, or support. Drawing on years of experience leading high-performing technology teams, Armstrong breaks down the challenges of IT leadership with real-world insights, practical frameworks, and battle-tested strategies.

This book is your crash course in mastering IT Management. Learn how to:

- **Build and manage a high-impact IT team**—from hiring and onboarding to retention and career development.
- **Navigate the shift from doer to leader**—avoid the common pitfalls that derail new managers.
- **Set priorities, delegate effectively, and drive results** without micromanaging or burning out.
- **Manage up, down, and across**—communicate with executives, gain stakeholder buy-in, and earn your team's trust.
- **Measure what matters**—ensure your team's work is recognized and valued by the business.

Packed with actionable advice, real-world examples, and insights from industry leaders, *Members, Methods, and Measures* is the ultimate playbook for IT professionals making the leap to management. Whether stepping into leadership for the first time or looking to refine your skills, this book will equip you with the tools, confidence, and strategies to build a thriving, high-performing team.

Thomas E. Armstrong is an IT executive specializing in business transformation, digital innovation, and enterprise architecture. With leadership roles spanning global firms like Deloitte, IBM, and PwC, he has helped top organizations streamline operations, enhance customer experiences, and drive strategic growth. Currently the Director of Strategy and Enterprise Architecture for the State of Connecticut, Tom also teaches IT at the graduate level. He holds degrees from Georgetown, Quinnipiac, and Fairfield University, along with certifications in cloud computing, IT service management, and enterprise architecture. When he's not tackling complex IT challenges, Tom enjoys life in Connecticut with his golden retriever, Doug.

Security, Audit and Leadership Series
Series Editor: Dan Swanson, Dan Swanson and Associates, Ltd., Winnipeg, Manitoba, Canada.

The scope and mandate for internal audit continue to evolve each year, as does the complexity of the business environment and the speed of the changing risk landscape in which it must operate. The fundamental goal of this exciting series is to produce leading-edge books on critical subjects facing security and audit executives and practitioners. Key topics addressed include Leadership, Cybersecurity, Security Leadership, Privacy, Strategic Risk Management, Auditing IT, Audit Management and Leadership, and Operational Auditing.

Evidence-Based Cybersecurity: Foundations, Research, and Practice
By Pierre-Luc Pomerleau, David Maimon

Operational Auditing: Principles and Techniques for a Changing World
By Hernan Murdock

The Security Leader's Communication Playbook: Bridging the Gap between Security and the Business
By Jeffrey W. Brown

The CISO 3.0: A Guide to Next-Generation Cybersecurity Leadership
By Walt Powell

Securing Talent: Building and Retaining High-Performance Cybersecurity Teams
By Kevin Lynn McLaughlin

Digitalization and Women's Rights: Volume 1
By Muharrem Kılıç and Sezer Bozkus Kahyaoglu

Analysis of Threat Perceptions: NATO and Türkiye's Cyber Terrorism Policies
By Mehmet Emin Erendor

Members, Methods, and Measures: Unlocking the Secrets of IT Leadership
By Thomas E. Armstrong

Members, Methods, and Measures

Unlocking the Secrets of IT Leadership

Thomas E. Armstrong

CRC Press
Taylor & Francis Group
Boca Raton London New York

CRC Press is an imprint of the
Taylor & Francis Group, an **informa** business

Designed cover image: Shutterstock images

First edition published 2026
by CRC Press
2385 NW Executive Center Drive, Suite 320, Boca Raton FL 33431

and by CRC Press
4 Park Square, Milton Park, Abingdon, Oxon, OX14 4RN

CRC Press is an imprint of Taylor & Francis Group, LLC

ISBN: 978-1-032-91054-3 (hbk)
ISBN: 978-1-032-91254-7 (pbk)
ISBN: 978-1-003-56216-0 (ebk)

DOI: 10.1201/9781003562160

Typeset in Sabon
by SPi Technologies India Pvt Ltd (Straive)

To Mom: Thank you for your unwavering encouragement (and occasional well-placed nagging) to write this book. Here it is! I couldn't have done it without you. They say every author writes with an ideal reader in mind—you are mine.

To Dad: You taught me to honor my commitments, do things the right way, and always treat people with respect. Those lessons have been the foundation of any success I've had. Sorry, I never quite mastered holding the flashlight steady.

To Mike: You are my biggest supporter, my fiercest defender, and my best friend. A big brother is the greatest gift in the world. No matter what happens, I know you'll always be there, cheering me on and keeping me grounded. (You're still wrong about Pepsi.)

Contents

Introduction

The awkward silence

The quiet shifted from merely uncomfortable to outright painful. Six highly paid, razor-sharp, and fiercely competitive consultants fixed their gazes on me. Some looked eager, others wary and guarded. Moments earlier, the client and partner had slipped out of the conference room, leaving me alone at the table with *my* team. Every eye was on me, waiting for direction. I shifted in my seat, suddenly very aware of the suit jacket I'd chosen that morning. Was I sweating through my shirt? Probably. My temples pounded in sync with my pulse. I like to think I don't panic, but in that moment, I was on the edge.

Seventy-two hours earlier, my phone rang. It was the staffing team with my next assignment. "You'll be leading the Fixed Assets workstream for an Oracle Implementation," they said. No fanfare, no discussion—just a casual directive that turned my world upside down.

I was a junior consultant, fresh enough that I still double-checked my email drafts before sending them to senior leaders. Now, suddenly, I was in charge of other consultants. It wasn't a promotion. I wasn't officially a manager. In the consulting world, they call this a "stretch assignment." I call it getting thrown into the deep end. "Here's your new role. Good luck."

I knew Oracle well enough. I had an accounting background, and fixed-asset accounting was familiar enough. So I did what any rational over-achiever would do—I crammed. The weekend before my first day, I buried myself in user guides, memorized Generally Accepted Accounting Principles, and reviewed every nuance of asset acquisition, amortization, and disposal. I convinced myself that if I mastered the technical details, I'd impress both the client and the partner.

No one would stump me with a question about straight-line depreciation versus double-declining balance. I'd know cold how to set up a mass transaction, configure the depreciation calendar, and transfer the data to the general ledger. I was hell-bent on proving I belonged.

And yet, sitting at that table, faced with six people waiting for me to lead, I realized I had prepped for all the wrong things. I was rewriting the music for a song I'd already performed instead of learning the next set. I had

DOI: 10.1201/9781003562160-1

over-prepared for the technical details but overlooked the real challenge—managing people.

Managing a team is nothing like being an individual contributor. My technical aptitude, my accounting knowledge, even my ability to bend a spreadsheet to my will—none of it mattered at that moment. The software, the rules, the regulations—I knew all of that. What I didn't know was how to lead a team.

This is the part no one tells you about when you step into a leadership role for the first time. There's an assumption, dangerous but common, that top performers will naturally become great managers. Companies promote the best engineers to lead engineering teams, the top developers to manage development groups, and the most organized project managers to run entire PMOs.

But, excelling as an individual contributor requires an entirely different skill set than leading a group. And in the fast-moving world of IT, where technical knowledge can sometimes feel like a lifeline, it's easy to fall into the trap of thinking that expertise alone will make you an effective manager. It won't.

Too many first-time managers are thrown into leadership roles with no formal training and no blueprint for success. Whether due to cost-cutting or sheer oversight, few companies invest in structured management development programs, especially for technical teams. They expect new leaders to figure it out as they go.

That's exactly what I was doing—figuring it out, one awkward silence at a time. My instincts screamed at me to fill the void with some authoritative statement, some confident directive that would establish my credibility. But what was I supposed to say? "Okay, team. Let's, uh, get started?"

Instead, I took a breath, looked around the room, and did the only thing I could think of.

I asked a question.

"What's the biggest challenge we're facing right now?"

It wasn't elegant, and it certainly wasn't what I'd envisioned as a moment of leadership brilliance. But it worked. One by one, the team started talking—about the client's expectations, about tight deadlines, about data integration concerns. Within minutes, the energy in the room shifted.

I wasn't lecturing. I was listening.

And that, I would later realize, was the first real lesson in leadership: People don't want a boss who knows everything. They want a leader who listens, who asks the right questions, who trusts the team to contribute.

My experience in that conference room was just the beginning. I made mistakes—plenty of them. But I also learned, adapted, and eventually found my footing. I wrote this book because I wish someone had handed me a guide before I walked into that room. A map to navigate the transition from high-performing individual contributor to effective leader.

The chapters ahead lay out the hard-won lessons I and many other IT leaders have learned through experience. We'll cover the common pitfalls, the essential skills, and the practical tools that make the difference between floundering and thriving in management. If you've ever felt like you were in over your head, if you've ever wondered why leading a team feels so much harder than you expected, you're not alone. And you're not doomed to struggle. Management is a skill, not an innate talent. And like any skill, it can be learned. Let's get started.

WHO THIS BOOK IS FOR

Good technology management has never been more important, yet it has never been more difficult. The rapid evolution of the IT landscape, combined with shifting workforce expectations, the rise of remote work, and a steady decline in structured management training, has made effective leadership a rare skill. Gone are the days when an employee joined a company fresh out of college and stayed until retirement. Careers are now built across multiple organizations, industries, and even geographies. More frequent job changes, whether by choice or necessity, have disrupted the traditional apprenticeship model that once developed future leaders. The managers who would have trained the next generation have moved on, and those stepping into leadership roles are often left to figure it out on their own.

The shift to hybrid and remote work has only exacerbated the problem. In the past, an aspiring leader could learn by observing a seasoned manager in action—sitting in on meetings, absorbing leadership behaviors, and picking up on office dynamics. That kind of informal learning is much harder when teams are distributed across time zones, interacting primarily through screens.

Making matters worse, companies no longer invest in leadership training the way they used to. Instead, someone decides that because you're a great software developer, network engineer, or project manager, you should also be responsible for leading a team. The problem? Managing people requires a different skill set than excelling as an individual contributor.

That's where this book comes in.

This book is for anyone who has found themselves managing an IT team, hopes to manage one someday, or is responsible for developing new IT leaders. Whether you're stepping into leadership for the first time, trying to get your bearings in a new role, or helping someone else navigate their transition, this book provides practical insights and a structured approach to making the shift successfully.

This book is divided into three parts, each tackling a critical aspect of IT leadership.

Part I is for new managers—or experienced managers who need a refresher on the fundamentals. These chapters focus on people management—arguably the hardest and most important aspect of the job. If you're wondering how to give effective feedback, structure a productive staff meeting, hire and onboard new team members, or build a strong relationship with your boss, this section provides concrete, actionable guidance.

Part II dives into the unique challenges of managing the work of technology teams. Leading an IT organization isn't just about managing people—it's about managing projects, security risks, emerging technology, and operational change. This section covers IT project execution, change control, cybersecurity strategy, and navigating the rapid shifts in enterprise technology. Each chapter starts with the basics, providing a framework for understanding the topic before moving into advanced strategies for leading high-performing teams that deliver real business value.

Part III explores how to measure and communicate the value your team creates. Leadership isn't just about execution—it's about making sure people understand why your team's work matters. This section covers how to ensure your team is working on the right priorities, how to develop meaningful metrics that showcase impact, and how to avoid the trap of drowning in spreadsheets and dashboards that don't actually drive results.

This book exists because most organizations *don't* teach people how to be good managers.

It's easy to assume that management is an innate skill—that some people are just natural leaders while others struggle. But that's not true. Leadership is a learnable skill, just like coding, networking, or cybersecurity. The problem is that most IT professionals are never given the opportunity to learn before they're expected to lead.

Decades ago, companies like General Electric, IBM, and Procter & Gamble were famous for their leadership development programs. GE, in particular, was known as a CEO factory, investing heavily in training that produced some of the most sought-after executives in the corporate world. But today, most organizations don't make that kind of investment. Instead, employees are promoted into leadership roles with little guidance and expected to "figure it out" as they go.

Think about how you trained for your technical career. If you're a software developer, you didn't write a fully functional application on day one. You started with "Hello, World!," struggling to get your first few lines of code to compile. You made mistakes, debugged your errors, and gradually built the skills to take on more complex projects. If you're a network engineer, your first exposure to configuring a router was probably a low-stakes environment—a lab, a test system, or a classroom. No one handed you the keys to a production data center and expected you to figure it out on the fly. We don't expect technical professionals to learn their craft through trial and error alone, so why do we expect new managers to? Leadership isn't magic. It's a skill that can be taught, practiced, and refined. That's what this book aims to do—provide a structured, practical approach to mastering IT leadership so that you can succeed without unnecessary trial and error.

Managing an IT team isn't the same as managing a sales team, a marketing team, or a finance department. IT teams are often made up of deeply technical specialists, working on complex, interdependent systems with high stakes. A poorly configured firewall rule can expose an entire company to a security breach. A single mismanaged cloud deployment can cause hours or days of downtime. A delayed software release can put millions of dollars in revenue at risk.

That's why IT managers need to balance technical awareness with leadership skills. You don't need to be the most technical person in the room, but you do need to understand how to lead a technical team effectively.

This means:

- Earning the respect of deeply technical employees without micromanaging their work.
- Navigating the tension between stability and innovation, ensuring that new technologies are introduced responsibly.
- Building a culture of accountability and continuous improvement, rather than reactive fire-fighting.

The skills that made you a great individual contributor won't necessarily make you a great leader. That's a hard reality for many first-time managers. But if you're willing to shift your mindset, invest in learning, and build new leadership muscles, you'll set yourself—and your team—up for long-term success.

WHO THIS BOOK IS REALLY FOR

If you've been promoted into a management role and thought, "I have no idea what I'm doing," this book is for you.

If you've ever watched a former colleague struggle after being promoted and wondered, "Why don't companies train new managers better?" this book is for you.

If you've ever had a boss who clearly had no idea how to manage people—and you're determined to be different—this book is for you.

Whether you're stepping into leadership for the first time or refining your management skills, the lessons in this book will help you navigate the transition, avoid common pitfalls, and become the kind of leader your team deserves.

THREE Ms OF IT LEADERSHIP

What does it mean to be a manager? Ask ten different people, and you'll get ten different answers. Some will say it's about supervising others. Others will describe it as achieving results through people. Some might mention coaching, delegation, or leadership. These definitions aren't wrong, but they're incomplete.

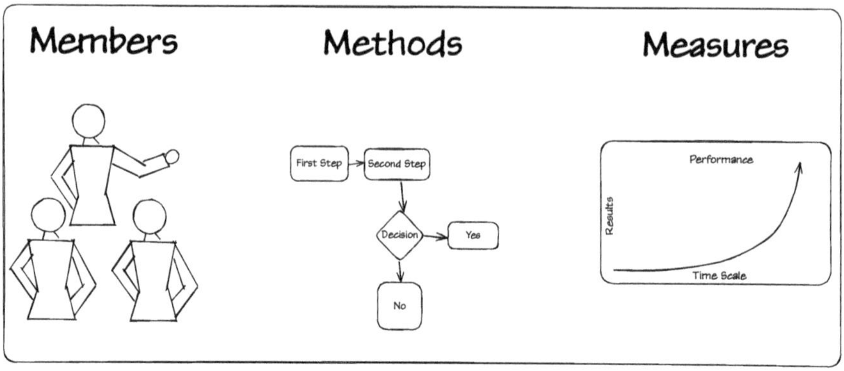

Figure I.1 Members, methods, and measures.

Good management, especially in IT, isn't just about telling people what to do or ensuring projects get delivered. It's about balancing three core elements: Members, Methods, and Measures. This is what I call the Three Ms of IT Management. Mastering these three pillars is the key to effective leadership in IT. Neglect one, and your team struggles. Focus on all three, and you create an environment where people perform at their best, workflows efficiently, and results are both measurable and meaningful (Figure I.1).

Members: The foundation of your success

At its core, management is about people. Your job is no longer about your personal technical expertise. It's about getting the best from your team.

Your success as a manager is directly tied to the success of your people. If your team thrives, so do you. If they struggle, you do too. That means your first priority is hiring the right people, ensuring they're working on the right things, and setting the right expectations.

Getting this right requires several key skills:

- Hiring & Firing: You must learn to identify great talent and, when necessary, make tough decisions about underperformers.
- Delegation: You can't do everything yourself anymore. Your job is to trust your team and distribute work effectively.
- Feedback & Development: Your team won't improve unless you provide clear, constructive feedback and opportunities for growth.
- Prioritization & Work Allocation: Even the best team will flounder if they're working on low-impact projects. Your job is to align their work with the company's biggest priorities.

You don't need to be perfect at these things from day one. Management is a journey, not a one-time promotion. But every day, you should be striving to get a little better at managing your people. In the next few chapters, we'll dive deeper into each of these areas—how to structure effective meetings, deliver useful feedback, and make smart hiring decisions.

For now, remember this: your team's success is your success.

Methods: How work gets done

If Members are the "who" of management, Methods are the "how." These are the systems, processes, and cultural norms that govern how your team works together.

Methods can be simple, like deciding that your team will work in the office on Tuesdays and Thursdays and remotely the rest of the week. Or they can be complex, like defining an entire software development lifecycle, setting up incident management workflows, or establishing rules for how major decisions get made.

As an individual contributor, you had the freedom to decide how you worked best. You had personal preferences for tackling projects, structuring your day, and solving problems. But as a manager, you have to think beyond yourself. You must define a consistent way of working for the entire team.

Without clear methods, chaos takes root. Imagine a software development team where:

- One developer stores their code in GitHub, another prefers Bitbucket, and a third uses Azure DevOps.
- Everyone tracks project tasks in different ways—some in Jira, some in spreadsheets, some in sticky notes.
- Status updates are shared inconsistently. Some people send weekly emails, others provide verbal updates, and some say nothing at all.

Without alignment on methods, things fall apart quickly. Work slows down, miscommunication becomes rampant, and frustration builds.

That's why process matters. Some people resist structure, believing that process equals bureaucracy. They worry that too many rules will stifle innovation. But the truth is, good processes don't slow teams down. They speed them up. When everyone knows how decisions get made, how work is tracked, and how issues get escalated, teams move faster, not slower. Part of your job as a manager is to find the balance—implementing just enough process to keep things running smoothly, but not so much that you suffocate creativity. In later chapters, we'll explore how to build the right level of structure without creating unnecessary bureaucracy.

For now, remember this: Without clear methods, even the best team will struggle.

Measures: Tracking and communicating value

The final pillar of IT management is Measures, the data you use to evaluate success, make decisions, and communicate your team's impact.

In IT, it's easy to focus on the wrong measures. Some managers track endless numbers without considering whether those numbers actually matter. Others ignore data entirely, leading to a lack of accountability and an inability to prove their team's value to the business. Great IT managers strike a balance. They track just enough data to make informed decisions, improve performance, and tell a compelling story about their team's contributions.

There are three key categories of measures you should consider:

- Technical Measures: These track the health of your infrastructure—server uptime, response times, database performance, and so on.
- Operational Measures: These assess how well your team is functioning—incident resolution times, project completion rates, employee retention, etc.
- Financial Measures: These help justify budgets and resources—cost savings, return on investment, and overall IT spending efficiency.

The key is to choose measures that align with your team's goals. Don't track numbers just for the sake of tracking. Focus on the data that tells a clear story about how you are driving value.

There's a well-known saying in management: "*What gets measured, gets managed.*" That's true, but what gets measured also gets manipulated. If your team knows they'll be judged on ticket resolution times, they might start closing tickets prematurely just to hit their targets. If developers are rewarded for the number of lines of code they write, they might start writing bloated, inefficient code.

That's why you shouldn't just track numbers. You need to ask the right questions, dig deeper when something looks off, and ensure that metrics drive the right behaviors, not just high scores on a dashboard. In later chapters, we'll explore how to choose the right measures, avoid common measurement traps, and use data to tell a compelling story about your team's impact.

For now, remember this: The right measures don't just track performance. They drive the right behaviors.

Mastering the Three Ms, Members, Methods, and Measures, is the foundation of great IT management.

- Members ensure you have the right people, working on the right things, with the right expectations.
- Methods create consistency, reduce friction, and allow teams to move quickly.
- Measures provide visibility into performance, guiding decisions and proving your team's value.

When you get these three things right, your team will thrive. They'll know what's expected of them, how to work effectively, and how their contributions impact the business. Focus on these three areas—and commit to getting just a little better every day—and you'll set yourself up for long-term success.

TRANSITION TO MANAGEMENT

Moving into management isn't a promotion, it's a career change. Transitioning from an individual contributor to a manager is so much more than a change in title. It is a profound transformation that demands new skills and new perspectives. As an individual contributor, you focused on your tasks, projects, and deadlines. However, as a manager, your work is often less tangible. Instead of directly completing tasks, you must facilitate your team members' success by planning, assigning tasks, setting deadlines, securing resources, and providing feedback and support. Your success will be measured by what your team achieves under your guidance.

This shift from *doing* to *managing* requires learning new skills like delegation, motivation, communication, prioritization, and conflict resolution. These skills can be learned just like technical skills. And just like technical skills, they require practice and patience to master, so be gentle with yourself as you navigate this learning curve.

The move from team member to team manager changes the nature of your relationships with your colleagues. As a peer, your relationships were primarily collegial. You collaborated on projects, lent each other support, and perhaps socialized outside work. As a manager, you must maintain positive relationships but keep a certain level of professional distance. You're now responsible for evaluating performance, providing feedback, and making tough decisions, like who gets promoted or who gets let go. This can be one of the most challenging aspects of the transition to management.

Along with changes in relationships comes a shift in how you spend your time. Instead of spending most of your time "head down" on specific tasks or projects, you'll spend much more time in team meetings—one-on-one meetings, staff meetings, meetings with other managers, and so on. These meetings are essential to your role as they allow you to stay informed, build relationships, and make decisions. However, they can also be time-consuming, so learning to prioritize and protect your time is critical.

Your role as a decision-maker also expands significantly as you transition into management. As an individual contributor, the majority of your decisions revolved around how to complete your tasks best. As a manager, the scope of your decision-making expands dramatically. You'll make decisions about resources, priorities, strategies, and people. You will rarely have all the information you think you need. Developing good judgment and decision-making skills is crucial to your new role.

Another crucial change is that you are now a bigger representative of the organization. This means you're responsible for upholding and enforcing the company's policies and values. You need to lead by example and maintain high standards, which can mean having difficult conversations when performance needs to be addressed.

Finally, transitioning from team member to manager comes with new challenges and pressures. You face higher expectations, scrutiny, and responsibility. You need to navigate the complexity of managing people with all their unique personalities and motivations. This can sometimes feel overwhelming. That's totally normal. It's all part of the journey of becoming an effective IT manager. Develop a strong support network of mentors, colleagues, or even a professional coach. They can provide advice and support when things get tough.

Common challenges in the transition

Becoming an IT manager can be an exciting but also challenging experience. Recognizing and understanding these challenges can help you overcome them. Here are some of the most common ones and some strategies to address them.

1. **Letting Go of the Technical Work:** This is what I call "Hands off, eyes on." As a manager, you *delegate* and *supervise* but less often *do* the actual work. Many IT professionals are passionate about the technical aspects of their work. It can be hard to let go of this hands-on work and focus on managerial duties. This challenge often manifests as micromanagement, where you struggle to delegate and become involved in tasks that your team should handle. To overcome this, remember that your role now is to facilitate your team's success rather than to do their work. Practice delegation and trust your team's abilities. You can keep your technical skills sharp but focus on using them strategically—such as making informed decisions or mentoring your team—rather than executing tasks.
2. **Managing Former Peers:** If you've been promoted within your team, you might manage people who were once your peers. This can create awkward dynamics, as you need to evaluate performance, mediate conflicts, and sometimes make unpopular decisions. Communicate openly about the change. Acknowledge the new dynamic and reassure your team that you'll be fair and respectful. Maintain professional boundaries but also keep the lines of communication open. Provide feedback and be open to receiving it.
3. **Balancing Priorities:** IT managers juggle numerous responsibilities, from which project to prioritize to who gets the bigger raise. This can be overwhelming, especially when everything seems important or urgent. Effective time management and prioritization are critical for handling this challenge. Use tools and techniques like task lists, project management software, and the Eisenhower Matrix to help

prioritize your tasks. Learn to differentiate between what's urgent and what's important, and don't be afraid to delegate tasks when appropriate.
4. **Navigating Organizational Politics:** Every organization has its politics. Navigating this landscape can be tricky. Building strong relationships across the organization can help you navigate politics. Understand the goals and pressures of different stakeholders, and learn to communicate and negotiate effectively. Be respectful and professional, even when conflicts arise.
5. **Balancing Technical and Management Skills:** While your role as an IT manager will likely place a greater emphasis on management skills, it's essential to maintain a balance. Both technical and management skills are critical for your effectiveness and success. As a manager, you don't need to be the most technically skilled person on your team. It's more important to have a solid understanding of the technical work your team does, along with the ability to make informed decisions, rather than being the one to execute the tasks.

Transitioning from an individual contributor to a manager requires a focus shift from technical to management skills. This shift doesn't mean leaving your technical expertise behind. Instead, it means leveraging it in new ways while developing additional skills to lead your team effectively and navigate the broader business landscape.

IMPOSTER SYNDROME

Imposter syndrome is like a sneaky little voice in your head that makes you question your own abilities and successes. It's like a party pooper that shows up just when you're about to celebrate a win, whispering that you don't really deserve it, that you just got lucky, or worse, that you've fooled everyone into thinking you're more intelligent or more capable than you really are.

The term was first coined by psychologists Pauline Rose Clance and Suzanne Imes back in 1978 as "imposter phenomenon." It's not an official mental health disorder. You won't find imposter syndrome listed in the DSM-5. But it's a real thing. It's a common problem that spans experience, careers, gender, or background.

Feeling like an impostor is normal, especially when stepping into a new role. Studies show that around 70% of people experience imposter syndrome, and the number is even higher for women. If you feel overwhelmed, ill-prepared, or as though you're on the verge of being found a fraud, acknowledge those feelings, but don't let them paralyze you.

"Their whole professional life is built on this shaky ground of self-doubt, which can be really disconcerting as they move into career paths where confidence and belief in oneself should be a powerful and positive motivator," says psychologist Becky Ponting.[1]

Share your feelings with friends, colleagues, or mentors who can offer support and encouragement. They might have been in your shoes before and can share their experiences. I've felt like an imposter in literally every job I've started. I've laid awake at 3 am, wondering when my new boss would realize they'd blundered by hiring me and how quickly they would correct their mistake.

In his book *Hidden Potential: The Science of Achieving Greater Things*,[2] organizational psychologist Adam Grant expresses the fundamental problem with imposter syndrome—it's a paradox. Think about the implications of Imposter Syndrome:

- You do not believe in yourself or trust your judgment.
- Other people believe in you.
- You don't believe other people's judgment about you, but instead believe your own judgment is better.

How does that make sense? If you doubt your judgment, shouldn't you also accept that you're not a good judge of your own abilities? You're saying you don't belong because everyone around you is smarter and more qualified, yet you assume they are wrong for trusting you. You more heavily weigh your own judgment about your lack of qualifications. This thinking is internally inconsistent. If you're not qualified, if your judgment is worse than that of your boss and peers, that everyone around you knows more, then maybe you should trust their assessment of you and give yourself a break.

Focus on your achievements, and remember that you were chosen for this role for a reason. Remember that you've accomplished a lot to get where you are today. Nobody's perfect! Embrace the fact that you're always learning and growing. It's okay not to have all the answers. Keep developing your skills, keep learning, and remain open to new ideas. You'll get better over time. Fake it 'til you make it is sometimes good advice, especially when experiencing imposter syndrome.

Set realistic expectations for yourself and be prepared to make mistakes. That's part of the learning process. Instead of getting down on yourself, try to learn from those experiences and improve. Regularly ask for feedback from your team and boss so you can understand your strengths and areas for improvement.

Celebrate your successes, both big and small, to help boost your confidence. And don't forget to be kind to yourself. Treat yourself with understanding and compassion when things don't go as planned. Building a support network of peers, mentors, and friends can make a huge difference as you navigate your new role.

Lastly, if your feelings of impostor syndrome become too overwhelming or start to affect your work and personal life, seek professional help from a therapist or counselor. Remember, dealing with impostor syndrome takes time and effort, but with persistence, you can overcome it and become a more confident and effective leader.

NOTES

1 Rutherford, G. (n.d.). *Up to 70 per cent of us feel like a fraud, says U of A psychologist.* https://www.ualberta.ca/en/folio/2020/02/up-to-70-per-cent-of-us-feel-like-a-fraud-says-u-of-a-psychologist.html.
2 Grant, A. (2023). *Hidden potential: the science of achieving greater things.* [New York, New York], Viking, an imprint of Penguin Random House LLC.

Part One

Members

We start this book by discussing Members because nothing impacts your success as a manager more than your team. A great team can make a mediocre manager look like a star, while a poor team can topple even a great manager. Good teams are characterized by accountability, cooperation, alignment toward a common mission, and camaraderie. Each member knows what they must do, has the tools and knowledge to do it, and shows a genuine commitment to the team's success. Bad teams, on the other hand, are plagued by misalignment, infighting, finger-pointing, and low morale. The team members are disengaged, work in silos, hoard information, and spend more time thinking about individual success rather than team success.

Good and bad teams don't just happen randomly. Just as your team members will determine your success, you will play a pivotal role in their success. The path to a high-performing team starts with mastering the basics. Your one-on-one meetings will form the foundation of your relationships with the people on your team. Your staff meetings will ensure the team stays aligned, engaged, and inspired. Delegation and prioritization will keep you sane and your team operating at peak efficiency.

Good teams are built on good feedback. Feedback to your team must be timely, clear, and actionable. You need to learn to praise in public while offering constructive feedback in private. You must also be open to receiving feedback from your team members.

In Part One, we'll also cover how to build the pieces of your team through recruiting, hiring, onboarding, and retention. Perhaps no decision a manager makes is more important than choosing whom to hire. Great hires elevate the entire team. Poor hires have the opposite effect. We'll talk about how to craft job descriptions, screen candidates, interview, and select the right people. We'll also talk about how to onboard them so they get off to a strong start and how to retain them for the long term.

DOI: 10.1201/9781003562160-2

Finally, we'll talk about managing some specific team members: your boss, your former peers, and those deeply technical people on your team. Each comes with opportunities and challenges. Each requires a certain level of nuance. Mastering these relationships will help you steer clear of potential issues.

* * *

Chapter 1

Brilliant at the basics

Becoming brilliant at the basics will establish a sound foundation for your management style. The rest of your management activity will build on these few items, so getting them right is critical. This process can't be rushed. Instead, you must discover your style gradually. Don't wait for some moment of enlightenment. Don't spend weeks or months planning the perfect management style. Dig in and begin the work of managing your team. Some parts of managing are essential if you're to succeed, regardless of your style. Your priority upon assuming your new role is to implement the basics into your routine and thinking. Begin to build the foundation.

ONE-ON-ONES

One-on-one meetings with your direct reports underpin all your other management activities. You use this time to build relationships with your staff, provide a forum for your team to bring ideas, updates, and concerns to your attention, and signal to your staff that they matter to you. If your team members observe you attending multiple meetings, but you're not scheduling any with them, they will feel neglected. By scheduling regular time with them, you're saying they are just as important as everything else you do.

An IT Manager lives and dies by her calendar. In a September 2022 report, Otter.ai found that managers of at least four direct reports spent an average of 22.5 hours weekly in meetings![1] My own experience suggests this number is low. I just counted meetings on my calendar. Over the last month, I averaged 46 meetings per week: staff meetings, project meetings, vendor meetings, procurement meetings, architecture meetings, and all-hands meetings. Everyone wants some of your time. Many meetings are optional. One-on-ones are not one of them.

One-on-ones aren't just about sacrificing time to benefit your team members. Managers benefit just as much as their reports. First, you build better relationships with each member of your team. This structured time gives you a chance to talk without other distractions. You can focus on the person in front of you. Second, research has shown that you regain time in your

DOI: 10.1201/9781003562160-3

week by having standing one-on-ones.[2] You avoid interruptions throughout the week. We're all too familiar with the do-you-have-a-minute drop-ins that never last a minute. Knowing that a regular one-on-one is around the coroner will drastically cut down on these drop-ins. Finally, you stay more up-to-date on your team's work. As you delegate more work downward, the one-on-one gives you a mechanism to check in on the progress of the delegated tasks.

To structure effective one-on-one meetings, start with three things:

1. block off a recurring time slot,
2. follow the same structure for each meeting, and
3. take notes.

Start with weekly, 30-minute meetings with each direct report. You can consider bi-weekly meetings if you have an unusually large team (over 15 direct reports). You lose some benefits of the one-on-one if you schedule bi-weekly vs. weekly, but it's better than nothing. As a new manager, a team larger than 15 is not likely, and even most senior leaders I've worked with tend not to have more than a dozen direct reports.

I like 30-minute meetings for two reasons. First, you are less likely to cancel or run into a conflict if your meeting is 30 minutes. They are just easier to schedule. Second, 30 minutes is enough to cover what you need to but short enough to ensure you are not wasting time. Remember, part of the goal is to recapture time in your week.

Once you have the meeting scheduled, stick to the meeting time. One-on-ones seem like the easiest meetings to reschedule because you only need to worry about two calendars. However, regularly rescheduling, or worse, canceling, one-on-ones sends the wrong message to your staff. Inevitably, you'll need to reschedule some of them throughout the year. But if you reschedule over 20% of the meetings, look for a better time.

I use a straightforward agenda for my one-on-one meetings taken from *The Effective Manager* by Mark Horstman. The first 10 minutes are "You Time," the next 10 minutes are "Me Time," and the final 10 minutes are "Us Time." The names might sound ridiculous, but it makes the expectations very clear. For the first 10 minutes of each meeting, we discuss whatever my staff wants to discuss. This can be last night's Yankee game, his weekend plans, or his work. Most of the time, my team wants to talk about their work. It's essential that your staff have the first part of the agenda. If you flip the order so that you're talking first, your directs will use their time to further expound on whatever you brought up.

"Me Time" is similarly straightforward. Those are my 10 minutes. I ask for updates on work, assign additional tasks, plan upcoming activities, and brainstorm. (Though, I've also lamented the lack of offensive production from the Yankees.) The final 10 minutes, "Us Time," is for long-term planning and career growth conversations. You don't need to cover these in every meeting. Most often, the first, second agenda topics, or both, will run long and take up the other 10 minutes. That's fine! Check in on long-term issues at least a few times a year.

The agenda is purposely very high-level. Don't ask your team to send you a list of topics beforehand; don't send them a list of what you plan to discuss. These are the only meetings where a formal agenda can do more harm than good. If I send my team a list of topics, it's almost guaranteed they will open "You Time" with those topics. I've now robbed them of their dedicated time on the agenda.

Conversely, if they send a list of topics, they might send me a sensitive or critical issue. I might be obligated to address it immediately rather than wait until our meeting. Remember, part of the goal is to streamline the communication flow. I open every meeting with "What's up?" and let them begin.

During these meetings, take notes. This signals to your team members that you're paying attention and that what they say matters. I prefer to take notes on paper with a pen. A laptop screen can block your view across the table or make you appear distracted. I've got separate sections of a notebook for each of my team members for one-on-one notes. Of course, digital notes are fine, too. The key is quick access to your notes to review the prior meeting before attending the next one. Here are some quick tips on note-taking that work well for me:

- I structure the pages in my notebook based on the Cornell Notes Template.[3] I leave a wide left margin for some shorthand, take the bulk of the notes on the right two-thirds of the page, and leave space at the bottom for a summary of key points I'll fill in after the meeting. I find this summary helps me remember better.
- I put an asterisk next to action items or deliverables I've promised someone. This is one of the shorthand notations that go in the left margin. You can also circle, underline, or highlight these—whatever works for you. Make sure you can quickly spot them. Your staff will not feel important if you're blowing off your follow-up actions.
- One-on-ones are a great place to provide and document constructive feedback. A quick notation like "Spoke to Molly about the need for code review before moving anything to production" is sufficient. Documentation doesn't need to be formal and drawn out. Quick, contemporaneous notes go a long way if HR ever needs to get involved. After a meeting, I'll usually underline these in red and put an "F" (for feedback) in the left margin so that I can find them at a glance.
- When I've delegated a task to someone, I'll put an arrow in the left margin next to that task. I also include the date it's due and any other milestones, for instance, if we agree to follow up in a week.

After the meeting, send a quick follow-up email summarizing what you discussed. You can use a template to make this easier or send over a few bullet points covering the highlights and any action items. This serves three purposes: it makes sure you're both clear on the meeting outcomes and who is responsible for what items, it memorializes the discussion in written form in case you need it later, and it reinforces that you paid attention during the meeting. As a bonus, typing the email also helps you remember what items to follow up on.

As I mentioned at the beginning of this chapter, you'll need to find your own style. My system works well for me and my team. That doesn't mean it will work best for you. As long as you're scheduling one-on-ones and keeping to that schedule most of the time, your one-on-ones will have a positive impact.

STAFF MEETINGS

After one-on-ones, your staff meeting is the most important meeting on your calendar. Without an effective, recurring staff meeting, you risk a team where members do not know what others are doing, where management does not know what staff are doing, and where essential tasks fall through the cracks. That doesn't sound like a fun place to work.

Staff meetings require a minimal investment of time yet generate massive returns. Staff meetings exist for a few key reasons: to keep everyone on the team informed, to collectively solve problems, and to help establish the culture of your team. Let's discuss each of the benefits of a staff meeting and how to structure one effectively.

You should regularly schedule your staff meeting for a time when all team members can attend. People may need to rearrange their calendars, or you may need to schedule the recurring meeting a few weeks out and use ad hoc meeting times in the short term. If you're a brand new manager, don't wait 2–3 weeks for your first staff meeting. Your team needs to get to know you in your new role, and staff meetings are a great time to show your leadership.

Currently, I schedule staff meetings every other week. In my previous jobs, I held weekly staff meetings. The frequency largely depends on your team size and your workload. Smaller teams should meet more frequently. These meetings are typically an hour long, though I've worked with some bosses who schedule 90 minutes and some who prefer 30 minutes. This is largely dependent on the type of work you do. Senior executive staff meetings might be 2 hours long as they need time to dive into thorny strategic issues, but for most teams, 60 minutes is the sweet spot. 90-minute meetings are long, regardless of how much we like our team, and 30 minutes will not leave enough time for everything you need to discuss. A weekly 60-minute time slot is ideal.

Unlike one-on-ones, your staff meeting needs an agenda! You can use standing agenda items to create a structure, but each meeting should have a specific list of topics for discussion. I solicit topics from my team a few days before each meeting and then add my own. Then I prioritize the list to place the most important items early in the meeting. This ensures you don't run out of time and cover the most important topics when your team's attention is the highest. Most of my agendas are bullet points emailed the night before the meeting. You don't need to be formal. You need to ensure you cover essential items and don't inadvertently forget anything.

I start every meeting with general announcements. These can be items from my boss's staff meeting that the team needs to know or from recent corporate announcements, earnings reports, or other newsworthy topics. Remember, you always have more information than your team. Even if something was on the front page of the paper and your company's home page, don't assume your team knows about it. Take a minute or two to inform them. Repetition never hurts.

I then move on to project-specific updates. You won't have time to cover every project, so focus on the most critical projects, those with upcoming milestones or those with announcements worth sharing. If you have nothing obvious in these categories, rotate through projects. You can also think about what team members need an opportunity to present to the group. You should ensure everyone contributes to the team regularly to build credibility and presentation skills. This will also help increase your team's cohesion. During these discussions, encourage questions and feedback from others in the room.

Be sure to pull in the quiet people—not everyone is comfortable speaking up in meetings. Watch for anyone sitting quietly who looks like they might have something to say. Pay attention to those with great insights in your one-on-ones but who rarely speak in group settings. Try to get them involved. Don't mistake the loudest or most talkative person in the room for the smartest person. It's hardly ever the case.

Once you've covered your announcements and project updates, you can use the rest of the time for a "go around." You can literally go around the table (or virtual room) and ask everyone to provide a brief update. You can also make this an open-forum time slot where you ask, "Who has another topic to discuss." The former option ensures everyone speaks but takes longer. The latter option is quicker, but you risk the same people speaking every time and crowding out the quieter members of your team. Try both and see what works best for you. If you find you never have time to get to this section of the meeting, you either need to tighten up the first two sections or schedule a longer meeting. This time is essential for your team to share updates, gather feedback, and feel heard.

Save the meeting's last 2–3 minutes to review action items and follow-ups. Don't end a meeting until everyone knows who is doing what and by when. Then ask someone on your team to send out a summary. I like to pick someone randomly at the end of each meeting as it helps incentivize everyone to pay attention, but you could create a schedule beforehand. Just make sure you're sharing the load among your team members. This is an area where unconscious biases slip in. I've seen too many managers assign the role of meeting minutes to the women on the team while unintentionally suggesting the men were too busy. Don't be that kind of manager.

Now that we've established the mechanics of an effective staff meeting, you need to consider the topics for each meeting. I like to open each meeting on a cheerful note. Share good news, praise a team member, remind them about an upcoming holiday, or find another way to set a positive tone for the meeting. This is a great time to "praise in public" by calling out a win someone on your team had that week. This boosts them up, sets an example for others, and helps you shape the culture. One of the most effective ways to do this is to praise people for behaviors you are trying to model. If you need to drive better collaboration on your team, call out the person who put their work aside to help a colleague. If you want to drive better accountability, call out the person who quickly notified you of an issue. These praiseworthy items will shift over time but are a great way to drive culture. Find your own themes and use your staff meeting to drive them.

Project updates in your meetings are equally important. They should not be a never-ending list of tasks. That type of discussion benefits no one, and you will quickly lose the attention of others in the room (this is doubly true if your meeting is virtual). Instead, they should focus on risks and issues, milestones, and collaboration.

- **Risks and Issues:** Someone in your meeting might have a creative solution or an idea worth pursuing, but you won't know if you don't candidly discuss issues. Do not encourage a culture that hides bad news.
- **Milestones:** Keep your entire team informed about upcoming milestones. Do you have a change freeze coming because Project Alpha has a move to production? Lay it out there! You can also use this time to celebrate recent milestone wins.
- **Collaboration:** Your team should tell the group what help they need or where their work will intersect with someone else's. If Jeff changed an API and Tracy is calling that API, she needs to know it changed. You have a formal change control procedure (which we'll discuss in more detail in Chapter 10), but these meetings effectively supplement that process.

My final tip to take your staff meeting to the next level: let your team run the meeting! You won't do this for the first few meetings as you're working to establish an agenda, build the culture, and set expectations. But once your team is accustomed to your expectations, designate someone else to run the staff meeting. You obviously need to attend and actively participate, but you can offload some of the preparation. This is beneficial for everyone. You free up some time, and people on your team get valuable experience. When preparing for the meeting, they will need to reach out to their peers for updates, set an agenda, and think about future projects. This will reinforce collaboration and planning. You should still be the first item on the agenda for updates and announcements but think about flipping your role to that of a participant while someone else manages the meeting.

A well-structured staff meeting, held regularly, will elevate your team's performance and improve your effectiveness as a manager. You will solve problems more efficiently, keep everyone informed, and inspire your team. By investing a little time every week, you will reap an outsized return.

DELEGATION

The most significant change that comes with management is your new responsibility for a team. You're no longer responsible solely for your own work. You will now be judged based on your team's outcomes and results. It's part of what makes management so tricky. It's essential to your success that you delegate intelligently. Failure to delegate is one of the most common mistakes I see with new managers. The instinct for most new managers is to continue doing those things that made them successful in the past. Don't do this. You will fail.

Stop me if you've heard this before: Jane is an excellent employee. Not only does she deliver high-quality work, but she asks for more. One day, Jane is promoted to manage her team. She takes on more work, stays late, works weekends, and continues to build her reputation as someone who "gets it done." Jane is rewarded with another promotion, this time to a director-level role overseeing four different departments. Three months later, Jane resigns to "pursue other opportunities."

What happened? Jane got buried under an increasing mountain of work and failed to delegate appropriately. Sadly, this happens all too often. Think about some of the changes that come with managing a team. You need to add 30 minutes of meetings per week for a one-on-one with each direct report, an hour per week for a staff meeting, and the time to prepare for and follow up on each meeting. This is in addition to whatever new responsibilities your boss piles on. The demands are higher than ever before. You simply can't do all the work yourself. Nor should you.

Delegation can be uncomfortable. Until now, you've gotten ahead by taking on more work and stepping up for extra assignments. Now, you need to figure out how to give work away. It's understandable to feel anxiety about relinquishing control and overwhelming your team, but it's important to remember that effective delegation benefits everyone involved. While it's natural to worry about your team's ability to perform the task as well as you, you can take steps to ensure that they are adequately trained and supported.

Delegation empowers you and the person receiving the work. That might sound odd. You might feel you're giving a busy person more work, but delegating correctly will increase their autonomy, improve their skillset, and help their career. Delegating correctly means you need to transfer ownership of something to another person. It's not assigning tasks and telling them how to perform them. That's micromanagement. Delegating says, "I'd like you to own this and complete it by the end of the week," and then expects them to figure out the best way to achieve the outcome. The freedom to choose how and when to complete the task within the assigned parameters makes delegation powerful.

There are three reasons you need to delegate.

- Your time is more valuable
- Team growth compounds
- It's the only way to survive

Your time is now more valuable. You are paid more than you were in your last role (I hope), which means you cost your company more. You have more experience than a junior person on your team, meaning you can take on more intractable problems and more challenging assignments. And, you have a broader scope. The result is that your time is more valuable. Imagine the CEO of a Fortune 500 company approving every expense report. They wouldn't last very long as CEO. The board wouldn't let it go on, as it wastes their top executive's valuable time. The CEO would also become a bottleneck; the reimbursement process would grind to a halt. The same outcome awaits if you don't delegate your tasks.

The second reason to delegate is that it helps your team learn. People grow by taking on challenging new assignments. If you're afraid to delegate because someone on your team isn't as good at a task as you are, they will never get the chance to improve. If you routinely do a task, the task gets done, and no one learns anything. If you delegate that task to a team member and they learn how to do it, you end up with two people who know how to complete that task. The work still gets done, but you've doubled the organizational capacity to complete it. Think about this like making a deposit in the growth bank. The more you deposit, the more it compounds. Your team gets stronger and stronger. The flip side is also true—when you do a task you could have delegated, you create a growth "debt" that compounds every bit as fast as a growth deposit.

The person completing the task for the first time might not do it as well as you would have. That's ok. The second time they do it, they will improve. The third time will be even better. And each time they complete it, the results will improve, they will get more efficient, and you will be free to work on something more substantial. You're building organizational capacity, training your team members, and liberating yourself to take on something new.

The last reason to delegate is that it's the only way to survive. If you don't delegate, you'll work more than ever. And you will burn out. You will end up resigning or getting fired.

Think about what your days are like in your new role. You're in more meetings than ever before, which means the only time to do "real work" is at the end of your day or very early before the work day starts. Your days get longer and longer. There is a strong correlation between lack of sleep and impaired executive function.[4] If you don't sleep enough, you'll have more trouble paying attention in meetings, analyzing information, and making sound decisions—three essential pieces of a manager's job. Delegation is crucial to your team's success and your personal success.

Luckily, delegation is not complicated. The process can be broken down into six simple steps:

- **Pick something to delegate:** This can be a single task: "Follow up with Heather from the network team about the status of the firewall change." It can also be a larger project, "Upgrade the mobile app." Depending on the makeup of your team, you're likely to have a mix of both types of delegations.
- **Pick a person:** Choose someone from your team to own the task, project, goal, or whatever you're delegating. "Own" is important here. They must understand that they need to see the item through to completion, pull in help when needed, raise issues and risks for resolution, work through blockers, etc.
- **Plan and guide:** Meet with the person you pick and create a plan. Explain the outcome you're looking for, the timeline you expect, and the context surrounding it. Is this a presentation for a big meeting? A key project with leadership visibility? What Quality vs. Speed tradeoffs are acceptable? Go over all the questions so that expectations are clear.
- **Execute:** The person you chose should execute the task, deliver the project, or work toward the goal. This is the step where you can turn your attention to other matters, trusting that your team has your back.
- **Monitor and coach:** Depending on the complexity of what you delegate and the experience of the person to whom you delegate, you likely need check-ins along the way. You can make this a standing agenda item during your one-on-ones, email check-ins weekly, or some other mechanism that works for both of you. But make sure you have some way to monitor progress and provide feedback.
- **Learn and improve:** Once the task is complete, you should take some time to debrief with your team member. Discuss what went well, what didn't, and what you can do better next time (Figure 1.1).

That's all there is to it. It isn't complicated. Yet, repeatedly, managers struggle with delegation.

There are a few things to watch out for that could derail your delegation efforts. First, you must be clear when delegating. Ensure the new owner understands what you're asking. Use the Plan and Guide step to be explicit

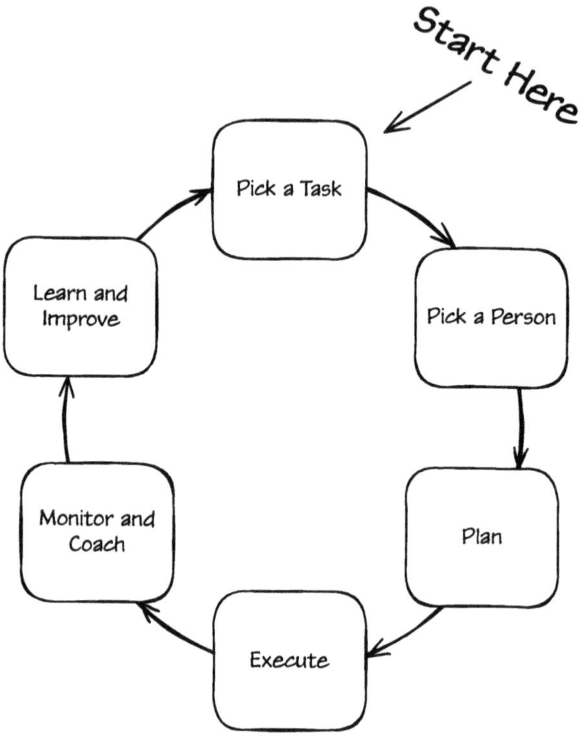

Figure 1.1 Delegation process.

about your expectations. I've left more than a few meetings in my career where I thought I'd delegated something, but a week later, the person I delegated to asked me how things were going! Be direct, get acknowledgment, and agree on expectations! It won't hurt to memorialize the delegation with an email, but it's not strictly necessary.

The second risk is not letting go after you delegate something. You need to empower the other person and then let them manage the work. I've had managers delegate to me but proofread every email, attend every meeting, and sign off on every deliverable. At that point, it would have been easier and faster for them to do it themselves. George Patton said, "Never tell people how to do things. Tell them what to do, and they will surprise you with their ingenuity."[5] Once you've delegated, move on to something else and trust that your team will handle their responsibilities.

Also, beware of your team delegating back to you! It's too easy for someone on your team to ask you to look over a document before they send it, to proofread an email to a key stakeholder, or to make too many decisions. Encourage them to work independently and come to you only if stuck. Expect to do a little more hand-holding with new people, but for your established team, set the expectation that they own their tasks.

The last risk is assuming your team is too busy. We are all busy, and your team will be no exception. You need to help them prioritize. If your team is at capacity such that you can delegate nothing else, you'll need to review your planning process and reassess priorities. Likely, there is something less critical you can push off until later or tasks you can stop doing altogether. We'll talk about prioritization in the next section, but make sure you focus on the most critical tasks. People tend to find time for the tasks they enjoy doing. Your job is to keep them focused on the highest priority items.

Delegating well is one trait that sets apart managers who continue to advance in their careers from those who get stuck at the current level (or worse). Review your priorities regularly and determine which items you can delegate to someone else. The more you can push down the organizational chart, the better. You free up your time to work on other things and improve your team's capacity and skill set. Pretty soon, you start to build self-reinforcing momentum.

PRIORITIZATION

In nearly every corporation, non-profit, government, NGO, or anywhere else you might find a job, the total work to be done may be limitless. Simply put, you will never have enough hours in the day to do everything that needs to be done. Every manager at every level sleeps at night with a mountain of unfinished work. The sooner you accept this and start prioritizing the most essential items, the sooner you can succeed.

I like to use an approach called Eliminate, Automate, and Delegate. I can't remember where I first heard about this approach, but it may have been in Tim Ferris's *The 4-Hour Work Week*.[6] The basic premise is that for every item on your to-do list, you decide to eliminate, automate, or delegate it. The tasks remaining are the ones you need to work on. It's essential to go through the list in that order. You don't want to waste time automating something you could eliminate, and you don't want to delegate something you could automate. You can, however, delegate the automation of a task.

When looking at everything you have to get done for the week, start with tasks that may not be necessary. Are you providing reports for a project no one cares about? Attending an irrelevant meeting? There's likely something no longer important enough to be worth your time. If you're unsure, check with your boss. Another approach is to stop doing it and see if anyone notices. Often, no one does. This approach is more effective but riskier.

After eliminating as much as possible, review the list and see what you can automate. Would an Excel macro save you 20 minutes on a task you do every week? Even if it took 2 hours to automate, your breakeven point is six weeks. I've seen too many people fail to automate tasks because "it would take too long," when, in reality, the breakeven point is relatively soon. Humans are not good at thinking in extended time frames.

Once you've automated everything you can, review the list a 3rd time and see what you can delegate. And remember from the last section; delegation is not getting someone else to *do* the task. It's getting someone to *own* the task. Make sure they own it in the future. You don't want to have to re-delegate the same task every week.

After you've gone through your list three times, whatever work remains is the work you must do. This is likely still more work than you can reasonably accomplish. So how do we tackle what's left? Use the Eisenhower Matrix. The name comes from a quote from Dwight Eisenhower, "I have two kinds of problems, the urgent and the important. The urgent are not important, and the important are never urgent."[7] I first read about the Eisenhower Matrix in Steven Covey's excellent *7 Habits of Highly Effective People*.[8] I can't recommend it strongly enough if you've never read it.

While Ike may not have dealt with issues that were both urgent and important, you will. The Matrix divides items into four quadrants. Those that are both urgent and important, we'll call Quadrant I problems using the following categorization:

- **Quadrant I**: These items need to be done and need to be done soon. There is no way to get out of doing this work, but spending too much time in this quadrant will lead to burnout, frustration, and higher attrition. If you're spending most of your time here, step back and figure out why.
- **Quadrant II**: These things are important but not urgent. We can also think of this as the planning quadrant. You want to spend most of your time here because it means you are working on important things that have not snuck up on you—things you will have space and time to address appropriately.
- **Quadrant III**: Things that are urgent but not important. It would be best if you delegate these items as much as possible.
- **Quadrant IV**: Items that are neither urgent nor important. Often, these are time wasters better left undone entirely. Unsolicited sales calls and emails from vendors will fall into this category.

Below is an example of a simple Eisenhower Matrix. The specific items in each quadrant will vary. Things in Quadrant II can easily make their way into Quadrant I if you do not give them attention. Think about planning for a quarterly business review meeting with the leadership team. If you procrastinate on this Quadrant II task, it will sneakily slide into Quadrant I about a week before the meeting.

Print out this matrix or one like it and put it on your wall. It can serve as a friendly reminder to refocus on important priorities (Figure 1.2).

Using the Eisenhower framework, the first step is to prioritize your calendar. Managers live and die by what's on their calendar for the day, week, and month. If it's not on your calendar, it may as well not exist. You need to

	Urgent	Not Urgent
Important	Quadrant I Deadline Driven Sev 1 Issues Security Incidents	Quadrant II Strategy Long-Term Planning Preventative Maintenance
Not Important	Quadrant III Emails, Calls, Slack Messages Many of Your Meetings Drop-Ins, Interruptions	Quadrant IV Busy Work Time Wasters Unsolicited Sales Calls Procrastination

Figure 1.2 Eisenhower matrix.

reevaluate your priorities and how you spend your time regularly. There is no panacea to excel at prioritization. It takes diligence, hard work, and attention. There are some tools you can use to make things easier.

First, schedule dedicated time for email and only look at emails during that time. The constant pinging of our inboxes can distract us from more important work. You can spend hours a day reading and responding to emails. But the beautiful thing about email is it's an asynchronous form of communication. Those messages will still be there waiting for you when you next open your inbox. Someone will call, text, or send a Slack if something is genuinely urgent. Even better, if you don't reply right away, one of the other six people copied might respond with an answer, and then you can eliminate it from your list.

Set some boundaries around when you check your email. I aim to spend 30 minutes each morning, 30 minutes just before or after lunch, and 30 minutes at the end of each day going through emails. I don't succeed, but that's my goal. There are some excellent resources on email management and "inbox zero" that you can read for more tips. When you're not in an email window, turn off the notifications. Nothing will distract you from your work, like 17 Outlook notifications in 5 minutes.

It's important to get each day off to a strong start. You can do this through planning. Before you shut down for the night, write out the top three things you need to accomplish the next day. If you get those three things done, consider it a good day. Longer lists lead people to focus on crossing off as many items as possible. Your goal is to make progress on your most important priorities. Start your day—before you check your email—by reviewing your list from the night before. You don't need to start working on the list, but review it and use those three things to set the tone for the day.

Skip the open-door policy. An open-door approach sounds like a good idea—everyone likes to pop into the boss's office. But it will lead to distractions throughout the day and interrupt your deep work. Instead, opt for "Office Hours," where you set aside a couple of hours per week to be available for questions. This is a great way to build rapport with your team and discuss things that arise between one-on-ones. Now that so many people are remote, I host my office hours via video call so everyone can attend. You can use this time for less formal discussions and to build relationships with team members, but don't be afraid to set boundaries. If the same person shows up every week to tell you about the golf shot he hit that weekend, it's ok to cut him off and explain that you need to get back to work.

Schedule time for deep work. Every manager needs time to do deep, focused work without interruptions. Block this time on your calendar in advance. It's hard to get into a flow state if you work in 15-minute increments between meetings. Even as you climb the career ladder and take a role as a CIO, you still need unbroken blocks of time to work. You need to prepare for Board Meetings, respond to regulators, review resumes, etc. Build good habits now and protect this time on your calendar.

Use your calendar to schedule all the important items in your week. This includes personal appointments (e.g., the doctor), family commitments, time for exercise, eating, and blocks for deep work. Keeping everything in one view makes you less likely to double-book yourself into a conflict and miss important events. When you look at your calendar, you should have a complete picture of your day. [Note: Don't let your work calendar be the only place you save personal appointments. I've seen a few times when someone was terminated suddenly. When they lost access to their work calendar, they lost all records of upcoming appointments. Put these appointments on your work calendar for visibility, but save them elsewhere!]

To be an effective manager, you need to be good at prioritization. There is too much to do in too little time. You'll need to be ruthless about prioritizing what gets done, when, and by whom. The alternative is frenetically rushing between tasks until you fail or burn out. Prioritization is difficult. It requires that you say "No" frequently. No, I can't attend that meeting as I have another priority. No, we can't take on that new task right now. No, I'm not interested in a sales demo of your new low-code platform. By saying no to these things, you're saying yes to the more important things in your world—and yes to a more productive, successful, and happier career.

NOTES

1 Morel, D. (2023, February 28). Stop these three pandemic habits that are hampering productivity. *Forbes*. https://www.forbes.com/sites/davidmorel/2023/01/30/stop-these-three-pandemic-habits-that-are-hampering-productivity/?sh=1b45ad4737e7.

2 Horstman, M. (2016). *The effective manager*. John Wiley & Sons.
3 *The Cornell Note Taking System – Learning Strategies Center*. (n.d.). https://lsc.cornell.edu/how-to-study/taking-notes/cornell-note-taking-system/.
4 Alhola, P., & Polo-Kantola, P. (2007). *Sleep deprivation: Impact on cognitive performance. Neuropsychiatric Disease and Treatment*, 3(5), 553–567. https://www.ncbi.nlm.nih.gov/pmc/articles/PMC2656292/.
5 Patton, G. S. (1995). *War as I knew it*. Houghton Mifflin Harcourt.
6 Ferriss, T. (2011). *The 4-hour work week: Escape the 9-5, live anywhere and join the new rich*. Random House.
7 Eisenhower, D. (1954). *Address at the Second Assembly of the World Council of Churches*. Archived from http://www.presidency.ucsb.edu/ws/?pid=9991 on 2015-04-02. Evanston, Illinois. (retrieved 28 February 2023).
8 Covey, S. R. (2004). *The 7 habits of highly effective people: Powerful lessons in personal change*. Simon and Schuster.

RECOMMENDED ADDITIONAL READING

Blanchard, K. H., & Johnson, S. (2004). *The One Minute Manager*. HarperCollins Publishers.
Drucker, P. F. (1985). *The Effective Executive*. HarperCollins Publishers.
Horstman, M. (2016). *The Effective Manager*. John Wiley & Sons.
Schmidt, E., Rosenberg, J., & Eagle, A. (2019). *Trillion Dollar Coach: The Leadership Playbook of Silicon Valley's Bill Campbell*. HarperBusiness.

Chapter 2

Feedback

Good feedback is critical to a healthy organization—it improves your employees' skills, drives better results for your team, and increases job satisfaction. The opposite is also true. Anyone who's been a part of a team with unclear expectations, who didn't know where they stood with the boss, or who was surprised when they got a bad review is a victim of an unhealthy organization. Managers need to give good feedback. You owe it to your staff to help them grow and develop. And you owe it to your employer to ensure they get the results they pay for.

Feedback helps ensure you and your team are aligned on expectations. It's as simple as that. Effective feedback happens in the context of pre-established goals. Goals should cascade from the top down. After you and your manager align on goals for your team, sit down and create individual plans for each of your staff. These mutually agreed-upon goals will form the basis of your annual evaluations for your team. Research shows that "effective feedback requires that the employee has a goal, takes action to achieve the goal, and receives goal-related feedback on their actions. The employee goals and performance...are directly linked to the key success factors."[1]

Feedback is simple but not easy. In its most basic form, it is information you convey to your employees about their performance, teamwork, or skills. Feedback can be delivered formally or informally at any time of the year. It can be verbal or written. It can happen one-on-one, via email, or in a group setting, though you should reserve negative feedback for a private setting.

GOOD FEEDBACK

Let's talk about bad feedback. I don't mean negative feedback—both positive and negative feedback can be bad. When I say bad feedback, I mean unhelpful feedback. The feedback that puts the other person on the defensive by being overly aggressive, feedback that glosses over problems and pretends like things are fine, or feedback that's given so far after the fact that it's useless. There are three ways you can give feedback that misses the mark:

DOI: 10.1201/9781003562160-4

- Feedback that glosses over anything negative and focuses only on the positive. This is typically the result of a manager who tries to avoid uncomfortable conversations. These managers hope that endless encouragement will magically convince their employees to improve. Employees who get this type of feedback are deprived of the opportunity to develop because their manager never tells them what needs to change. Giving a weak employee this type of feedback ensures the problems will grow. Giving a good employee this kind of feedback makes it much more likely they will grow disengaged, frustrated, and unhappy.
- Feedback that focuses only on the negative. You're at risk of this kind of feedback when you decide an employee is beyond help. If you're at a point in your relationship where you can't see any positive contributions from an employee, you've waited too long to give them feedback. Employees who receive only negative feedback are likely to either burn out or find another job.
- Feedback that is neutral and offers neither positive reinforcement nor constructive suggestions for improvement is useless for the employee receiving it. Employees who receive only this kind of feedback will disengage.

The other big mistake managers make is waiting too long to give feedback. Some bosses only provide feedback during an annual review, which is way too late and far too infrequent. Even waiting until your next one-on-one could be too long to wait to provide feedback.

The US Office of Personnel Management uses a great example of a children's game to illustrate this point. "'You're cold! Now you're getting warmer! You're HOT!' Even children playing the popular 'Hot or Cold' game know that to perform well people need to be told how they're doing."[2] Imagine only saying "hotter" or "colder" once every 15 minutes. The game would take forever, the players would get frustrated, and everyone would quit. The same principle applies to your staff. If you can provide feedback on a presentation immediately after the meeting ends, you're more likely to give specific, actionable, and relevant advice. Your employee can immediately apply your feedback to their next presentation.

There are many ways to give bad feedback, but there are only a few ways to give good feedback. Good feedback should be timely, clear, and empathetic. It also needs to be based on trust. I emphasize the importance of one-on-ones because they are fundamental to building that trust. If your team feels supported, they will be more receptive to feedback.

NEGATIVE FEEDBACK

Early in my career as a manager, I thought I was "being nice" by softening the negative feedback. I remember saying to one person on my team, "I've noticed how much effort you've been putting in, and I really appreciate it. In the future, I'd like it if you could update me more often on your status." What I meant was, "I'm completely in the dark about what you were spending all that time doing," but because I wasn't clear, he didn't know that. I left the meeting with a different understanding of the feedback than my subordinate. This didn't help either one of us. They didn't get a chance to improve, and I dealt with the same performance issue for far longer than I should have. In the worst-case scenario, if something like this continues, the employee ends up in a meeting where HR explains that he's been fired, yet he has no idea why! Clear feedback is so important!

So, what does clear feedback look like? It looks like being harsh, unfortunately. Bluntness and meanness are very different things, though you might feel mean while being blunt. To give effective negative feedback, you need to be blunt. You need to ensure that the other person understands the problem and how they can fix it. You need to remove room for ambiguity—the mental escape hatch we all use when we interpret events in a way that casts ourselves in the best light.

You should start by informing the person that you are providing feedback on their performance. "I need to talk to you about your performance lately. I know this conversation may be unpleasant, but your career is too important for me not to say anything. Your current performance is unacceptable." You can bet you'll have their attention at this point. Then be as clear and as specific as possible about the issue. "You're dismissive of ideas from the team, and no one wants to work with you. You must find a way to get along better with your teammates." Notice that I removed any language around "I think" or "I'd like to see." Present your feedback as a fact. State the action the employee needs to take to improve. Remove the ambiguity. There is no way to make conversations like this pleasant, so don't try. Be professional. Be polite. But, above all, be clear!

Of course, not all feedback needs to be so harsh. The above example is meant for an employee with a consistent performance issue. If you can address a problem early, you can often avoid the need for conversations like this. For example, if you witness an employee acting like a jerk, pull them aside as soon as possible. "Hey, Kevin, your comments to Sam were out of line in that meeting. It's fine to disagree. I encourage vigorous debate. But you need to be more respectful." or "Mark, you came across as unprepared for that meeting. Your presentation had obvious mistakes, and you could not answer most questions. You need to prepare more for meetings. Let's chat tomorrow about how to approach the next meeting." These are both easy conversations. Early intervention can stave off more significant problems down the road.

Part of the reason so many managers struggle to give good feedback is that they want to seem friendly. They want their team to know they care. They worry that shocking someone with negative feedback will make them look uncaring. I get it. I spent way too long in my career doing the same thing. But I learned that the best way to care is to be completely, even brutally honest. If you genuinely care for the people on your team, and you should, then you should care about their performance, and you should care about their careers. You need to care about the outcome. You need to care that your feedback is received and that they understand its importance. Too many managers care only about being liked, but that's selfish. Care more about the success of your team than about your feelings.

I follow a six-step guide to giving thoughtful negative feedback. Eventually, you'll find your own style, but if it is your first time giving negative feedback, this can provide a helpful guide:

1) Find someplace private to have the conversation. Private doesn't have to mean secret. You don't need to lock yourself in a conference room. If you work in a cubicle with standard, head-high walls, that would be fine. But don't give negative feedback when there are other people within earshot.
2) Tell the other person that you want to provide feedback. This removes ambiguity about what's happening and ensures you're both on the same page. For lower-stakes feedback, like simple suggestions for improvement or a quick correction from a meeting, you can ask, "Hey, do you mind if I give you some quick feedback?" I've never had someone say no to this question, and it lowers the tension a bit. However, when someone's career is in jeopardy, just say it. "I need to give you some unpleasant feedback. It's important that you listen and understand what I'm saying."
3) State what you observed with as much specific detail as possible. Make sure that you have observed the behavior. If someone complains to you about a team member, you'll need to investigate to confirm that the complaint is accurate before acting on it. But when you've observed the behavior, state it as fact. "Twice in the last month, you've made a production change without proper approval. This violates our change control process and can't happen again."
4) Explain the impact. Ensure your employee understands why the behavior is problematic for them and the organization. You want to convey that you're not picking on them because you don't like them but because their behavior is a concern. "The change control process exists to make sure that everyone is aware of upcoming changes, to prevent unnecessary outages, and to help with troubleshooting if anything goes wrong. By skipping the process, you're putting the entire environment at risk. You're also putting your career at risk."
5) Establish specific actions to fix the situation. Once you've clarified the problem, the most critical part of giving feedback is establishing steps to fix what's wrong. If the concern is a lack of preparation, put some processes in place to help them prepare. You can ask them to send

you a copy of the presentations a few days ahead of time, you can ask them to get another team member to review their work, or you can come up with something else. The key is to make the remediating actions as specific as possible.

6) Ask for their questions, suggestions, and concerns. Make sure this is a two-way conversation. You don't want feedback sessions to turn into lectures where the other party sits passively, saying nothing. Asking for their suggestions will ensure they understand the feedback and leave the meeting with a clear idea of how to improve. You're not there to give them a hard time; you want to ensure they understand what's expected and how to meet those expectations.

My last piece of advice when giving negative feedback, especially summative feedback when someone's career or job is at risk, is to prepare in advance. These are tough conversations, regardless of how many times you've done this before. Spend 15 or 20 minutes and think about what you want the other person to take away from the meeting. Start with the desired outcome and work backward to what you will say. I do not recommend reading from a script, but having a few notes can be helpful. [Note: If you end up in a conversation terminating an employee, HR may have a script to follow. You should work closely with HR and follow their guidelines.]

Conflict is stressful. I've never met a manager who enjoyed providing negative feedback. It's also an essential part of managing effectively. There's a quote a colleague of mine uses that gets to the heart of it: conflict deferred is conflict compounded. The longer you ignore a problem, the more likely the problem is to get bigger. You help yourself and your team when you tackle challenging situations head-on.

POSITIVE FEEDBACK

That's enough negativity. Managing people is rewarding, and the good moments vastly outweigh the bad. Most discussions about giving feedback focus on providing tough, constructive feedback. This makes sense because giving such feedback is harder for most of us. No one wants to be the "bad guy"; everyone wants to be liked, and many of us fear conflict. Luckily, giving positive feedback is a lot more fun! For starters, the other person will not resist hearing good feedback, so you won't have to work through that resistance. You can and should also provide positive feedback in public. Calling out good behavior when you see it will help reinforce the behaviors and culture you're trying to build with your team. Public praise boosts confidence for the person receiving the feedback and raises overall team morale. Just be sure you're not playing favorites. Be objective with your feedback and spread the love. Staff meetings are a great time to celebrate professional success.

The biggest impediment to giving positive feedback is that we often forget. We expect good work from our teams, and we're so wrapped up in the next crisis that we move on too quickly from things that go well. Unfortunately, bad events and feedback have greater power over our emotions than good ones. Some studies, including a well-known study from John Gottman in 1994, show that we need five positive interactions to have the same effect as one negative interaction.[3] Gottman studied marriages specifically, but other research has consistently demonstrated that negative interactions and negative feedback have a much more significant impact on our emotions than positive feedback.[4] For this reason, you need to praise your team frequently and consistently.

You can follow the same broad guidelines for positive feedback: Tell the other person you are going to give them feedback, state what you observed, explain the impact, and establish some follow-up behavior. There are minor tweaks you should make for positive feedback. First, you don't need to find someplace private, although you can certainly use one-on-ones or other private conversations. Additionally, you can relay comments or feedback from someone else when providing positive feedback.

> Christine, I got some great feedback from Marketing that I wanted to share. They were impressed with how you kept the website redesign on track despite delays on their end. Your efforts helped us launch before the end of Q4, which got us a lot of goodwill with our investors. Great work!

Note how I started by telling Christine that I wanted to relay some feedback, then I provided some specific examples and explained the impact of her work. You need to highlight particular behaviors so the other person understands correctly what's prompting the feedback. With negative feedback, you're looking for them to change their behavior. In this instance, you're looking to reinforce the behavior so that they can build on it. It's essential that you are sincere in your feedback. Fake, vacuous feedback doesn't help anyone. People will sniff out insincere feedback every time.

Another point to consider: keep your positive feedback positive! I'm sure I'm not the only manager taught the "sandwich method" when you say something positive, then something negative, and then close with someone else positive. In my experience, this is a terrible way to give feedback. Some people hear only the good and miss the negative part, while others fixate on the negative and miss the positive feedback entirely. Worse, you can come across as insincere since the other person will think you're sprinkling in some positive feedback to soften the blow of what you really wanted to say. When you give someone kudos for a job well done, leave it at that. If there's other constructive feedback you need to provide, schedule another time when you can focus on that feedback. Allow them to enjoy the positive feedback unmarred by anything else.

Because positive feedback can be publicly given, feel free to get creative about it. One of my employers had a "Wall of Win," where we would hang up customer emails praising someone on the team. You can also create a Slack channel dedicated to providing kudos. Get creative. The payback is incredible.

Positive feedback is easier to give but no less essential. Like all feedback, it should be timely and specific. It can motivate employees to do better work, help someone who is having a rough stretch, and emphasize positive examples for the rest of your team. There's no reason to be stingy with positive feedback.

TWO-WAY FEEDBACK

Two-way feedback flips the traditional manager-employee feedback model on its head. Ask your staff for feedback. You can do this informally. "Hey, how do you think that meeting went? I'm not sure that I was clear enough about our upcoming work." Or you can use part of your one-on-one time to ask for feedback. I generally like to set the stage in the meeting prior. "Mike, I'm always looking to improve as a manager. It would really help me if you could think about ways I can better help you. If you're comfortable, let's discuss this in our next one-on-one."

There are a couple of tricks to doing this right. First, you need to be open to feedback. Don't ask for it if you're going to get upset when someone points out something you're not doing well. You can't get angry. You can't retaliate if you don't like what they say. Second, ensure you've invested time and effort to build trusted relationships with your team. Giving your boss feedback can be scary (and potentially career-limiting) for staff. Don't put your team on the spot until you're sure they trust you not to react badly. Third, make sure you establish that the other person will be helping you. This isn't a test to see how good they are at feedback. This is one instance where there's no such thing as bad feedback.

The final way you should solicit feedback from your staff is a periodic survey. Use Survey Monkey or a similarly easy tool. Your organization might even have a formal process for this (often called 360-degree feedback). Make use of it. Make it anonymous so people will be honest. We all have blind spots. This is a great way to shine some light on them and help you improve as a manager. Remember, you have a career to manage as well.

When you've collected your feedback, set aside a few hours to review it. Some of what you hear will likely come as a surprise. You might have a visceral defensive or angry reaction. Acknowledge your feelings, but do not let them cloud your rational judgment. Some of the feedback you get from your team will miss the mark. They'll complain about things well outside your control. They'll disagree with your decisions, even if those decisions are sound. Find a way to filter out the noise and focus on actionable items.

If you see patterns in the feedback, pay special attention. I once found out my team thought I was terrible at responding to emails. When I reflected as objectively as I could, they were correct. This made my team feel as though they were not a priority. I put an action plan in place that included 15 minutes at the end of each day to review my inbox for messages from my team. I then shared this action plan with my team and asked them to hold me accountable. Try to find at least a few things in the feedback you can publicly commit to acting on.

CONCLUSION

In a perfect world, your team would do everything you want. They'd nail all their work, learn new skills just because they wanted to, and never have issues with colleagues. But we don't live in a perfect world. We live in the real world. If you manage a team, you need to give feedback. If you want to be a *good* manager, you need to give *good* feedback. By following the six-step process in this chapter, you will deliver meaningful feedback. As you grow, you can develop your own style by noting what works and what doesn't. Keep the effective parts and discard the rest.

Employees with unaddressed performance issues are a drag on your team. Too many managers live with the status quo because they prefer to avoid uncomfortable conversations. Embrace the discomfort. A half-hour of unpleasant conversation can get your employee back on track and signal to the rest of your team that performance matters. Avoiding the conversation is selfish and counter-productive.

Similarly, your employees deserve recognition and praise when they perform well. As you establish a culture for your team, praise those who support the culture. As you set standards, praise the people who exceed the standard. Both positive and negative feedback are critical tools to build the team you need to succeed.

When done well, feedback will improve your team's performance, engagement, and morale. It will make you a more effective leader. There is no alternative.

NOTES

1 Nikolić, T. M. (n.d.). *The role of feedback as a management tool in Performance Management Program - ProQuest*. https://www.proquest.com/openview/d9a56e3a1639ac315027698de325eadb/1?pq-origsite=gscholar&cbl=1046413.

2 *Feedback is Critical to Improving Performance*. (n.d.). U.S. Office of Personnel Management. https://www.opm.gov/policy-data-oversight/performance-management/performance-management-cycle/monitoring/feedback-is-critical-to-improving-performance/.

3 Gottman, J. M., & Silver, N. (1994). *Why marriages succeed or fail: What you can learn from the breakthrough research to make your marriage last.* New York, Simon & Schuster.
4 Baumeister, R. F., Bratslavsky, E., Finkenauer, C., & Vohs, K. D. (2001). Bad is Stronger than Good. *Review of General Psychology*, *5*(4), 323–370. https://doi.org/10.1037/1089-2680.5.4.323.

RECOMMENDED ADDITIONAL READING

Carnegie, Dale. (2009). *How to Win Friends and Influence People.* Simon & Schuster.
McCord, P. (2018). *Powerful: Building a Culture of Freedom and Responsibility.* Silicon Guild.
Scott, K. M. (2017). *Radical Candor: How to Get What You Want by Saying What You Mean.* Macmillan.

Chapter 3

Recruiting and hiring

Hiring is one of the most essential parts of every manager's job. Get this right, and your team will flourish. Get it wrong, and you will struggle constantly. The cost of a bad hire is staggering. Not only do you risk getting poor work from a bad hire, but the impact on the morale of the rest of your team is toxic. Tony Hsieh, the late CEO of Zappos, estimated in 2016 that bad hires cost his company more than $100 Million.[1] All new hires take time to get fully up to speed. But if your new hire does not have the right skills or has a bad attitude, they may never get up to speed. You'll risk burning out your existing team and being forced to remove your newly hired employee.

How do you give yourself the best odds of hiring the right person? Process and discipline. Be intentional about how you evaluate candidates, dedicate enough time to review resumes, and prepare thoroughly for interviews. When actively searching for a candidate, I spend 30% to 50% of my time reviewing resumes, preparing for interviews, meeting candidates, and debriefing with my team. My time commitment reflects the importance of this task. Do not assume you'll magically find the time. Be intentional and block your calendar. You may need to delegate some tasks to others on your team (see Chapter 1), but make sure you protect this time to focus on hiring.

No manager can be successful without a good team. It should come as no surprise, then, that one of your most important responsibilities is to find, recruit, and hire staff. In this chapter, we explore the hiring process from the first time you recognize you need a new role through to making an offer. In the next chapter, we'll discuss how to effectively onboard a new employee and how to retain your existing employees. Getting these three pieces correct will make your life as a manager much easier.

It's worth noting that your autonomy in selecting your team may be limited, especially for new managers. At many large organizations, hiring is overseen by a dedicated recruiting team that creates a job description, posts the job where others can find it, interviews candidates, makes offers, and even handles a big part of onboarding. As a first-time manager, you may also find that your boss directs much of the hiring process. That's ok. You are not expected to do it all on your own, but it's helpful to understand how it

DOI: 10.1201/9781003562160-5

works. At a minimum, make sure you're interviewing candidates. After all, if you don't get along with them during the interview or see the skill fit, it will be difficult to trust them later when you need to work together.

The recruiting and hiring process can be broken down into just a few high-level steps: identify a need, craft a job description, recruit for the role, evaluate candidates, and make an offer. Let's take each of these in order.

IDENTIFY THE NEED

Before you can hire someone, you need to identify a need that will justify the time and expense that goes into this process. Sometimes the justification is simple. If your star database administrator resigns and their work is critical to your success, it's pretty easy to make a case to replace them. Similarly, if your company is growing quickly and you've been tasked with a major new initiative, it's not hard to justify bringing on additional people to complete the project.

At other times, it can be extremely difficult to hire new people. I've worked in places with hiring freezes where the Chief Operating Officer (COO) had to approve every new role. The scrutiny each request received caused many managers to abandon the idea of hiring altogether. Other scenarios where it can be difficult to hire include working in the non-profit sector, where budgets are always constrained, working at a company struggling financially, or working on a project that isn't seen as strategically important. It's possible to hire in these situations, but you will have to work harder.

Support your request with hard data. If you don't have data, go find some. You can show that the number of projects has increased by X% over the last six months, that you've onboarded Y new customers, or that you've expanded your support hours.

It's always nice to be in a position to talk about new headcounts in terms of growth, as everyone likes a happy conversation. "If we add three more software engineers, we can ship code faster and iterate on these new features that marketing has been asking for." Of course, sometimes you need to hire to avoid bad outcomes instead. "Our defect rate has been increasing, and every time we test a new feature, we find more bugs. We're unlikely to hit our release schedule if we don't bring in some help."

This is a perfectly acceptable reason to hire additional people; just be sure that you've explored all other possibilities before you have this conversation. Review your processes, code review, testing procedures, planning, etc., because your boss is sure to ask about all of them. Also, make sure your work intake process or project intake governance is working correctly. You can't fix prioritization problems by hiring more. This is something that should be addressed with your leadership team. Carefully prioritizing what you take on and when is a big part of a manager's role. Don't accept a new project if you don't have the staff to get it done.

CRAFT THE JOB DESCRIPTION

Typically, before hiring someone, you need to post the job somewhere to attract candidates. Some positions get filled via referrals and word of mouth, but most require a posting. This posting begins with a job description. Start by thinking critically about the work that needs to get done. Remember that you don't always need to replace a vacant position with the same kind of resource. If you have a database administrator who quit, but you have three others who can handle the work, you might be better served by bringing on an analytics SME or a data engineer. If you have a Java Developer quit, think about how much Java development your team needs. Do you need a Python dev instead? Or an analyst instead of a developer?

Once you've determined the work your team needs to get done, start thinking about the skill set a new person will need to succeed on your team. Your Java developer needs to know Java, but do they also need Agile experience? Do they need experience working with a globally distributed team? How much industry expertise do you want? If you work in insurance, and they spent a career working in consumer packaged goods, will that matter?

One key to drafting effective requirements is to think about the outcomes this person will be responsible for. If they will single-handedly maintain your server environment, you're going to need someone who's done that work before. You can't afford a junior SysAdmin. If someone will be one of 20 developers, maybe a junior resource is fine. Create a list of these outcomes and then fill in other requirements around them.

Write down everything you can think of. This is just a brainstorming exercise when you've got a list, run it by a few team members to get their input. Be upfront and candid about what role you're hiring for because everyone on your team will have their own ideas about what you need. "I've decided to hire a new DevOps Engineer with whom you'll work closely. I've brainstormed a list of skills and attributes I think the successful candidate needs, and I'd like your feedback." By tapping into your team's collective experience and wisdom, you will almost certainly come up with some items you didn't think of. Gather feedback on skills, but don't feel obligated to debate the role.

As you're writing the job description, pay attention to requirements that are not actually requirements. IT is notorious for requiring certifications, college degrees, and years of experience that are not truly necessary. There's a viral example from Sebastian Ramirez, who saw an ad for a job requiring four or more years of experience in FastAPI. He couldn't apply for the role because he *created* FastAPI only 18 months prior. No one could have four years of experience.[2]

While this is an egregious example, it happens all the time. A common requirement is "BS in Computer Science, Software Engineering or related field required." Ask yourself, "What if I got a resume from someone who built two start-ups and was a senior dev at Google for five years but didn't go to college?" If you would still want to interview that person, then a college degree is probably not a requirement. Throw it in the preferred section instead. I call this the "What If" game. Many organizations erect too many requirements for job postings. This discourages otherwise qualified candidates. These same companies complain about an inability to find qualified people. Too many requirements can also hamper diversity efforts.

Keep your requirements concise and your job descriptions tight. Your best candidates don't want to wade through line after line of bogus requirements. The worst outcome you'll get is too many resumes. That's certainly better than the alternative.

Once your boss agrees on your hiring need, you should quickly create a job description and work with HR to get it posted. "Quickly" may vary by organization, but keep the process moving. I've seen too many times when someone got a role approved, but conditions changed before the role was filled and the job was pulled. Don't risk this. Move quickly.

FINDING CANDIDATES

You've got an open role and the job description to go with it. Now comes the hard part. You need to get the position in front of enough people to generate qualified applicants. There are a number of ways to go about doing this. You should absolutely utilize more than one.

The most straightforward and obvious is to get the job on your organization's website. I assume HR will handle this for you, but don't let it slip through the cracks. People interested in working at your company enough to check the job board have some built-in advantages. For one, you don't need to sell them on it being a good place to work. They wouldn't be stalking the website if they did not already want to work there. Bear in mind this can be a double-edged sword. When I was working in higher education, many people wanted to work at my university because we offered free tuition for their children. This led to lots of unqualified applicants. You'll need to dig through some resumes, so let HR help screen out the completely unqualified people.

Another obvious way to get your job out there is to post it to your LinkedIn Profile. If you've been building a network in your industry—and you should—you likely have many connections who might be interested in the role. Furthermore, when your network interacts with the posting by liking or commenting, their network also gets visibility. Most jobs I've posted on LinkedIn got several thousand views in the first week. The easiest way is to post a link to the job posting from your organization's website. Encourage your coworkers to "repost" your post to increase visibility.

You can also use larger job boards like Indeed or Monster.com. This is an excellent way for thousands of people to see your role and ensure you get the broadest possible reach. But this approach comes with some tradeoffs.

First, posting a job on these sites often costs money. Your HR department may already have a contract and may do this as a standard part of job postings. Be sure to check with them.

The other downside is that when tens of thousands of people see your role, you will get many unqualified applicants who take a "spray and pray" approach to finding a job. If you don't have a good HR partner filtering through resumes, you'll be buried in applicants and waste a lot of time. Make sure you can handle the deluge of applicants.

If your industry has a specific job board, that's a great place to post the role. For instance, I know of job boards dedicated to higher education, engineering, and hospitality roles.[3] There is a good chance there's a job board dedicated to your industry.

The last option is to work with a dedicated recruiter. Larger companies may have recruiters in-house, but you can also contract with an external recruiter (often called a headhunter) who will work through their network to find qualified candidates for your role. There are plenty of resources on effectively utilizing a recruiter, so I will not go into too much detail here. However, it's an avenue worth pursuing for specialized, hard-to-fill roles.

There are two types of recruiters—retained and contingent. Retained recruiters get hired like any other consultant. You agree on a fee for the search, and they find you a candidate. These recruiters are generally geared toward executive job searches, as they tend to be pretty expensive. Contingent recruiters only get paid if they place a candidate. Generally, the fee is between 10% and 30% of the first year's salary and bonus. This isn't a cheap option, but if you're struggling to find a suitable candidate or are too busy to weed through resumes, this can be an excellent avenue to pursue. Recruiters can be especially helpful if you need to fill multiple roles quickly or if you need specialized, hard-to-find skills.

You aim to get your job in front of as many qualified candidates as possible to increase your chances of finding a perfect fit. Work with your HR department and talk to your peers. You aren't the first manager to hire. Find out what's worked for your company in the past—there's no value in reinventing the wheel.

RESUME REVIEW

If you did the right work in crafting the job description, you already have a prioritized list of requirements and nice-to-haves for this role. Start by going through all the resumes. Start with a quick scan of every resume. This should only take around 90 seconds each. This is a filtering mechanism to discard the candidates who are clearly not qualified. Are you hiring a network engineer but seeing a resume for a carpenter with no relevant skills? You can move it to the "no" pile and move on (yes, this is a real example from my experience). You don't need to dig deep at this step to eliminate roughly half the resumes you're looking at. I'll usually have HR notify these people that they are no longer in the running. I don't want to leave candidates in limbo when they have no hope of getting the role. Sometimes HR will do this initial screen. If you're working with a recruiter, they will certainly do this for you.

Then take a second look at those resumes not yet discarded. This is when you'll start to dig a little deeper. It's vital in this step to pay attention to the details. If a candidate lists Java in their skills section, do you see a role and associated accomplishments demonstrating Java expertise? Have they articulated their position on the team and the outcomes they achieved? Can you see solid career progression that leads them to where they are today? At this stage, I typically sort the candidates into the "This person looks like an excellent option" pile and the "probably not, but let's not completely rule them out yet" pile.

I then take yet another pass through the pile I like and begin looking for those candidates who stand out. Here I'm looking for exceptional accomplishments, experience at companies with a good track record for turning out the skills I need, and, in some cases, even the candidate's educational background. I also pay attention to location if this will be an on-site role. Some candidates are willing to relocate, but it reduces friction in the negotiation and hiring if the candidate is already within commuting distance of your workplace. I try to narrow down my top 3–5 choices from this list.

If there is no clear subset of front-runners, I'll also forward the resumes to my team for feedback. Since your team will work closely with the person you hire, it's a good idea to involve them as much as possible. In the next section, we'll talk more about how to get them involved in interviews and how to gather their feedback, but it never hurts to get extra sets of eyes on resumes.

INTERVIEWS

Once you narrow down the candidates to the small group you want to interview, work with HR to schedule the interviews. Interviewing candidates is the single most important part of hiring.

Today, most first-round interviews are scheduled via video conference using a tool like Zoom or Microsoft Teams. HR will conduct the first round of interviews in some organizations but use these for informational purposes only. Do not let HR disqualify a candidate until you've had a chance to meet them. You've done a lot of work to narrow down the pool. Trust your process.

Before interviewing candidates, you should have a good grasp of their resumes and a set of questions you want each candidate to answer. I don't like reading off a list during the interview as I think it can make the process stilted and awkward, but I keep a checklist of questions. I refer to it during the interview to keep on track. I try to craft that list so that the questions will take approximately half the time allotted for the interview. This leaves time upfront for introductions and time at the end so the candidates can ask any questions they have.

I also share this list of questions with my team before interviews begin and ask them to provide feedback. They often think of questions I failed to consider. If your team has reviewed the resumes and has a chance to give input on the questions, you're well on your way to creating alignment around the hiring process and increasing your chances of a good outcome.

During the interview, you need to manage your time carefully. Some candidates, especially when nervous, will become very talkative. Encourage these candidates to answer the questions succinctly. If they ramble too long, interrupt them to move on to the next question.

One approach for candidates during an interview is the STAR method.[4] This is a great way to structure answers during a behavioral interview. Not every candidate knows or uses the STAR method. If you find a candidate rambling too long or, conversely, not adequately answering your questions, it's a good idea to suggest it. STAR stands for:

- **Situation:** The candidate describes the background or context of a specific situation they faced in the past.
- **Task:** The candidate explains what they needed to accomplish or what goal they were trying to achieve in that situation.
- **Action:** The candidate describes their actions to address the situation and accomplish the task.
- **Result:** The candidate explains the outcome of their actions and the impact they had on the situation and task.

An exchange like this should take no more than a few minutes. From it, you'll get a good idea of the candidate's knowledge of the systems they use, their thought process when faced with a challenge, and their ability to communicate clearly. That's a lot of value for a three-minute answer.

There's a balance and art to conducting good interviews. Make sure you leave each one with a good sense of the candidate and their potential fit for your role, but don't worry about being perfect.

INCLUDE YOUR TEAM

I love to include my team in interviews. They need to work with the new hire day to day, so it's critical we select someone they can work with. They're also closer to the work and can offer a different perspective. Bring the 1–2 team members who will work most closely with this person. Meet with those people ahead of time to ensure everyone has reviewed the resume. It's easy to tell when you're in an interview with someone who has not prepared, and it can turn off candidates. Make sure your team is as well-prepared as you are. The second reason to meet ahead of time is to plan how you will approach the interview.

Avoid overly large group interviews. Don't bring your entire team. No candidate likes to interview with ten people on the other side of the table. The more people who need to ask questions, the less chance each will have for follow-up. Interviews with too many people often result in an awkward cadence where everyone fires questions at the candidate. It makes it hard to have any real back and forth, ask follow-up questions, or seek clarification when an answer is ambiguous. It begins to look like a press conference. Worse, the nine people who aren't speaking often lose focus and start checking their phones.

Since this is your interview, you should be the primary questioner. Go through your interview topic by topic. Your team can ask follow-up questions if they need clarification. Before moving on to a new topic, check in with your team to see if they have any additional questions. This way, you'll keep the interview on track and assess what kind of rapport you develop with the candidate.

Immediately after the interview, pull your team back together to debrief. Compare notes and document what each of you liked and disliked about the candidate. Don't let your team vote on whether to move forward or make an offer to a candidate. That's your decision alone. You should listen carefully to your team's feedback and ensure you didn't miss a red flag or selling point during the interview. However, do not delegate the responsibility to make the ultimate decision. Everyone gets a voice, but not everyone gets a vote. You should wrap up this debrief by asking your team to email you their impressions of the candidate and add these notes to your documentation.

LEGAL AND ETHICAL CONSIDERATIONS

As a new manager, knowing the legal and ethical obligations accompanying the process is important. This is an area where HR can be helpful to you. But you should get familiar with these obligations before you start hiring.

Many federal, state, and local laws related to discrimination govern the hiring process, including the Civil Rights Act, the Americans with Disabilities Act, and the Age Discrimination in Employment Act. You do not need to become an expert, but understanding the basics can help you avoid landing in hot water later. Specifically, it's a good idea to understand protected classes, which include race, ethnicity, gender, religion, age, national origin, sexual orientation, and disability, among others.

When you develop the job description, ensure the requirements and qualifications are directly related. Starting with a solid job description, you can establish evaluation criteria for the candidates. By using consistent evaluation criteria to review resumes and a consistent set of questions during the interviews, you can ensure the process is fair for everyone.

Avoid asking questions that are irrelevant to the work, especially those that may be prohibited by law. It's generally a bad idea to ask candidates questions about their age (this can include indirect questions about age such as "What year did you graduate?"), their religion, or their family status. While asking, in and of itself, may not be illegal (though in some jurisdictions it is), you can open yourself up to a discrimination suit later on. Plus, these questions are rarely relevant to the job at hand.

Finally, keep good records, including job descriptions, copies of the postings, resumes, interview notes, and candidate evaluations. Keeping accurate and comprehensive documentation during the hiring process can help you demonstrate that the process was fair, consistent, and non-discriminatory.

MAKE AN OFFER

Once you've narrowed the resumes, conducted interviews, and assessed each candidate, it's time to move forward with an offer. Given that you are a new manager and this may be your first time hiring someone, meet with your boss to review the offer you intend to make. You want to confirm it's within budget and allow your boss to meet the candidate first if they choose to do so. You don't want to hire someone your boss is going to hate.

Every organization will have a different culture about extending offers. In some companies, the hiring manager will call the candidate directly and negotiate. In others, HR will negotiate on behalf of the company within the parameters given by the hiring manager. There are benefits to each approach. When you make the call, you benefit from:

- Building a relationship with the soon-to-be employee as early as possible. Hopefully, your new hire is excited about the offer, so it's nice to be the one to share the good news.
- You are closer to the budget and other details and can be better positioned to negotiate quickly to close a deal. You won't need to play phone tag with HR to work out the final salary, signing bonus, start date, etc.
- You can answer any last-minute questions the candidate has. Some candidates will hold questions until after they get an offer for fear of screwing up the interview process. Something like the dress code or what time the team starts their day might be "trivial" during the interview but important before a candidate starts.

Allowing HR to negotiate on behalf of the company also has benefits:

- HR is likely more experienced in extending offers and less likely to make mistakes.
- HR may be more familiar with company-wide policies such as vacation time, test or probation periods, health care benefits, etc.

Allowing HR to negotiate creates some breathing room in the process. Perhaps you make an offer, and the candidate asks for 20% more than you hoped to pay. HR will need to check with you and call the candidate back. This allows you the time and space to consider if this candidate is worth a higher offer.

There is no right or wrong method here, and you'll be well served to follow the existing practice at your organization. As you grow in your career and if you're ever in the position to hire more senior employees, you'll be better off making the offer yourself. A personal touch can help land a candidate who is weighing competing offers. But at this stage, I would say just go with the flow. If you are uncomfortable making the offer, don't be afraid to ask for help. HR can either make it for you or coach you through the process.

On the flip side, I urge you to have HR notify the candidates who were not hired. As discussed in the sections on ethics and the law, all kinds of pitfalls are possible, and HR is better equipped to handle those. You want to make sure you don't say anything that could be misconstrued as biased or discriminatory. Avoid any of these issues and let HR make those calls. Plus, you never know when you might someday look to hire the same candidate for a different role. Let HR be the bad guy.

HR'S ROLE

While I recommend delegating the task of notifying the people you will not be hiring, recognize that you own the hiring process. The specific roles and responsibilities may vary depending on the size and structure of the organization, but you own the outcome.

HR can be very helpful in the process and likely has far more experience interviewing candidates than you, so it's important to partner with them. They can help create job descriptions, post ads, review resumes, screen candidates, and conduct background checks. They can also guide you on legal and ethical issues related to hiring, including discrimination, compensation, and benefits. And, as previously mentioned, you can let them play the bad cop.

But don't let HR dictate who you hire. I once got a call from HR telling me I wasn't allowed to hire a candidate because they "had a very concerning social media presence." I was caught off guard. This person interviewed very well, had a stellar resume, and checked all the boxes I was seeking for this role. Their references were excellent as well. When I probed deeper with HR, it turned out they were very concerned because of a seven-year-old Facebook photo of this person doing a keg stand. I don't condone binge-drinking and irresponsible behavior, but seven years ago, the candidate was in college. I'm happy I graduated before everyone started carrying a camera in their pocket with a direct link to social media!

I talked HR off the ledge, and the candidate agreed to remove this photo from Facebook. This person turned into one of my best hires. They worked for me for five years, during which time they were promoted twice.

I don't fault HR. They are responsible for protecting the company from risk, and that's a difficult job. However, they are not accountable for my goals, and one of my goals was to field the best team possible. In many cases, HR and hiring managers work together to ensure the hiring process is efficient, effective, and compliant with legal and ethical standards. Partner closely with HR, but don't let them own the process.

NOTES

1 Wei, W. (2011, January 28). *Tony Hsieh: Bad hires have cost Zappos over $100 million*. Business Insider. https://www.businessinsider.com/tony-hsieh-making-the-right-hires-2010-10.
2 *X.com*. (n.d.). X (Formerly Twitter). https://twitter.com/tiangolo/status/1281946592459853830?lang=en.
3 Hospitality Jobs at https://www.hotelleriejobs.com/en.
4 *Using the STAR method for your next behavioral interview (worksheet included)*. (2023, August 30). Career Advising & Professional Development | MIT. https://capd.mit.edu/resources/the-star-method-for-behavioral-interviews/.

RECOMMENDED ADDITIONAL READING

Miller, M. (2011). *The Secret of Teams: What Great Teams Know and Do*. Berrett-Koehler Publishers.
Nelson, D. (2019). *Talk to Me: How to Ask Better Questions, Get Better Answers, and Interview Anyone Like a Pro*. HarperCollins.
Smart, G., & Street, R. (2008). *Who: The A Method for Hiring*. Ballantine Books.

Chapter 4

Onboarding

Because your employee is new, these first impressions set the tone for their entire experience. Little problems during onboarding can appear more significant and calcify in the employee's mind. Up to 20% of turnover happens in the first 45 days of employment,[1] and 40–60% of new hires fail in the first 18 months. Bad onboarding is to blame. Conversely, a strong onboarding experience can boost retention by 82% and improve performance by 70%.[2]

Onboarding starts before your employee joins the company. As part of your offer package, you and the candidate will have agreed on a start date. Reach out to your new hire before their first day. A quick text or email to reiterate how excited you are and to see if they have any questions about what to expect on day one can help put them at ease. Remember, starting a new job is stressful.

The new employee needs to know where to go to get questions answered and how to manage all the logistical details—how do they submit a time card? Are there different time codes for various projects? Where should they obtain an ID and parking pass? These may seem like minor details, but if a new employee gets stuck on them, they cannot focus on the work you hired them to do.

Employees may start by attending a company-wide training and orientation. At large firms, this can last up to a couple of weeks and may be held off-site where all new employees are together (the cohort model). If this is the case for your organization, make sure to reach out to your new hire via phone or email during this time and welcome them to the team one more time. Also, make sure you have a plan for when they return from training.

If your organization does not have a centralized, formal orientation, ensure you're prepared for their first day. Properly onboarding a new hire can make or break that employee's experience. Getting off to a good start and feeling supported by the surrounding team will help a new person get up to speed faster, have higher engagement and job satisfaction, and make them feel welcome. Getting this process wrong or failing to onboard at all can undo all your hard work in recruiting, interviewing, and hiring.

DOI: 10.1201/9781003562160-6

DAY ONE

If your location allows, it's best to meet in person on the first day, even for primarily remote jobs. At a minimum, your new employee must pick up their computer and other required equipment. Do your best to meet them at the office. A personal touch goes a long way and can help speed up the relationship-building process. If you can't get together in person, at least schedule a video call for shortly after the start of the workday. Send the invite to the employee's corporate and personal email. If they have trouble logging into the systems on their first day, you can still connect.

While you should plan out the first 5, 10, and 30 days of onboarding activities for your new employee, be careful not to overwhelm them on day one. Use the initial meeting to get to know them before you bombard them with project details, milestones, and deliverables. This is the first interaction where you will be on the same team—the interview and negotiation can sometimes feel adversarial. Lay out the broad strokes of your team's work, highlight some key priorities, and ensure they have your team meeting invites on their calendars. This is also an excellent time to establish a cadence for regular check-ins.

Regarding check-ins, while I recommend weekly or bi-weekly 1-1s with the people on your team, you'll need to get together more often with a new employee. Depending on their experience level, plan to meet daily for the first week or two. Especially if your new hire is straight out of college or this is their first professional experience, you don't want them to sit too long with questions. More experienced employees will be OK with meeting less frequently, but I would still plan for 2–3 check-ins in the first couple of weeks. These can be as short as 15–30 minutes, but it's good to reserve the time so they know they have an opportunity to get help.

MAKE INTRODUCTIONS

Don't forget to introduce your new hire around the office (or around the virtual office). Hopefully, they met one or two of your team members during the interview but introduce them again. Interviews are stressful, so the new hire may not remember names or roles. You should ensure the key people on your team and those with whom the new hire will be working most closely have blocked some time on the first day for these meetings. 1-1s are usually best, but small group meetings are fine, too, if that's what the schedule allows.

These should be informal meetings. You want the team members to get to know one another as people as well as professionals. Each team member might spend a few minutes talking about themselves, and then spend a little time going over their role and responsibilities. Hopefully, each meeting will end with an offer to answer additional questions when they come up.

You should also take your new hire around to meet people from other teams. Since they don't know anyone, helping them put faces with names and roles means they will better understand the overall business and how their work fits in. A good practice is to introduce them to at least one other person from all the teams who also report to your manager. So if your manager has five managers reporting to him, introduce your new hire to someone from each of those five teams. Ideally, you would introduce them to your peers, but that may be harder, depending on schedules. It may have to wait until later in their first or second week.

If your organization is primarily remote, think about blocking an hour for short, speed-dating type video calls. Get each of your peers to set aside 10 minutes to hop on and off the same video conference. This is enough time for a quick introduction and to help your new hires feel like they are becoming part of the team.

If your new hire is working from an office, introduce them to the people who sit near them, regardless of team structure. We all like to know the people around us. Plus, when the copier runs out of paper, or they need to figure out the coffee machine, it's far easier to ask the person two desks over.

LOGISTICS

Dedicate someone to oversee logistics for your new hire's first day. If you have an office manager or a shared executive assistant, this person can take responsibility for these tasks. It's not important *who* takes charge, just that someone does. Don't leave these things until the last minute, and don't assume they will magically happen:

- Badge/ID—most organizations have a process to provide an employee ID. Depending on where you work, these may be more or less critical. Government agencies, hospitals, and schools often require employees to wear their badge visibly while on site. Even if your workplace is more relaxed, getting a badge can help your new employee feel "official."
- Parking Permit/Pass—if your employer provides a dedicated parking area, ensure your new employee gets a parking pass. If you work in a large city, taking public transportation might be more common, so tell the new hire about any benefits or programs to defray the cost.
- Computer Equipment—make sure someone is coordinating to have a computer ready on day one. This means a laptop is ordered, imaged, and waiting at their workspace (or shipped to their house if they will be remote). There are few things worse than stepping into a new role and coming into an empty desk.
- Swag—if your company offers things like shirts, jackets, stickers, or water bottles, make sure to have some waiting for your new employee. This helps create a welcoming atmosphere.

- Paperwork—HR will likely take care of the paperwork, but depending on your organization, you may also need to help out here. Spend time on day one to ensure your new employee is squared away with tax forms, benefit elections, and any other necessary paperwork. Note: be careful not to give tax, legal, or financial advice.
- Tour—whether you work at a multi-building campus, a massive office tower, or a tiny office, give your new hire a tour. Show them where the bathrooms are, how to use the copier and the coffee machine, and make sure they can get from their desk to your desk if they have questions.
- Virtual Tour—navigating your intranet can be overwhelming for new hires. They likely don't want to bother someone every time they have a question, and you want to get them self-sufficient as soon as possible, so show them how to access your knowledge base. Do you have a git repo? Make sure they have access and know how to find it. Do you use confluence for documentation and sprint management? Step them through the structure. Depending on the size of your organization, you might even create documentation about how to navigate your documentation. A 2–3 page document with links to critical systems, files, and websites can help accelerate your employee's learning process. Also, make sure they have access to the systems they'll need.

BACKUP PLAN

Hopefully, you've planned an exciting, informative first day. But what happens if you end up sick that day or some other emergency comes up, and you can't be in the office? Have a backup plan.

I may be overly cautious, but I've lived this experience. In 2022, I was scheduled to meet a new employee at 9 am to welcome them to the team. I'd gathered the swag, confirmed their computer was ready, and laid out a full day of meetings, tours, and introductions. Then I woke up feeling awful and tested positive for COVID-19. The best-laid plans, right? Luckily, in this instance, I had a trusted lieutenant who ably stepped in for me. Everything went seamlessly. I felt well enough the next day to get on a video call with the new hires and check in on their progress while I finished my time in quarantine.

I also recognize that I was extremely fortunate in this instance. You won't always be lucky enough to have a deputy who can do your job better than you can. But you should have a contingency plan. It doesn't need to be elaborate, but make sure someone can step in for you if you can't make it. This could be a person on your team (like it was for) or one of your peers.

Because the first day is mainly about culture, introductions, and the big picture, your stand-in does not need to know the details of your team's work. Instead, they should know where your team fits into the bigger picture and know the key players. Your backup plan is all about having a friendly face who knows their way around the organization. It doesn't need to be perfect; just make sure your new hire won't be sitting in the parking lot trying to find someone to let them into the building.

DAY TWO AND BEYOND

After making a good first impression and ensuring your new employee starts on the right foot, you must build on that momentum. A check-in meeting first thing the following morning will allow them to ask any questions they thought of overnight and allow you to share anything you forgot or held back on day one. You can now settle into your everyday working mode, whether in-person, remote, or hybrid.

Keep the same focus on communication and collaboration, but add a touch of patience. No matter how good your hire is, it will take them time to get up to speed. They are busy meeting new people, learning new systems, and generally trying to find their way around. We often refer to this as "drinking from the fire hose." This phase may last only a week or two for someone coming from a similar role at another company, but for a new graduate or someone transitioning from a different industry, it could last a couple of months or longer. Hopefully, you will see steady improvement but don't expect miracles.

Now is an excellent time to start setting expectations and norms. Setting clear expectations from the beginning will help you both. An easy place to start is with expected behaviors. Cover weekly status reports and explain where they can find the template. Are there key relationships this person needs to build? Now is the time to lay them out. Explain what criteria you will use to judge their success at the end of the performance review period. This is good practice for all your employees, but with a new hire, you can establish these before they form any bad habits.

Your goal during this onboarding phase is to get your new hire to a place where they are a productive team member. The quicker they can get up to speed, the faster they provide relief to your existing team, and the quicker you can get back to the other parts of your job. Invest some time early in the process. It will pay dividends later on.

NOTES

1 *An onboarding checklist for success* | *O.C. Tanner*. (n.d.). https://www.octanner.com/insights/articles/2018/9/14/an_onboarding_checkl.html.

2 Laurano, M. (2015). *The true cost of a bad hire*. Brandon Hall Group. https://web.archive.org/web/20240706220857/https://b2b-assets.glassdoor.com/the-true-cost-of-a-bad-hire.pdf.

RECOMMENDED ADDITIONAL READING

Buckingham, M., & Coffman, C. (1999). *First, Break All The Rules: What the Worlds Greatest Managers Do Differently*. Simon and Schuster.

Hsieh, T. (2010). *Delivering Happiness: A Path to Profits, Passion, and Purpose.* Hachette UK.

Watkins, M. D. (2013). *The First 90 Days, Updated and Expanded: Proven Strategies for Getting Up to Speed Faster and Smarter*. Harvard Business Review Press.

Chapter 5

Retention

During and after the COVID-19 pandemic, employees resigned in unprecedented numbers. This was partly driven by accelerated hiring at many technology companies that grew during the pandemic. Companies like Google, Meta (Facebook), Microsoft, and Netflix saw a rise in earnings during 2020–2022 and used that growth to fund new hiring. Employees were lured by remote work and higher salaries, especially when so many businesses were cutting pay and hours. But the great resignation was more than a chance to earn more money. The pandemic caused employees everywhere to reevaluate what was important to them. Companies that adapted to the changing expectations of their people thrived, while those that tried to pretend it was still 2019 struggled to attract and retain the people they needed.

Immense time, effort, and expense go into hiring and onboarding new employees. Now that your new hire is on board, ensure they stick around. According to Gallup, employee turnover costs between 50% and 200% of the employee's annual pay. Retention is a growing problem, especially in information technology (IT) jobs. Demand for highly skilled IT workers is unlikely to wane anytime soon.

Not everyone will love their job. People often look for new roles to earn more money, take on more responsibility, and grow their careers in ways they don't think they can at their current company. Your goal is not to prevent everyone from leaving. That's not realistic. Some level of turnover is healthy. Jack Welch, once named the Manager of the Century by Fortune,[1] used to cull the bottom 10% of his workforce. Gallup has also said that 10% is a healthy rate of turnover. Some turnover benefits a company, especially if poor performers leave. It provides an opportunity to hire more skilled workers. It's an excellent way to bring in people with a fresh perspective on your issues. Too much turnover, however, means your team is never fully staffed. You are stuck in a constant recruiting cycle, taking you away from other work you need to do.

DOI: 10.1201/9781003562160-7

WHY DO EMPLOYEES LEAVE

There's an adage that "Employees don't leave bad jobs. They leave bad bosses." This is true, but it's only part of the equation. If you're a terrible manager, you can expect to have a difficult time keeping people on your team. They'll look outside the company, or they'll look to transfer internally, but they won't stick around if they have other options. What's worse is that your best employees will be the first to leave because they'll have the easiest time finding something else. The lesson is clear: be a good boss.

However, employees also leave because they don't feel they're making enough money or are no longer challenged in their current roles. They can leave because the commute is too long or because they do not like their coworkers. There are many reasons someone will decide they don't want a job and thus look for something new.

Employees sometimes leave for reasons only tangentially related to their current jobs. Harvard Business Review found that employees are 12% more likely to look for work around a birthday and 16% more likely to job hunt after a class reunion.[2] These milestone events create an opportunity to reevaluate where they are in life and reassess what they want.

With all these potential reasons for turnover and an ongoing battle for the best talent, how can you keep your team? There are five simple behaviors you can employ. Simple doesn't mean easy, but no one said this job would be easy.

- **Be Connected:** The most significant thing you can do to reduce turnover and boost retention on your team is to stay connected to your employees as individuals.
- **Be Empathetic:** Empathetic leadership focuses on identifying with others and understanding their points of view. Empathy and accountability are not mutually exclusive. You must ensure your people hit their targets, but you can do so while being empathetic.
- **Be Flexible:** Whether you work 100 hours per week at a new startup or 35 hours per week at your local college, having some control over your schedule, tasks, and mode of work will lead to dramatically higher job satisfaction and retention rates.
- **Be A Coach:** Being a coach means providing more support and guidance to your team and less direction. Employees prefer this type of management and are more productive when working for this type of manager. Plus, it will make your life easier.
- **Be Inspiring:** You don't need to be Winston Churchill or Barack Obama to inspire your team. Inspiration isn't big speeches. It's finding how much to push your team, taking opportunities to praise them, and placing their work in the proper context.

We'll explore these five items in more detail in the following sections.

BE CONNECTED

Human beings are social creatures. We want connection—to feel a part of something. This extends to our lives at work as much as our family and social lives. The biggest thing you can do to reduce turnover on your team is to stay connected to your employees. Team cohesion is important, but don't lose sight of the fact that your team is a collection of individual people, each with their fears, desires, and quirks.

Get to know the people on your team, including your new hires. Losing ourselves to urgent tasks, important meetings, and fast-approaching deadlines is easy. Dedicate focused time to checking in on your team. Learn their birthdays, the names of their spouses, kids, and pets, and what they do for fun when they aren't working. What defines them as people? Most of us don't define ourselves based solely on our jobs. Create a culture of trust and make an effort to actively listen and care about what they tell you. I promise just about everyone will open up.

Keep a finger on the pulse of their job satisfaction. Is everyone on your team engaged, or is someone just going through the motions? Understand the rhythm of your team. Is someone who's always on time suddenly coming in late? Check-in. Make sure everything is ok. One potential tip-off that someone is interviewing elsewhere is if they disappear for a couple of hours in the middle of the day a few times over a few weeks. This might be a good time to check how that employee is doing. Maybe they're unhappy with their job or having an issue outside of work, but in either event, show you care. If they're unhappy at work, discuss what changes you might make. If it's a problem at home, offer some added flexibility. The golden rule is golden for a reason.

Another way to stay connected is to have regular, honest conversations about career paths. These conversations should be a standing agenda item during your 1-1s. Take the time to understand what they want out of their current role and what role they imagine next for themselves. You'll find that some people are perfectly happy and don't want to climb the career ladder. Others are eager for more responsibility and that next promotion. And some don't know what they want. That's ok too.

When you know where each individual is, you can work with them to cocreate career plans. For the employee who is content where they are, ensure they continue receiving interesting assignments. Help protect their time outside of work. For the person who wants to take the next step, lay out a development plan that covers the skills they'll need for promotion. And for team members who aren't sure what they want, try to find varied assignments to expose them to different things. Then schedule regular touchpoints to see how they felt about each one. Careers are as individual as the people who live them. Don't assume one size fits all.

BE EMPATHETIC

Empathy is one of the critical skills you need as a manager. It helps you connect with your staff, peers, boss, and customers. It will make you a better manager. Empathy and accountability are not mutually exclusive. You must ensure your people hit their targets, but you can do so while being compassionate, considerate, and empathetic.

With your staff, this starts by listening to their problems in their own words. When you can, offer solutions. If they are struggling to complete a project, do you have someone else on the team who can spare a few hours a week to help? Or maybe they've been wrestling with the same bug for the last three days and can't make any progress. Paired programming or a second set of eyes might solve this quickly. Employees should proactively speak up, but many won't. Take it upon yourself to ask, listen, and offer suggestions.

Listening to your team's concerns is worthwhile, even when you are powerless to fix them. You can acknowledge their feelings without having a solution. "I can see you're upset. Help me understand why and if we can work together to fix it." Right away, you're "on their side" without committing to anything other than listening. Of course, if you can fix the issue, do so.

But expect some of the complaints to be beyond your ability to solve. Maybe an employee doesn't like a corporate policy. We're seeing a lot of this right now with Return to Office plans. Most IT managers will have very little influence over enterprise-wide HR policies. As a manager, part of your job is to advocate for decisions from above. You may disagree with a Return to Office policy, but once that decision has been made and communicated, you must get on board. It's part of the job.

Amazon has a leadership principle that says: "Have Backbone; Disagree and Commit... *Once a decision is determined, they commit wholly*."[3]

The last part of the principle is key, and this is where the balance between empathy and accountability comes into play. You may have spent the previous week uncomfortably, exhaustively, and tenaciously trying to convince your boss to go a different direction. But once a decision is made, it's your job to see that it gets carried out. While you can – and should – listen to your team's problems, don't make it worse by cosigning their complaints.

If you reinforce their concern by saying, "I know. It's idiotic. I don't understand why we're doing that," you risk hurting morale. Your employees will now feel like "I was right," but they'll feel even more stuck because you can't help them. You also risk your career if word gets back that you've been badmouthing the company's decisions. Instead, let your employee vent, and then search for positives you can pull out of the situation. "I appreciate you sharing your concerns with me. We're a much stronger team when we are open with each other. Here's my perspective on the issue..."

If you're struggling to come up with a way to turn the conversation around, or if you can't articulate support for a leadership decision, take a step back. Turn the focus to long-term growth. Providing some perspective to your team can help any situation. "I know you disagree with this decision. It's important to remember this is one decision in thousands you'll encounter throughout your career. Finding a way to "make it work" even when you disagree is a valuable skill. Having this arrow in your quiver will help later in your career." Your employees may not leave happy, but at least they'll leave with a new perspective.

The final way to be empathetic with your team is to accept their feedback. You should seek their input on projects and the work you collectively accomplish. But, more importantly, be open to feedback about your performance. You work closely with your team, so they have good insight into your performance. Accept this feedback and find ways to act on it. Make sure your team knows that you're open to feedback.

I've managed a few teams that were particularly resistant to "criticizing the boss," so I created anonymous 360 feedback surveys. They took about 15 minutes to set up in a tool like Survey Monkey. Each person on my staff spent less than 20 minutes completing their review. At my next staff meeting, I shared the results and a 30-day plan to address the immediate concerns. About 30 days later, I presented a status report to my team on my progress against that plan. I accomplished two valuable things: I objectively improved as a manager and showed the team that I valued their perspective.

BE FLEXIBLE

No one wants to feel like a drone who punches a clock between 8 am and 5 pm every day, pretending the world outside the office doesn't exist. Whether grinding at a new startup or toiling inside a massive bureaucracy, having some control over your schedule, tasks, and work mode will lead to higher job satisfaction and retention rates.

There are limits to your flexibility. Your company may not allow remote or hybrid work, for instance. However, I encourage you to think creatively about the flexibility you can offer. Consider that small changes can have big impacts on your staff.

If you have an employee with school-age children who needs to handle morning drop-off, you'd be amazed at the stress you can relieve by allowing them to start their day at 9:00 or 9:30 instead of 8:30, like everyone else. Similarly, if they need to be home to take the kids to soccer practice, allowing them to start and end earlier could make their lives easier. The key is to find what works for both of you. They need to get the work done. You need to meet the business needs. But you can be creative in how you make that happen. Minor schedule tweaks might make your employees more productive.

If you work at an organization with more latitude, you could consider more extensive schedule changes. I once worked for a company that had "Core Hours." Everyone had to be at their desk between 10 am and 3 pm

Monday to Friday (with an hour for lunch). Outside of those 5 hours, each team was empowered to create their own schedules. Some people chose to work 6 am to 3 pm. Others came in at 10 am and worked until 7 pm. One person even worked 9 am to 4 pm, left to coach his son's little league team, and then got back online after the kids were asleep to finish his day. This company did a great job balancing collaboration during core hours with time for focused work the rest of the day.

Flexibility extends beyond scheduling. Another way to offer flexibility is to give employees some autonomy in what they work on. Variety is the spice of life, as they say. Find ways to add variety to people's work day. When planning a new project, think about the existing workload of your team and find a way to mix things up a little. Even better, ask your team what they want to work on. Someone may be tired of updating Gantt charts for 25 hours a week and would like to get more hands-on with development work. Perhaps one of your developers wants to use a new library she recently heard about. Can you make some room for her to try it in the next sprint? The business needs to come first, but if you look, you'll find more flexibility than you may have thought.

The key to being flexible is to find what works for the individuals on your team within the constraints required to achieve your goals. For a time, Best Buy, the electronics retailer, rolled out a Results Only Workplace Environment (ROWE).[4] The promise of ROWE was that employees could work wherever and whenever they wanted as long as they delivered results. This is an extreme version of flexibility that's likely beyond the ability of any single manager to implement. Still, if you focus on results rather than inputs, impact instead of hours, and outcomes as opposed to actions, you'll keep your team and boss happy!

BE A COACH

Over the last few decades, there's been a marked shift from a command-and-control management style to one where managers provide more support and guidance but less direction. This coaching-style management is driven, in part, by the growing complexity of IT. It's simply not possible for a manager to be an expert in all aspects of the ever-changing technology landscape. As such, they must focus on setting a direction and delegating responsibility to their team to determine how to achieve the outcomes. The other reason for this shift is that we've learned that employees prefer this type of management and are more productive when working for this type of manager.

Command-and-control management stems from early industrialization, where efficiency and consistency were essential for success. Decisions were made at the top, pushed down through layers of middle management, and workers at the bottom completed the tasks they were assigned by following explicit, detailed instructors. Workers didn't solve problems. When they encountered a problem, they called their boss, who handed down a solution. A command-and-control manager is needed to instruct, monitor, and ensure compliance.

A coaching manager believes that employees are more satisfied and productive when they are empowered, guided, and developed. This coaching style encourages collaborative decision-making. Managers guide their teams to solutions rather than providing directives. Some decisions may still be made at the top, but more authority is delegated to frontline workers, who are encouraged to find creative ways to solve problems. This coaching style promotes a more agile organization.

When working with your team, a shared understanding of your vision and goals forms the foundation to succeed as a coach. A shared vision ensures your team members are all working toward the same future. The vision and the culture you build around it help your employees make the right choices when faced with critical decisions. It helps them work more independently. It gives them a greater sense of ownership. Your team's vision should be based on the organization's overall goals. Put your work in context so your team can see how their efforts influence the company's overall success.

Once you've established how your team's efforts fit into the organization's overall picture, look at your team's strengths and weaknesses. This helps you assign each team member the correct roles to leverage their strengths. You can also plan to address any weaknesses through hiring and upskilling. With these items in place, you can work collaboratively with your team to establish a shared vision. Your vision should encompass the company's goals, your team's abilities, and your shared values. At the end of the process, try to boil the vision down to a concise statement you can document and refer back to on occasion. In short, you need to answer, "Why do we exist?"

That's your framework. With this shared vision, your team should understand their work, anticipate issues, and feel empowered to make decisions. This allows you to focus on guidance, development, and feedback and frees you from the need to micromanage. Try it with your team, and you'll be amazed at how the tone of meetings changes.

BE INSPIRING

Connectedness, empathy, flexibility, and coaching play significant roles in retaining your team, but nothing has as much impact as inspiring them. Inspiration means they wake each morning with a desire to perform well. If you've ever worked on a kick-ass team, you know this feeling. You leap out of bed, ready to take on the world. Think back to that time. You likely had an inspiring manager.

You don't need to be Tony Robbins to inspire your team. It's not about eloquence or grand speeches. It's about finding the right level to push your team and finding the right opportunities to praise them.

If you think about pressure as a bell curve, there's a section to the left of the peak where there isn't enough pressure to motivate your team. This is the boredom zone. Employees in this area have too much free time. They lack challenging problems. This is where you find the stereotypical office drone just going through the motions, watching the clock until they can quit for the day.

There's a portion on the right side of the peak where there's so much pressure your team is liable to crumble. I call this the burnout zone. Here expectations and resources are so misaligned that your team constantly fights fires and misses deadlines. You can endure short stints in this zone, often before big project deadlines. But if you spend too much time here, you'll notice an uptick in turnover and a drop off in performance.

You aim to push enough to keep them in the middle of the bell curve. You need to learn when to dial it up and when to protect your team from burning out (Figure 5.1).

When your team sees that you're challenging them fairly and shielding them when needed, they will rise to the challenge. And when they do, your job is to praise them. Look for opportunities to recognize your team for their excellent work. For big things and small things, recognition goes a long way. A quick call out during a staff meeting, an email with your boss copied, or an announcement at an IT All Hands meeting are great examples of informal praise you can give your team. Some people thrive on positive feedback; you should provide it liberally to get the best from them. Even those who find their inner satisfaction elsewhere and care less about being told "Good job!" will benefit from praise.

Finally, you can help your team find inspiration by reminding them of the impact of their work. There's a famous story, maybe even a true story, of

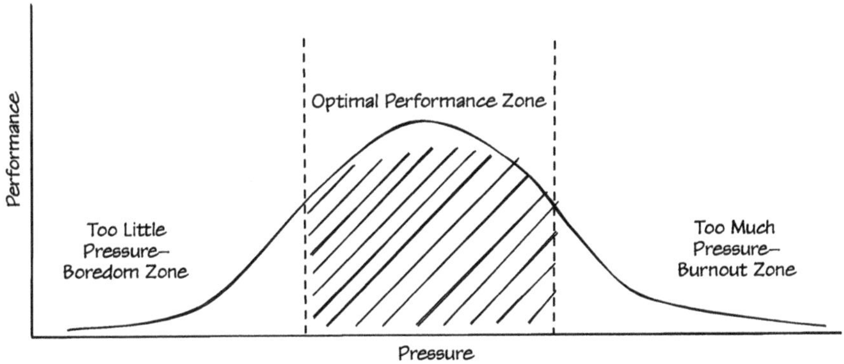

Figure 5.1 Pressure vs. performance.

John F. Kennedy on a visit to NASA during the space program. Seeing a janitor in the hallway, JFK asked him what he did at NASA. The man replied, "I'm helping put a man on the moon." Real or not, this person understood how to connect his work to the mission.

If you work for a mission-driven organization, like a university or a non-profit, it should be easy to see the organization's impact. You need to tie your team's work to the success of that mission. But even for profit-driven companies, there's something you can point to. Work for a large investment bank? Your team is helping to ensure the efficient functioning of the capital markets and providing much-needed funds to American businesses. Pharmaceutical companies are helping to cure diseases and relieve suffering. Airlines, railroads, and automakers help connect people and move critical goods around the country. Find the larger purpose.

If you need help, ask. Your boss expects you to inspire your team, so ask during your next meeting. "I'm trying to find ways to tie my team's work to the company's broader goals, but I'm struggling. Can you suggest some language I could use in my next staff meeting?" By putting everyday tasks and projects in a larger context, you will help your team find meaning in their work.

Inspiration isn't about grand gestures or big speeches. It's about the little things. Apply the right amount of pressure, praise your team when they rise to the challenge, and contextualize their work. Do it consistently, and you might be surprised by the lengths your team will go to succeed.

NOTES

1 *FORTUNE selects Henry Ford BUSINESSMAN OF THE CENTURY.* (1999, November 1). https://web.archive.org/web/20081121120100.http://www.timewarner.com/corp/newsroom/pr/0,20812,667526,00.html.
2 *Why people quit their jobs.* (2016, August 23). Harvard Business Review. https://hbr.org/2016/09/why-people-quit-their-jobs.
3 *Leadership principles.* (n.d.). amazon.jobs. https://www.amazon.jobs/content/en/our-workplace/leadership-principles.
4 Valcour, M. (2014, August 7). *The end of "Results only" at best buy is bad news.* Harvard Business Review. https://hbr.org/2013/03/goodbye-to-flexible-work-at-be.

RECOMMENDED ADDITIONAL READING

Pink, D. H. (2011). *Drive: The Surprising Truth about What Motivates Us.* Penguin.
Sinek, S. (2014). *Leaders Eat Last: Why Some Teams Pull Together and Others Don't.* Penguin.
Stringer, L. (2016). *The Healthy Workplace: How to Improve the Well-Being of Your Employees---and Boost Your Company's Bottom Line.* AMACOM.

Chapter 6

Managing peers

People take many different paths to management. Some join from the outside directly as managers. Others are promoted from within. Some compete to replace a departing employee. Others step into newly created roles. Internal promotions and external hires face different challenges. Those from outside need to learn the business, meet everyone, and figure out the culture. Those who are promoted from within face a different challenge. They know the business, understand the culture, and have relationships with the people. But the nature of those relationships changes when they're promoted. If this describes your new role, read on to learn how to navigate the transition.

An internal job opening can lead to a scenario where you and your peers compete for the same position. Only one person can get the job. If that's you, you might find yourself in the uncomfortable experience of managing people who were your peers just a short while ago. Managing peers presents unique challenges. In the best-case scenario, you have a close relationship with them, and they are genuinely happy you got promoted. They may even think you are the most deserving of the job.

Unfortunately, it doesn't always work out this way. At least one person likely resents that you got the job. They think they are more qualified. They wanted the job. They're convinced they can do the job better than you. Maybe they didn't like you when you worked together, and now they really don't like having to work for you. Employees like this must be managed carefully, as they can undermine your new authority.

Even peers with whom you have a great relationship need attention in your first few weeks as their new boss. These may be your regular happy hour crew, the people you used to vent to about the latest idiocy from senior management, the people you gossiped with, and even some true friends. The new power dynamic can be tricky to manage, leading to awkward interactions as everyone adjusts. Let's look at a few approaches to handle this situation to keep your career on track and your friendships intact.

DOI: 10.1201/9781003562160-8

SET EXPECTATIONS

The key to any successful transition begins by setting the right tone. You need clear communication about the changes and clear expectations for how everyone will work together in the future.

Ideally, your boss or HR will announce that you've been promoted to fill a position. Most companies have a process to do this. However, I've worked for at least one organization that was a fan of stealth promotions. People would take on new roles and titles, but no announcements accompanied the changes. If you work at one of these places, please tell your new team. Avoid an "I'm in charge now" email. Instead, schedule a group meeting or a series of one-on-ones and let your team members know that you've been given a new role. Don't let your team hear about the transition from the rumor mill. And there's always a rumor mill, especially about internal politics and promotions.

There's a great quote from Sheryl Sandberg, former COO of Meta (Facebook). She says, "Once I addressed the elephant, we were able to kick him out of the room."[1] Moving from a peer relationship to a manager/employee relationship will be awkward. There's no way to avoid it. Address the awkwardness head-on. Use your first one-on-one with each employee. Start by saying something like,

> I know it might be awkward now that our relationship is different. I can't pretend nothing will change, but I value you as a colleague. I have some thoughts on how we can work effectively, but I'd like to hear what you're thinking. Do you have any questions, concerns, or issues you'd like to raise?

This recognizes the new dynamic and allows the employee to say what's on their mind. Many people simply want to be heard. They may vent frustration about not getting the job, question how this change will affect their friendship, or raise concerns about their leadership abilities. All of these are normal reactions to a change like this. Hear them out. Use this first meeting to clear the air and get started on the right foot.

If you approach this conversation with an open mind and listen attentively to what the other person has to say, you might learn something. If you know that they applied for the job and were not selected, you can also mention that. "I know you were hoping for this role, and I'm sure you believed you were a strong candidate. I'd love to hear your ideas for improving the department." Invite collaboration. You'll gain an ally and valuable insights in the process.

This conversation also sets the tone for your leadership style. It reassures the other person that you're open to input, don't have all the answers, and value their perspective on the challenges you'll face together. You also demonstrate that you're unafraid to tackle challenging issues head-on. This is a great way to begin building your new manager/employee relationship.

You need to create some boundaries in your new role that likely didn't exist before. It's ok to be friends with the people you work with, and I firmly believe you can be friends with people you manage. But you need to establish some ground rules. You also need to accept that some things have to change. Michael Watkins, author of *The First 90 Days*, put it this way to Harvard Business Review, "You can't continue to have relationships in the way you did before. This is a loss for everybody, but it's part of the deal."[2]

If you have genuinely close friends on your team, pull them aside individually. Enlist their help in the transition. Explain that you need to be professional and focused on the job when you're at work—your friendship takes a backseat at the office. You may have joked around before or discussed upcoming weekend plans. Doing so now that you're the boss can signal to others that you're playing favorites. You must remain objective and impartial at work.

Establishing a "no work" rule when socializing with this person outside of work is also a good idea. When you're not at work, don't discuss work. It can be easy for someone to lobby for a plum assignment or push for a raise when you're sitting around sharing a few beers. Keep yourself out of this position by setting clear boundaries upfront.

You're no longer "one of the guys" (or girls). When your team heads to the weekly happy hour, find an excuse to be elsewhere. This helps establish some distance between you and the team. Remember, these are people to whom you assign work, who you evaluate, determine raises for, award bonuses to, and potentially fire. This also gives the team a chance to bond without you. Anyone who's been to happy hour with their boss knows that, while it can be fun, it's not as relaxing as blowing off steam with your coworkers. Give your team the space to socialize without you. "If you're not feeling a little bit lonely and left out, that can be a sign that you're not distancing yourself enough," says Robert Sutton, Professor of Management Science at Stanford University.[3]

START SLOW TO MOVE QUICKLY

Spend the first few weeks in your new role focused on communication, relationship building, and listening. You will be tempted to fix every problem you see. This temptation intensifies when you've worked on the team for a while, with a strong perspective on where the team should be heading. Resist the urge to make changes too quickly. Unless you've been told explicitly that you must turn around the team swiftly, take some time to get established. Start small. Set up a meeting cadence for your one-on-ones and staff meeting. Explain your expectations around status reporting and communication. Hold a meeting to cocreate new goals with your team. You're looking for quick wins that will avoid stepping on too many toes or damaging existing relationships. Quick wins will help build your authority without alienating your team.

As these quick wins build, so will your momentum. If you're having the elephant-in-the-room conversations and establishing clear ground rules, you can soon move on to more significant, impactful changes. Allow your team some time to adjust and give yourself time to settle in and gather information. You might find that your perspective as a team member differs significantly from your perspective as the team leader.

Navy SEALs have a saying, "Slow is smooth, smooth is fast." Use this mantra as you ramp up. It's about not rushing into the wrong things. It's about the power of thinking strategically and acting deliberately. As you slow down, think beyond your first good idea, and challenge your assumptions, you'll begin to make better decisions. These decisions will compound, ultimately leading to better execution.

Don't rush into decisions that will be painful to undo. The spotlight is brightest when you're new. Your former peers will be watching for every misstep. Balance action with contemplation. You have more time than you think. Use it wisely.

BUILT-IN EDGE

Jumping from team member to team manager means you already know the people on your team. While your relationship with them will change, it's unlikely that their strengths and weaknesses shift because you're now their manager. You can use this to your advantage and theirs. You already know which team members can handle more autonomy and which need additional oversight. Likewise, you can delegate tasks that play to individual strengths. People perform best and find the most satisfaction at work when they work within their area of expertise. You want to challenge them, but make sure they are successful most of the time. Research suggests we grow the most when we're successful 85% of the time.[4] So load them up with tasks they're good at.

You've also worked hard to build trust with your team members. Use this to your advantage as well. Find people you trust and use them to solicit feedback. These people will tell you, honestly, when you've screwed up. They'll push back on your bad ideas. They'll point out when another team member is struggling or unhappy. Solicit their feedback and use it to improve. Using your one-on-ones, let them know you're open to feedback, value their opinion and insight, and want them to help you stay on track.

Your final advantage is that you know the politics of your workplace already. One of the more difficult tasks for someone new to any company is to learn the lay of the land. Who has influence over your boss? Do requests from marketing get more attention than those from the warehouse team? Who are the users that will complain no matter what you do? Use this inside knowledge to build your political base. Win over those demanding customers with some extra attention. Politics might not be the prettiest game in town, but it's real and impacts us all. You can't sit out office politics. Use your insider knowledge to start strong in your new role.

As an insider, you must deal with shifting relationships, lingering bitterness, and extra attention. You can offset these added burdens by capitalizing on your built-in edge to get up to speed more quickly while consolidating your base of support. Don't waste this opportunity.

SOME PEOPLE MAY NEED TO MOVE ON

Even if you do everything right, follow the advice above, and excel as a new manager, some people will not get past the fact that you were promoted instead of them. If they are too bitter to get over it—too bitter to work constructively with you as their boss—you may need to help them move on. Managing those who used to be your peers is incredibly challenging. It doesn't always work out for everyone on the team. There are things you can do to ease the transition, but the other person has to meet you halfway. If they aren't willing to, you're going to have to get rid of them. Don't take it personally. Don't blame yourself. And don't write anyone off too soon.

If the person in question was a rival for your job, they probably have some things to work through. Give it a few months in the new dynamic. Model good behavior to show them that you're willing to help. If they see you helping others and working to lift the entire team, you may yet get them on board with what you're trying to do.

But if, after a few months, you have an employee who seems unwilling to put in the effort to make the new situation work, you need to call them out. Use one of your one-on-one meetings and have a candid, blunt conversation. I would phrase it like this,

> It's clear to me that you're not happy with this new arrangement. Things don't seem to be working out. I'm willing to put in the work to help you succeed here, but I need you to meet me halfway. If you don't want to, I understand. I'm also happy to help you find something else that's a better fit for you.

You can't tolerate a toxic, unhappy, or disengaged employee who isn't pulling their weight. Toxicity spreads like a virus on teams. One disgruntled employee is bad enough, especially if you have a small team already, but that attitude and behavior will rub off on others. A single, poorly performing employee will affect the entire team. One conversation should serve as a wake-up call. If that doesn't work, your following conversation needs to be about them applying for other jobs. In parallel, start the process with HR to have them let go.

This is the worst part of managing people. I've spent many sleepless nights searching for solutions to bad employees. It never feels good to affect someone's livelihood. However, managers are obligated to put the needs of the team and business ahead of personal feelings. Focus on your other team members. What message does it send if you allow a disgruntled employee to remain disruptive? As you build a culture of accountability, you need to move forward with those employees who buy in. The rest need to find someplace else to work.

HAVE COURAGE

Making the transition to lead a group of peers is difficult. It requires awkward conversations. It necessitates changing your relationship with people who might be friends. It means moving slowly so that you can act quickly. You must build new relationships with your new peer group and other managers. You need to juggle all this while finding a way to deliver results. You must tell people things they don't want to hear. You need to care deeply about your team while learning to worry less about what they think of you. Dick Costolo, the former CEO of Twitter, said it well,

> The way you build trust with your team and your people is by being forthright with them from day one. Not, 'I hope they leave the room feeling good.' You may think people are fooled if you tell them what they want to hear. They are not fooled. As a leader, you are totally transparent. Your people are looking at you all the time.[5]

Stepping up to lead former peers is intimidating. Imposter Syndrome will rear its ugly head. You'll question your selection for the job and your ability to do it well. Take comfort from the fact that every manager that's come before you—at least every good manager—has felt the same. Embrace the challenge. Trust yourself.

NOTES

1 Sandberg, S. (2015, June 3). *One of my favorite cartoons of all time has an elephant in a room answering the phone, saying, "It's the elephant." Once I addressed the elephant, we were able to kick him out of the room.* Facebook. https://www.facebook.com/sheryl/posts/10155617891025177:0.
2 Gallo, A. (2024, November 11). *How to manage your former peers.* Harvard Business Review. https://hbr.org/2012/12/how-to-manage-your-former-peer.
3 Gallo, A. (2024b, November 11). *How to manage your former peers.* Harvard Business Review. https://hbr.org/2012/12/how-to-manage-your-former-peer.
4 Wilson, R. C., Shenhav, A., Straccia, M., & Cohen, J. D. (2019). The Eighty Five Percent Rule for optimal learning. *Nature Communications*, *10*(1). https://doi.org/10.1038/s41467-019-12552-4.
5 TechCrunch. (2013, September 9). *Follow the Leader with Dick Costolo | Disrupt SF 2013* [Video]. YouTube. https://www.youtube.com/watch?v=Tbpd6vVdNQ0.

RECOMMENDED ADDITIONAL READING

Bradberry, T., & Greaves, J. (2009). *Emotional Intelligence 2.0.* TalentSmart.
Eikenberry, K., & Harris, G. (2011). *From Bud to Boss: Secrets to a Successful Transition to Remarkable Leadership.* John Wiley & Sons.
Winters, G. (2013). *Managing Friends and Former Peers.*

Chapter 7

Managing your boss

Your relationship with your boss will be your most important professional relationship. With support from your boss, you can take on that next big project, increase your budget, hire more people, and get recognized for all your great work. The fastest path to promotion is to have a boss who advocates for you.

Invest time early to get to know your boss. Understand their style and approach to work. Do they prefer lots of details, or do they want only the big picture? Do they prefer to communicate via email, instant message, text, or phone? Are they open to drop-ins, or should you schedule a formal appointment if you need some of their time? These are all critical questions early in your relationship. The best way to answer them is to ask. Too many people make assumptions about their boss's preferences. Instead, ask directly. You might be surprised by the answers.

Without support from your boss, you'll be swimming upstream. Your decisions will be second-guessed, important projects will get reassigned, and your life will become more difficult. I've had the unfortunate experience of working for a couple of bosses I struggled to connect with. For whatever reason, we never figured out a way to work well together and were rarely on the same page. Sometimes it felt like we weren't even in the same book.

If you're in this situation, and you can't establish any kind of personal bond, you should work hard to understand why. Are you communicating effectively? Did you establish expectations clearly? Did you follow up on the feedback your boss gave you? Take ownership of this situation and treat it as urgent. No one is as invested in your success as you, so it's on you to find a solution.

If the situation does not improve over time, you should start exploring other options. Whether out of malice or otherwise, your boss can torpedo your success. There are a lot of great organizations out there and lots of great leaders. If you find yourself in a situation that just isn't working out, be honest with yourself and start looking for something better.[1]

DOI: 10.1201/9781003562160-9

STATUS REPORTS AND ONE-ON-ONES

Ensure your boss is regularly kept in the loop about your activities, accomplishments, issues, and any help you need. You'll use two primary mechanisms to achieve this—your status report and your one-on-one.

Create a weekly status report and share it with them. You can approach a status report one of two ways, depending on the nature of your work. I've often used a project dashboard approach where I list the projects my team is working on, a brief description of each (no more than one or two sentences focusing on the business impact), and any significant issues or risks on those projects. I then add a simple green, yellow, or red status for each.

Be sure to define what green, yellow, and red mean—green to indicate no issues with a project's scope, schedule, or budget. We're on pace to deliver the expected results on time and within budget. Yellow indicates an issue with scope, schedule, or budget, from which we can recover with corrective action. Red indicates a problem that will impact delivery. This is pretty consistent across organizations, but defining it in a key/legend for your first few status reports is helpful.

The key to this kind of report is to keep it concise. One page in PowerPoint is plenty. Your boss should be able to review this in a few minutes and get an overall view of the portfolio. If you need to add more detail, save it for project update meetings or include additional slides in an appendix. Don't let your status report turn into a chore for your boss.

At the bottom of each status report, include a link to the prior report. This allows your boss to look back at prior reports if they have a question or want to see progress. This also helps you hold yourself accountable to make progress on your various initiatives. Small touches will help establish your credibility and build trust with your boss.

I've also used a less formal method in a few places. I would send an email with headings for the following:

- "Accomplished This Week"—these should be actual accomplishments. The goal is to show progress on your key priorities, not to demonstrate how busy you are.
- "Upcoming Activities"—Use this section for planned activities for the next week or two. I always add meetings with critical stakeholders outside IT so my boss is aware, but they don't need to know about every meeting on your team's calendar. This section can also include project milestones (e.g., finishing User Acceptance Testing), new hire start dates, etc. Again, focus on significant milestones and activities. This is not a task list.
- "Issues/Roadblocks"—These should be areas that you either need to bring to your boss's attention or areas where you need your boss's help. An excellent example of this would be, "We're still waiting on feedback from Marketing for the product launch. I've followed up on

> March 3rd, March 10th, and March 15th. I need your help to escalate." Remember, part of your boss's job is to remove roadblocks for their team. They're busy, so it's your job to ask for the help you need. We'll discuss these types of requests in the Managing Up section a bit later.

Keep this email short. Your boss should be able to scan through it on their phone without scrolling endlessly. The goal is to provide just enough information so your boss is informed. If they want more information, they will ask.

Your one-on-one with your boss will hopefully follow a similar format to the meetings you have with your team. Your boss might have a different style. That's fine. We all do. But make sure that you have an opportunity to update your boss about your work via a discussion. You need this time to share your successes and issues and hear about their priorities. If you don't have a regularly scheduled 1-1 (at least every other week), request one. Remember, this is your most important professional relationship. You and your boss need to invest the time to ensure it's successful.

Block off 30 minutes before your one-on-one. Use this time to plan your updates. Your status report should be your starting point, but there are likely things you didn't put in writing. There will be items that occurred after you sent your status report. You'll have limited time with your boss, so prepare and prioritize what you need to discuss. Effective one-on-ones will demonstrate that you are on top of your responsibilities and will reflect well on you as a leader.

BE PROACTIVELY TRANSPARENT

In addition to your status report and regular one-on-one, be aware of times when you need to provide an ad-hoc update to your boss. As a leader, there's nothing worse than hearing about a problem in your area from someone else. Don't let your boss hear about an issue for the first time when they get pulled aside by their boss. Keep them in the loop on the important stuff. This is a good practice at all times, but it is especially critical if your boss is heading to a significant meeting. Ensure they are armed with the information to respond appropriately.

Shooting off a quick message to your boss is a good habit when you become aware of a potentially significant issue. The 2021 security issue in Log4J is a perfect example. There was a critical security vulnerability in a widely used piece of software. This is one of those ubiquitous utilities we all use without really thinking about. I was alerted by a vendor around 7 pm on a Thursday to let me know that one of our core systems was at risk because of this vulnerability. I took 15 minutes to read the alerts and talk with my team. I then sent my boss a short text message that said something like,

> We were just made aware of a critical security vulnerability in ABC System. My team is reviewing our exposure and working on options to mitigate and remediate. I'll share more when I have it, but no later than 8 am tomorrow.

With that text, at least he knew enough that if asked, he could truthfully tell people we were on top of it. In this case, my boss called me 3 minutes later, and we chatted about what I knew and what specific actions we were taking. It turned out that he had an 8 am staff meeting with his boss. If I hadn't texted, he would have walked in blind.

These updates need to be factual, not speculative. It's easy to make too many assumptions, especially when issues are still new and the impact is not fully understood. You can assume everything will be fine, and the matter will be resolved in a few hours. It's similarly easy to assume the worst and catastrophize. Neither reaction is helpful. Focus on what you know at that point in time and share only that. Here's what we know now and what we're doing. If you're pressed for opinions, estimates, or flat-out guesses, be explicit about what's fact and what's speculation.

At the same time, don't wait too long to communicate. It can be uncomfortable to approach your boss when you don't completely grasp the issue. But there are times when an imperfect update right now is better than a perfect update when it's too late. Your boss can shift resources to help you with an issue. They can alert vendors, pull in other departments, and so on. If you wait for perfect clarity, it will be too late.

It's also helpful to ensure your boss knows when your team has achieved a big win. Your boss is in meetings all day with peers from other departments. They will appreciate having some good news to share that reflects well on the IT team. When sharing this news, make sure to focus on the business impact:

> We just completed the Virtual Desktop rollout to the final group, and we're ready to close the project. This will save $600,000 per year in hardware costs and reduce our cybersecurity risk.

That's an update your boss can share with the IT Security Team, the CFO, the board, or anyone in between. You can add detail during your next one-on-one. Keep the interim updates concise and focused on impact. Helping your boss look good is part of making your team look good. The more collective success you have, the better for everyone.

Transparency helps build trust with your boss and fosters open collaboration. Be transparent about your team's successes and challenges. Keep your manager informed rather than waiting to be asked. You'll be surprised by how quickly your manager will reciprocate. And now you're on your way to a productive, effective relationship.

MAKE THEIR LIVES EASIER

Your boss has the same focus on their team and career as you have on yours. They have annual goals, career aspirations, a boss to please, and deadlines to meet. Like you, they have an endless list of priorities and limited time to accomplish all of them. Helping your boss succeed is like a cheat code to career growth.

While it might be hard to imagine, your boss is busier than you are. As you climb the organizational hierarchy, your scope of responsibility expands dramatically. As a new manager, you might be responsible for ten people working on six projects. Your boss might be accountable for eight managers, each with 10 direct reports. That's 80 people for whom they're responsible. Just because you don't see them in every meeting (and sometimes might not see them all week), don't assume they aren't swamped.

When meeting with our boss, our instinct is to focus on ourselves—our priorities, our updates, our careers. These are important. But I also encourage you to spend some of that time finding your boss's priorities. What are they thinking about? What's keeping them up at night? What is *their* boss asking about? Look for areas where you can help. This can be taking on a project outside your typical scope, offering insight into a problem, relaying feedback from a key stakeholder, or acting as a sounding board to discuss strategy.

This creates a win-win. If you can take on a project outside your scope, you enhance your career, gain additional exposure to people you don't work with regularly, and learn new skills. At the same time, by taking something off your boss's plate, you free them up to tackle one of the endless items on their to-do list and, thus, make them more effective. Bosses tend to remember that. Former Amazon VP Ethan Evans calls this the Magic Loop.[2] He writes, "The magic in the loop is building a collaborative, mutually beneficial relationship."

The best way to achieve this is to delegate tasks to yourself. When you see something to be done, volunteer. If you and your boss are on the same meeting invite, let them know that you can handle the meeting and report back on anything important. If they have an upcoming deliverable, volunteer to create an initial draft. Every item you take off their plate frees them up to work on something else. Soon, they'll recognize your desire to help them succeed.

Be sure your house is in order before you do this. You'll get no bonus points if you take on an additional assignment while your team misses its deadlines, fails to deliver, or suffers other issues. Taking on stretch goals is a great way to grow, but make sure you're not setting yourself up for failure. This is an idea for when you're a few months into your new role, not something to bring up in your first week. Give your boss time to build confidence in your abilities.

MANAGE UP

Sometimes you need to push your boss to get something done. You may need them to open that extra headcount, sign off on a new contract, or intervene to resolve a project stalemate. Managing up begins with understanding your audience. You need to establish a relationship and learn about your boss's preferences before you can manage effectively. Know if they're more receptive to ideas during face-to-face meetings than they are over email (or vice versa). Know how direct you can be. I've worked for leaders who would prefer that I pull them aside and say something like, "You're blocking my progress. I need you to do this by the day's end so we can move forward." I've worked for others who would not react well to feedback like that.

Make the request easy for your boss to act on. Managing up is not the same as delegating up—generally, something to avoid. If there's a decision they need to make, lay out the options clearly and provide your recommendation. If they need to call someone on your behalf, clearly explain who and why they're calling, and provide the phone number. If you need them to send a note to a peer or a customer, provide them with a draft of the communication.

Managing up is not the same as managing down. You might give someone on your team an ambiguous task and rely on them to figure out the details. Here's the outcome I need, you go figure out the best way to make it happen. This is *not* the approach to take with your boss. Make it simple, make it easy, and make it as frictionless as possible.

Of course, as a leader, we should take action on vague requests from our team. We should ask clarifying questions, push for details, and then get it done. But, bosses are busy. I'm as guilty as anyone of seeing a poorly formed or complicated request from my team in my inbox and simply marking it as "to do later." The easier you make it, the more likely it will get done. If you've pre-written an email you want me to send, there's a good chance I'll cut, paste, and send it before moving on to the next thing. If I need to make a decision, then write an email, then run the email by you to make sure it aligns with what you need, then send it; I'm far more likely to put it off until later.

In the vein of making it easy for your boss, part of being a leader is getting comfortable moving from providing *options* to providing *opinions*. We expect leaders to make decisions within their scope. 80% of the time, when someone on my team comes to me to make a decision, I'll turn around and ask them what they think. And roughly 95% of those times, we move forward with their recommendation.

You are closer to the facts on the ground. You're steeped in the process, the people, the technology, and the issues. Barring some information your boss has not yet shared; you are usually in a better position to decide. You may not be authorized to make it independently, but you're empowered—even expected—to make a recommendation. Like everyone else, bosses suffer from decision fatigue, so make it easy for them. Take ownership, be proactive, and lead.

There is one other note about managing up. Like all of us, bosses are human. And each human has a unique rhythm. Some of us are night owls, and some of us are early birds. Some prefer to catch up on emails Sunday night before the chaos of the week starts, and some of us need to unplug all weekend to start fresh on Monday morning. Figure out your boss's rhythm and use it to your advantage. If they frequently log in to work for an hour or two after dinner, consider sending your request at the end of the day so it's near the top of their inbox when they settle in. If they are an early bird and like to clear their inbox first thing, then think about sending it at 6 am. Most email clients allow you to schedule when your message gets sent, so you don't need to mimic your boss's timetable. Just schedule the message for a time that makes sense.

LEVEL OF DETAIL

IT is plagued with technical jargon and impenetrable acronyms. We have a whole alphabet soup to communicate with one another—DDOS, API, TCP/IP, FTP, MFA, AES, WAN, etc. The acronyms serve as a specific, detailed short-hand. Our shared understanding forms the foundation for this house of abbreviations. But your meaning is lost when you talk to someone without this shared understanding.

You may find yourself working for a boss who is not an expert in your field. As we climb the career ladder, our ability to deliver results will depend less on our technical skills and more on other attributes. Are we effective people managers? Can we budget well and meet deadlines? Are we strategic thinkers? How is our business acumen? These things will play a more significant role the more senior we get. This also means that when organizations hire senior-level managers, they screen less for technical skills. I've worked for more than one person who could barely spell some of the systems I managed.

You must communicate in a way that your boss can understand. No one will be impressed by your level of technical detail or how many acronyms you know if they can't understand you. It's important to ensure your language makes sense to your boss. If I sent my boss a status report that said, "We ran into a spanning tree error because one 2960XR was running 802.1D instead of Per-VLAN RSTP," he wouldn't have any idea what I meant. If you're a network engineer, that sentence probably makes perfect sense. But if you rose through the ranks as a Project Manager, it might as well be written in Sanskrit. Instead, say, "We had a network outage due to a misconfigured switch." All the relevant details are there, but you're less likely to need to answer 17 questions that boil down to "What the heck are you talking about?"

Find the right level of detail when you communicate with your boss. Because of their broader scope, they can't have the same detailed understanding of everything in your domain that you have. This isn't a shortcoming on their part. It's a necessary part of scaling their time and responsibilities. I've seen too many people get upset when their boss doesn't understand a problem at a detailed level, yet that's not the boss's job. That would be akin to your boss getting mad that you didn't have a detailed understanding of what was happening on a different team. You need to share enough detail for them to help without burying them in every facet of the problem.

This skill is equally important as you communicate outside the department. The folks in Accounting don't care why the network went down. They just want to know when they can send emails again. When communicating about an incident, a project status, or a new initiative, make sure to choose language and a level of detail appropriate for your audience. As Jeffrey Brown says in *The Security Leader's Communication Playbook*, "Your knowledge doesn't matter if the listener has no idea what you're saying."[3]

ACCEPT FEEDBACK

Feedback is a gift. One of the most important things you can do in your career at any level is to seek feedback from your manager. Your boss is taking the time to provide his insight and evaluation so that you can improve and be more successful.

Step one to receiving feedback is to get in the proper mindset. Check your ego at the door and remain open to hearing things you may not like to hear. There is a Japanese word, Uketamo,[4] that's often translated as "I humbly accept with an open heart." I'm not an expert in philosophy, but I think this is the perfect attitude to adopt before receiving feedback. We've all heard the saying, "Perception is reality," so if your boss is giving you feedback about something, you should assume they are, at least partially, right.

You're likely working very hard, you're doing the best work you can, and you're learning and growing each day. It can be jarring to hear something negative about your performance. But do your best not to get defensive. Listen carefully to the feedback. Try to understand your boss's point of view. Ask for clarity or examples if you don't understand the feedback. Once you understand, or feel like you've exhausted further clarification, thank your boss. And I don't mean just offer up some platitude before you scurry out the door. I mean, genuinely thank them for caring enough to provide feedback. Commit to reflecting on what you heard and set a time to revisit the topic.

If you disagree with the feedback, keep your opinion to yourself at the moment. After the meeting, reflect on the feedback with an open mind. Do you have blind spots? Most of us do. Does your boss have a different understanding of expectations or priorities? Was there something you could have communicated better? If there is a demonstrably incorrect set of facts, you should gather evidence and schedule a follow-up. But these instances have been rare in my career. Giving negative feedback is almost as unpleasant as receiving it, so most people do their homework before having such a conversation.

Once you've accepted the feedback, it's time to put together an action plan. Think about what you heard and what you can do to improve or otherwise address the feedback. Shortly after the meeting (a day or two is best, but no more than a week), send your boss a brief email. Start by thanking them again for the feedback and lay out your plan to address it. You may not get a response to this email, but it's important to send it. Show that you heard and understood the message and that you're taking action.

OWN THE OUTCOME

Hearing that your team missed expectations can be jarring. You're working hard, putting in long hours, learning new skills, only to find out your boss isn't happy with the team's performance. It sucks. When you get this kind of feedback, never pass the buck—never blame someone on your team.

You are responsible for your team. Their shortcomings are your fault. Sometimes it's not fair, but that's the job. As Jocko Willink says in his book *Extreme Ownership*, "Leaders must own everything in their world. There is no one else to blame."[5] If you have a performance problem with an employee, you need to deal with it. It's no good to complain after the fact that so-and-so didn't pull their weight. Regardless of the underlying cause, a team failure is your failure.

For an excellent example, look at General Dwight Eisenhower's "In Case of Failure" letter about the Normandy Invasion on D-Day: "The troops, the air, and the Navy did all that Bravery and devotion to duty could do. *If any blame or fault attaches to the attempt, it is mine alone*."[6] [emphasis added]

Thankfully, Ike didn't have to send this letter, and his troops went on to liberate Europe. But this is what ownership is all about. When you succeed, share the credit liberally. When you fail, take personal responsibility. Build a reputation for integrity. Everyone makes mistakes. We all miss deadlines from time to time. What separates those who succeed is how they react. Be accountable, learn from the situation, and do better next time. That's what every leader wants to see.

NOTES

1 Note: I'm not talking about a rough patch. Everyone has tough times at work. Maybe your boss is under a lot of pressure to get a project completed or launch a new feature. Maybe he recently received bad feedback from his boss, and he's not handling it well. These situations are a normal part of navigating a career.

If you've had a good relationship with your manager and it hits a rough patch, work through it. You can be candid and say something like, "It seems like we're not on the same page lately. Should I be doing something different? We used to be in sync, but I wonder if I'm no longer meeting your expectations. I'd love to understand what I can do to improve.".

2 Evans, E. (2023, September 19). The Magic Loop. *Lenny's Newsletter*. https://www.lennysnewsletter.com/p/the-magic-loop.
3 Brown, J. (2021). *The security Leader's communication playbook: Bridging the Gap Between Security and the Business*. CRC Press.
4 Kimball, D. (2023, August 25). *Uketamo (I Accept) | Training with the Dewa Sanzan Yamabushi*. A Different Side of Japan. https://donnykimball.com/yamabushi-dewa-sanzan-f724a057d7a4.
5 Willink, J., & Babin, L. (2018). *Extreme ownership*. Macmillan Publishers Aus.
6 Simon, S. (2013, June 8). The speech Eisenhower never gave on the Normandy invasion. *NPR*. https://www.npr.org/2013/06/08/189535104/the-speech-eisenhower-never-gave-on-the-normandy-invasion.

RECOMMENDED ADDITIONAL READING

Abbajay, M. (2018). *Managing Up: How to Move Up, Win at Work, and Succeed with Any Type of Boss*. John Wiley & Sons.

Bing, S. (2009). *Throwing the Elephant: Zen and the Art of Managing Up*. Harper Collins.

Brown, B. (2018). *Dare to Lead: Brave Work. Tough Conversations. Whole Hearts*. Random House.

Chapter 8

Managing technical talent

You will lead teams of people who know far more about a specific subject than you do. This might be unique to IT. It's rare that an accounting manager would be inexpert in Generally Accepted Accounting Principles (GAAP) rules or that a payroll manager would have gaps in her knowledge about state laws regarding employee pay. But in IT, partially because it changes so fast and partially because it's become a vast field, you may be asked to lead a team outside your area of expertise. Maybe you manage a network team, but your last role was in charge of firewalls, so you don't have deep expertise in Cisco switches. While some of your knowledge is transferable, some will not apply. Accept the knowledge gap.

Your job is to drive outcomes, not solve every technical issue. You need to focus on what your business partners expect from IT, what your customers need, and what your boss expects from you. I think you'll find these rarely include "solve an interesting fresh problem" or "play with this cool new technology to see what it can do." However, you'll have people on your team who want to do just that. Keep them on task without stifling their creativity.

The other big challenge you'll face is estimating workload and pace. While some disciplines have standard tasks (some would say repetitive), technical tasks are more complicated to forecast. Your finance team knows closing the books will take eight days every year. Facilities know it takes five months to outfit and prepare a newly leased space. But how long will it take to get the network back online during an outage? How long should you plan to create that new application? How long to fix that bug? These are more challenging questions because they often involve taking five wrong paths before you land on the right one. We discuss how to estimate your projects and why throwing more people at an issue is unlikely to make it go faster.

Everything that applies to managing *employees* applies to managing *technical employees*. However, these added nuances will make you more effective. Ultimately, successful leadership depends on effective communication, mutual respect, and a shared commitment to the project.

DOI: 10.1201/9781003562160-10

IT PROFESSIONAL PERSONALITIES

Technical people often have unique personalities. Like everything else in life, you encounter all kinds of people in IT, and I don't want to stereotype. But there seems to be an embarrassment of riches regarding "interesting" people in IT. Part of it is likely selection bias. It takes a unique personality to debug C++ code for hours on end. To figure out what that GCC compiler is trying to tell you and where you have an issue in the thousands of lines of code. Whether from an innate trait or from years of practice, we in IT will bang our heads against a wall for weeks for that rush when we finally solve a problem. People who find this type of work soul-crushing will likely seek alternate career paths.

Indeed, the scientific literature supports the idea that people in IT are wired differently. In a 2014 paper, researchers from the University of Tennessee found quantifiable differences in the personalities of IT professionals vs. professionals in other parts of organizations. IT folks show higher levels of tough-mindedness.[1] You see this in action when a team is tracing the root cause of an outage or trying to debug code, tasks that require significant analytical skills and dogged determination. This will not surprise anyone who's spent a few years in an IT organization.

What might be more surprising is that IT professionals also scored higher on Agreeableness. The same authors define agreeableness as "Preference for and comfort with cooperation;... satisfaction with teamwork."[2] This might shock you if you've ever worked with a curmudgeonly system administrator. Technical people sometimes cultivate the image of the lone nerd working away all night in his cubicle, wearing noise-canceling headphones to block out the world. To be sure, there are people like this, but most of us enjoy working with teams and want to contribute to group efforts—even if we won't show up in any HR team-building videos. Ever notice that most startups have a small team rather than a single founder? Jobs had Wozniak. Larry Paige had Sergey Brin. Reed Hastings and Marc Randolph founded Netflix. Technical people work better in teams.

Conversely, IT professionals show lower levels of extroversion and conscientiousness, defined as "organized, orderly, methodical, detail-minded, dependable, and rule-following."[3] You might work with a few people who don't exactly fit the definition of orderly. Have you ever talked to a developer who wrote some legacy code and asked him to explain it? More than once, I've heard, "I don't know why it works, but it works. Just leave it alone." The real driver here is that IT work requires tremendous flexibility and creativity. You'll find many non-linear thinkers in IT, which probably contributes to lower scores in conscientiousness.

The personality traits presented here are at the population level. They can inform how you work with *IT people*, but they should not dictate how you interact with an individual IT person. As with any profession, there will always be outliers and unique personalities, and it is essential to approach everyone with an open mind and a willingness to work together toward a common goal.

ASSESSING TECHNICAL PROFESSIONALS

Theory and academic research are great, but you picked up this book because you've got a team to manage. Let's discuss how to get the most from your IT team, building on, but not beholden to, the personality traits of IT Professionals. There are many different ways to approach this endeavor. It's helpful to start by thinking about the makeup of your team and their different skill sets. These six competencies[4] are most helpful:

1. Technical competence
2. Personal productivity
3. Ability to juggle multiple tasks
4. Understanding of the business context
5. Ability to manage ambiguity
6. Time management

Technical competence is what we generally think of when we think, "Is this person any good?". It has two dimensions—breadth and depth. Breadth describes a person's technical knowledge across technologies, domains, and teams. Someone who can build an Oracle database schema, code a web app, and help troubleshoot a firewall issue has excellent breadth. Depth is their specific expertise within a narrow subject. Someone with a Cisco Certified Internetwork Expert (CCIE) certification and 25 years of experience configuring Cisco networks has deep expertise. They might also know something about Aruba or Juniper, but they likely won't know anything about Oracle databases. Most IT professionals have a "T" model of competence. They have some breadth across a range of topics and deep expertise in a single area. You're fortunate if you have a mix of "jack of all trades" and deep experts on your team.

Relevance is essential when evaluating technical competence. IT people like learning new technology. They also like jargon. Some managers get bulldozed by team members who overwhelm them with irrelevant facts and incomprehensible jargon. They are so lost partway through a discussion that they accede to whatever their team member suggests. You aren't going to do that. When you meet with your team, make sure you understand what they're saying and how it's relevant to the goals you're trying to achieve. Keep asking questions until you do. It's part of their job to explain things in a way that makes sense to you, just like it's your job to do the same for your boss.

Technical certifications can be a good way to demonstrate knowledge, but they are rarely sufficient. Taking a test is not the same thing as applying that knowledge. When managing your team, you need to assess who has "book smarts" and who can actually do the job. Some people are good at taking tests but struggle to contextualize what they've learned in a way that can be useful at work. You'll see this reflected in their personal productivity.

Personal productivity is how I evaluate how much work each person gets done. It's an imprecise measure of their total deliverable output. Whether they are writing code, documenting test procedures, building project plans, or installing network switches, you'll have some people on your team who accomplish more than everyone else. Of course, a measure of quality is embedded here—doing lots of bad work doesn't help anyone. But those who can produce more work at a high standard are more productive.

There's no one right way to manage productivity. This is where you'll need to get to know your team and their rhythms. Some people work in short bursts. It will seem like they do nothing for two weeks, then they get a month's work done in the next three days. Others are "Steady Eddies" who produce consistent, predictable work every day. Neither is better, but trying to force them all into a single mode of productivity can be detrimental. If they are hitting deadlines and your team is on schedule, it's best not to muck around too much here. If you have work you're falling behind on, a better idea is to focus on prioritization and removing distractions from your team.

Some of your team members will be excellent at **juggling multiple tasks**. They will structure their days and weeks to dedicate the appropriate amount of time to each priority and stay on track. Others will struggle when their plate gets too full. Imagine a developer with excellent technical competence and good productivity who simply cannot take on multiple projects simultaneously. The moment you add a second item to their plate, they crumble. They overanalyze how to prioritize their time. They feel overwhelmed and turn to procrastination. Or they switch tasks too often to be effective. You need to spoon-feed projects one at a time. As a manager, this is less than ideal. You should provide coaching on prioritization and multitasking. Your productivity and their career growth will both benefit if they learn to juggle competing priorities.

Another way to improve your productivity is getting your team to understand the business context. It's easy to think that an app is an app. Java doesn't care if the application is used to register students for a training course or to process expense reimbursements. But your team should care about the context, as it's the only way to prioritize. Because most of your team will come from technology backgrounds, they will likely overvalue the technical context and undervalue the business context. I'm guilty of this at times. I see a technical problem, and I want to fix it. I get bothered when systems don't work as well as I know they could. But sometimes, you need to accept that fixing a specific problem isn't a priority.

Look at **understanding business context** as a continuum. At the far left is a person with a limited understanding of the business. They might be able to articulate the goals of the project they are working on, but more likely, they

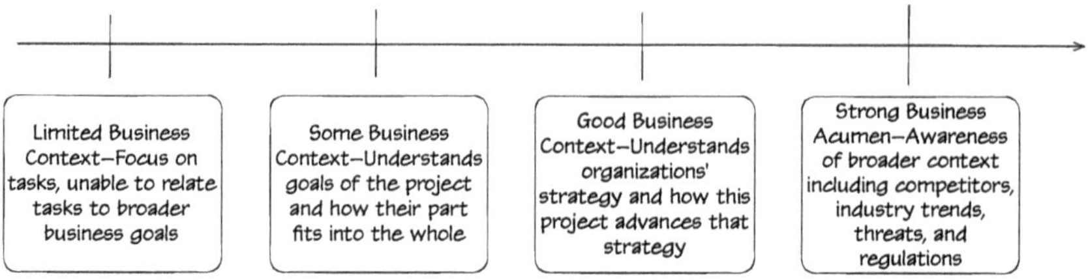

Figure 8.1 Business context continuum.

are focused on what feature they're building or what problem they are trying to solve, regardless of how it helps the business. A step further to the right is someone who understands the project's goals and how their piece fits into the broader whole. Moving further along the continuum is someone who can see how this project's goals fit into the organization's larger strategy. How this project complements the other projects at the organization and how they'll all come together to create value. At the far right end is someone who understands their organization's strategy and how it fits into the overall market. They can talk about competitors, industry challenges, and the regulatory environment. Strive to help your team move along this continuum. You'll have more credibility when you can understand and articulate the business context of your work (Figure 8.1).

When your team can think in terms of the business context of their work, they can begin to make tradeoffs necessary for prioritization. How big is the opportunity for Project A vs. Project B? If one is a back-office process optimization and the other is critical to launching a new line of business, the priority becomes clear. More experienced employees generally think more broadly about business context. Junior engineers and recent graduates have enough on their plate trying to figure out the technical pieces of their work. But someone who's been through it all before and has the battle scars to prove it will likely think more broadly. As their manager, your job is to help everyone on your team improve their business acumen. These are great topics for your one-on-ones and staff meetings.

Your staff must also **manage ambiguity**. Technology and IT projects are fraught with layers of uncertainty. The best planning process does not remove ambiguity from your projects. It only helps lower it. You'll encounter unexpected bugs, realize that your requirements weren't as clear as you hoped, find that two systems that should integrate easily don't play nicely together, and have stakeholders change their minds on critical features. Ambiguity is a fact of life in IT. That's why we say, "We're building the ship while trying to sail it."

Some of your staff will handle this well; others will struggle. Staff who can manage this ambiguity and remain productive are more effective. These are the people to whom you can delegate large chunks of projects and still sleep well at night. Others require you to break down their tasks more specifically while you manage the ambiguity for them.

Finally, we come to **time management**. Parkinson's Law says the work will expand to fill the available time. If you assign two weeks to a task, it will take two weeks. If you can somehow stretch the deadline to a month, the task will suddenly take a month. The most effective employees give themselves interim deadlines, build in buffers for when they hit a blocker, and find ways to finish work on time. Those who are less effective will assume their work will proceed linearly. Then they inevitably finish late because of some problem they could not foresee. Focus on this second group, help them build buffers, and set interim deadlines.

I had one employee who did fantastic work. Her code was clean and elegant, her solutions were creative, and her documentation was excellent. I would have liked her to work on every project. But, in the time we worked together, I don't think she met a single deadline. Her work was always late. This severely limited her effectiveness. I was forced to give her small pieces of work and tight deadlines with my own internal buffer. This led to more work for me and less opportunity for her. I'm sure as she grows, she will improve, but employees like this demand a lot of coaching.

These six factors—technical competence, personal productivity, ability to juggle multiple tasks, understanding of business context, ability to manage ambiguity, and time management—can help you assess the strengths and weaknesses of your team. You'll be lucky to have individuals strong in a few of these areas and very lucky to have even one person who excels at all six competencies. As you focus on coaching, highlight where they can improve and how it will help the team and their career. When you have an open role to fill, give some thought to these competencies as well as the technical skills you need. In the next section, we'll discuss helpful hacks to get the most from your team.

HELPFUL HACKS

Once you understand how to assess technical talent, you're left to figure out how to get the most out of the people on your team. I offer some Helpful Hacks that have worked well in my career. Experiment with some or all of these and see what works for your team. The advice offered in this section has worked across teams, companies, and industries, but each must be adapted for the individual.

Mentoring program

Implement a mentoring program. Pair your junior staff with more senior employees in a similar role—a junior engineer with a staff engineer or a new project manager with a seasoned program manager. Mentors will help your staff gain skills, whether in a specific programming language, a new technology, or a problem-solving approach. A good mentor will suggest resources, blogs, forums, and other avenues for the mentee to learn. They can provide career guidance by sharing their story, choices, and what they might do differently if given the chance again. Mentors also provide your staff with an enhanced network by introducing their mentees to peers and colleagues outside the department. Finally, mentors can support, motivate, and encourage more junior employees. The stakes are low because the mentor is not evaluating the employee. This leads employees to ask more questions and makes them more likely to seek help. Mentorship also helps sustain the culture of your department.

The benefits extend to the mentors as well. Mentorship lets senior technical resources hone their leadership ability. They help drive the culture they want to see and the required technical frameworks and standards. They gain a fresh perspective from their mentees' backgrounds, experiences, and skill sets.

Learning is a two-way street. A famous quote often attributed to Albert Einstein says, "If you can't explain something simply, you don't know it well enough." Whether Einstein actually said it, there's a lot of truth in that statement. The mentor will learn more about a topic by breaking down their technical knowledge to explain it to a mentee. You'll find the mentor gets as much fulfillment and satisfaction from the relationship as the mentee. Just don't ask the most overworked, burned-out person on the team to take on the role.

Discovery time

Carve out some time for your team to pursue their own creative outlets in technology. Google famously encouraged its employees to spend 20% of their time on side projects. From their Initial Public Offering (IPO) letter:

> We encourage our employees, in addition to their regular projects, to spend 20% of their time working on what they think will most benefit Google. This empowers them to be more creative and innovative. Many of our significant advances have happened in this manner. For example, AdSense for content and Google News were both prototyped in "20% time." Most risky projects fizzle, often teaching us something. Others succeed and become attractive businesses.[5]

Twenty percent is probably too much for you to offer. But free up a few hours each week to let your team flex their creative muscle. Most projects will lead to nothing, but you and your team will learn even in the failures. You'll learn how to implement new technologies, you'll learn how to evaluate them quickly, and you'll learn skills that can be brought to your existing work. You'll also find that your team's satisfaction and engagement will increase if they can self-direct at least some of their efforts. Ensure they have time to pursue paths that may not directly move a project forward.

Where you can, ensure your team has access to some of the latest tools and technology in your field. Even if you're supporting legacy systems, there's likely to be new development tools, a new vendor, or something getting buzz in your industry. Let your team take advantage of these opportunities to keep their skills fresh. You don't want to invest heavily just because something is new and shiny but look for ways to run pilots or proofs-of-concept. Inviting vendors for a demo can help satisfy the need. Remember, technical people like new technology.

Learning opportunities

Encourage your staff to participate in professional development activities. Find some money to let them attend a conference or workshop. If you can't find room in the budget, look for free offerings for virtual conferences from vendors. Seek training opportunities that fit with their career goals. In an ideal scenario, find something that lets them get out of the office for a few days. The costs for in-person conferences and training will be higher, but the benefits of time to focus, free from the distractions of their daily work, are well worth the investment. Conferences and training classes are also an excellent way for your team to expand their networks and learn from what other organizations are doing.

Encourage everyone on your team to suggest a few professional development opportunities for the coming year. Some will offer training classes, others a conference, and some want to pursue a degree or certification. Do your best to fund as many as possible. These are obvious win-win situations as your team's skills grow and your employee retention increases.

Flexible schedules

Lastly, and the most important thing you can do to keep your team engaged and performing at their best, is to provide flexible work arrangements. Today, that generally means remote or hybrid work. But look at other kinds of flexibility as well. I've worked with many engineers who, simply put, were not morning people. They preferred to start their days at 10 am and often worked long after everyone else had gone home. Because "early bird" and "night owl" are primarily determined by our chronotypes (genetics),[6] there's a risk in forcing someone outside their normal rhythm.

We all know that person who seems to have brain fog until noon but gets super-productive from 10 pm to 2 am. If you can provide flexibility, everyone will benefit. Your late risers will be happier and more productive, and the people around them won't have to deal with their half-awake zombie state. Even if this isn't a formal arrangement, consider allowing some flexibility to start and end times. No one wants to work for a manager who cares more about watching the clock than getting work done.

Also, consider if you can offer alternate scheduled days. Some organizations have successfully implemented a schedule with four ten-hour days and Fridays off. I've seen others do 9/80 scheduling where a person works nine hours daily Monday to Thursday, 8 hours the first Friday, and zero hours the alternating Friday. They work 80 hours every two weeks but get every other Friday off. This works well because the longer days provide more opportunity to do "deep work," and the extra day off helps them disconnect, run errands, etc.

You will need approval from your boss before implementing alternate work schedules, so don't overpromise if someone requests one. These arrangements only work if your team is hitting its goals, meeting deadlines, and delivering high quality. Ensure you've built your credibility before suggesting this.

These ideas will help you get the most from your team. Many of them can be positioned as benefits to the employee, but, in practice, the organization and the employee will both benefit. Of course, things like flexible schedules, training opportunities, and self-directed work are all predicated on your team members getting their job done. No one should ask to take a week out of the office to attend a conference if they've missed all their deliverable deadlines this year. Use your judgment, but when in doubt, err on the side of the employee.

NOTES

1 John W. Lounsbury., Eric Sundstrom., Jacob J. Levy & Lucy W. Gibson. (2014) "Distinctive Traits of Information Technology Professionals" *Computer and Information Science*, 7(3), 38. doi:10.5539/cis.v7n3p38.
2 John W. Lounsbury., Eric Sundstrom., Jacob J. Levy & Lucy W. Gibson. (2014) "Distinctive Traits of Information Technology Professionals" *Computer and Information Science*, 7(3), 38. doi:10.5539/cis.v7n3p38.
3 John W. Lounsbury., Eric Sundstrom., Jacob J. Levy & Lucy W. Gibson. (2014) "Distinctive Traits of Information Technology Professionals" *Computer and Information Science*, 7(3), 38. doi:10.5539/cis.v7n3p38.
4 Glen, P. (2002). *Leading geeks: How to Manage and Lead the People Who Deliver Technology*. John Wiley & Sons.
5 *Founders' IPO letter*. (n.d.). Alphabet Investor Relations. https://abc.xyz/investor/founders-letters/2004-ipo-letter/.
6 Fischer, D., Lombardi, D. A., Marucci-Wellman, H., & Roenneberg, T. (2017). Chronotypes in the US – Influence of age and sex. *PLoS ONE*, *12*(6), e0178782. https://doi.org/10.1371/journal.pone.0178782.

RECOMMENDED ADDITIONAL READING

Glen, P. (2003). *Leading Geeks: How to Manage and Lead the People Who Deliver Technology*. John Wiley & Sons.

Larson, W. (2019). *An elegant Puzzle: Systems of Engineering Management*. Stripe Press.

Ross-Munro, G. (2018). *Herding Cats and Coders: Software Development for Non-Techies*.

Part Two

Methods

Shared methods are the secret sauce of every successful team. Your team could be stacked with more talent than the 1927 Yankees, but if it isn't coordinated and pulling in the same direction, it will never reach its full potential. Part of managing methods is setting ground rules and expectations—this is how we deliver projects, this is how we manage changes, etc. It's also about collaborating effectively so that each team member understands what they should be doing, when, and how. A team that lacks coordination and a unified direction is like a ship without a rudder—it may move, but it will be aimless and without purpose.

Of course, you don't want to micromanage every task or decision. That would be entirely counterproductive, leading to frustration and resentment among team members. Instead, it's important to create the right structures and processes within which your team can thrive. This means defining how decisions are made, who has the authority to make them, and when they should be escalated to a higher level.

By putting these structures and processes in place, you empower your team to work together towards a common goal while still maintaining the flexibility and autonomy they need to succeed. Managing methods is all about finding the right balance between structure and freedom so that everyone on your team feels empowered and motivated to do their best work.

* * *

DOI: 10.1201/9781003562160-11

Chapter 9

Project management

After managing your team, your biggest challenge will be managing projects. Disciplined project execution is the lifeblood of an IT organization. You'll implement new applications, replace aging hardware, enable new capabilities, and find ways to reduce costs. Each will be managed as a project with a defined scope, schedule, and budget. If strategy is the blueprint that envisions the future and technology is the foundation that enables innovation, project management is the construction crew that turns vision into reality—brick by brick and step by step.

There are as many ways to manage a project as there are companies in the world. I've had the good fortune to work at dozens of top-flight companies, each managing their projects differently. Some used a rigidly structured, planning-heavy approach with tremendous time spent up front to detail requirements and a strict change control process to govern changes. Others were far more relaxed, with primary objectives defined and a team assigned to figure out the details. Your company will have its preferred approach.

Most of these approaches can be grouped into two overarching styles: waterfall and agile. Each approach has its own set of benefits. To help you make the right decision, let's look at the differences between these two methods.

Agile is an iterative approach that puts a focus on collaboration and flexibility. It's often used by smaller teams who need to adjust plans quickly as they go along—something that's hard to do in waterfall. With agile, team members are encouraged to give continuous feedback and work together towards common goals. Scrum is a well-known flavor of agile that focuses on cross-functional teams working collaboratively in short sprints to deliver high-quality results. It's based on breaking down complex tasks into smaller, incremental chunks, which can then be tested and rapidly adjusted to meet changing requirements. This allows the team to remain flexible and stay on track with minimal disruption. Other agile types include Lean Development, which seeks to reduce waste from the system, and Kanban, which uses visual workflows to minimize work-in-progress.

Conversely, waterfall is more structured and plan-driven, with well-defined stages from start to finish. This makes it ideal for larger projects that

DOI: 10.1201/9781003562160-12

require greater oversight and control. Waterfall follows the traditional phases of requirements gathering, analysis, design, implementation, testing, deployment, and maintenance. Waterfall tends to be more rigid, and changes to requirements later in the process are costly and time-consuming.

Both methodologies require planning, testing, execution, reporting, and risk management. The differences are in how they approach these items. Your choice of methods may be determined by your organization's culture or the types of projects you manage. Agile has been gaining popularity for decades, and most organizations claim to embrace some form of agile development. But, agile is not suitable for every project.

Ultimately, no project management method is perfect—it's all about finding what works best for your team and project goals. With the proper techniques, you can ensure that your team stays organized and delivers results on time, on budget, and with minimal disruption.

WATERFALL

Waterfall can be thought of as "traditional" project management. This methodology has been used for decades to deliver IT systems, large and small. Waterfall uses a sequential approach emphasizing detailed planning, requirements analysis, design, and testing. The phases happen one after the other, and the project moves in only one direction. It gets its name because the phases look like a waterfall when you draw out the steps on a Gantt chart (Figure 9.1).

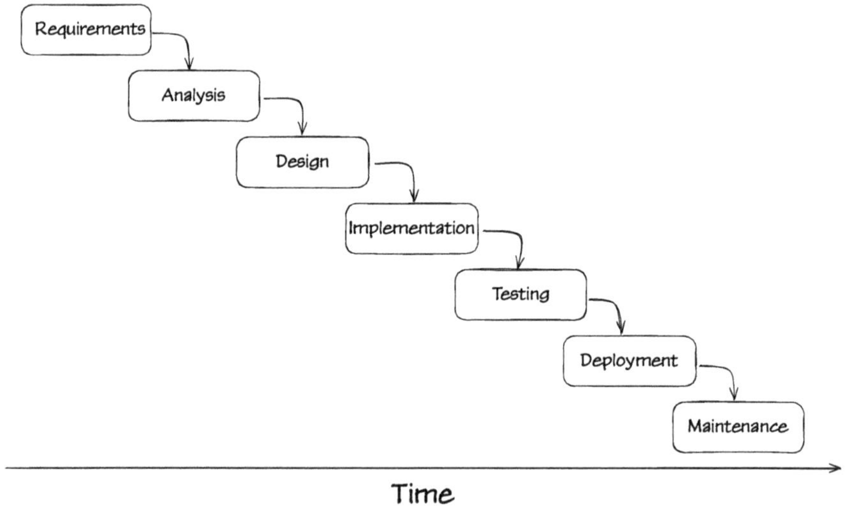

Figure 9.1 Waterfall project management.

- **Requirements gathering:** The project team collaborates with stakeholders to define the project goals, scope, and requirements. This information is then used to create a detailed project plan.
- **Analysis:** All relevant stakeholders and documents are reviewed to develop a clear project vision and goals. The analysis phase also involves gathering information on how the project will be completed, such as identifying resources, determining task schedules and dependencies, estimating budgets, and creating an action plan.
- **Design:** Based on the requirements, the team designs the project architecture, including technical specifications, user interface design, and other details. This phase aims to create a clear and detailed blueprint of the entire project.
- **Implementation:** Once the design is complete, the team moves on to the implementation phase, where software developers code the system following the technical specifications created in the design phase.
- **Testing:** After developing the system, it is tested to ensure it meets all the requirements and works correctly.
- **Deployment:** Once the system has met all the requirements and passed the testing phase, it can be deployed in a live environment.
- **Maintenance:** The maintenance phase involves ongoing support and maintenance of the system to keep it running efficiently and effectively.

Waterfall projects are planned in advance, with strict milestones and deadlines for each phase. This approach is often used for large projects, where a clear plan and upfront requirements are essential to completing the project on time and within budget. Although it is less flexible than agile methodologies, it is still widely used across many industries.

There are some projects where a waterfall absolutely makes sense. But for others, it is slower and more costly. Changes late in a project will incur high costs as you need to move back to a prior phase and likely discard work already done. If you've ever managed a waterfall project, you're probably familiar with a change order. This is a formal artifact to record a change and the costs of making that change. Due to its linear structure and lack of flexibility, complex projects with multiple moving parts can be challenging to manage with a waterfall.

The other big drawback to waterfall projects is that code gets tested and released in big blocks. When you find a problem in testing, you need to analyze the cause of the defect and then go back and redo that part. This can cause dependencies in other project areas and lead to a cycle of changing, testing, changing again, retesting, and on and on and on. Further, because you release the product all at once, there is no opportunity to gain user feedback until the end. If your requirements gathering missed a key detail, or your analysis was off, you will not know until you've exhausted the timeline, budget, and team when it's too late to course-correct.

I might sound too negative about waterfall project management, but it can be effective. It's still the most common type of project management I've encountered throughout my career. More places are moving to agile, which we'll discuss next, but it's a transition filled with missteps. You'll be well-served to understand waterfall and know how to use it to manage a project.

AGILE

Agile project management has quickly become the go-to method for managing IT projects. It offers a more dynamic, adaptive approach to project planning and execution, which is becoming increasingly important as the world of IT speeds up. This section explores agile project management and how to employ it in your projects.

Agile utilizes a collaborative process that adapts rapidly to changing requirements during a project. It emphasizes continuous improvement and adaptation based on feedback from stakeholders, team members, and customers. This allows for greater flexibility and responsiveness and improved customer satisfaction with the end product or service. It also allows you to pivot more quickly to capture new opportunities.

Compared to traditional waterfall project management, agile approaches often lead to cost and time savings while delivering higher-quality outcomes. Agile promotes collaboration between team members by breaking tasks into small pieces and seeking and providing frequent feedback throughout the process. This helps ensure that each task is completed accurately and on time without impacting the overall timeline or budget of the project.

Since progress can be easily tracked at any point during a project, team members can identify potential issues early on when they're still relatively easy to address. Agile promotes stakeholder communication by including user stories and customer feedback loops throughout development. This helps ensure that everyone understands what's being accomplished and how it fits into their overall objectives for the final product.

Finally, agile methodologies promote creativity among IT teams, emphasizing continuous learning and improvement over rigidly following predetermined plans or processes. This means that teams can experiment with different approaches or technologies until they find the most effective solution for their situation while remaining within their allotted budget or timeframe constraints. As a result, these teams can often come up with innovative solutions that wouldn't have been possible through traditional project management methods.

By taking advantage of its flexible nature and emphasis on frequent communication between stakeholders, projects managed via an agile approach can often be completed faster with better quality outcomes than those undertaken using traditional methods such as waterfall-based models. This is why more organizations are turning to agile.

But how do we use agile in an enterprise setting? You'll need to understand a few key processes and artifacts to use agile with your teams. Before we get to those, know that agile is built around a specific philosophy for delivering projects. It relies on iterative, incremental changes that bring about evolutionary progress.

Each iteration, often called a **sprint**, is time-boxed anywhere from 1 to 4 weeks. During each sprint, a cross-functional team works to deliver specific features. These teams include people for planning, analysis, design, development, and testing. There's a focus on short feedback cycles. You build something, test it, and show it to the end users, who then provide feedback. This feedback informs your next iteration so you can make the product better.

Agile also relies on the "Minimum Viable Product" (MVP). An MVP is "that version of a new product which allows a team to collect the maximum amount of validated learning about customers with the least effort."[1] Think about the 80/20 rule. You're in a great spot if you can capture 80% of the learning from only 20% of the effort.

Once you decide to use agile, you need to begin planning. Agile planning is different from traditional project planning. Rather than trying to document all of your requirements upfront, you're instead going to create a project vision. What are the high-level overview, the project's goals, and the outcomes you will measure yourselves against?

From there, create a **backlog**. Backlog is a very *"agile-y"* word. It's just a prioritized list of tasks necessary to achieve the vision. Prioritize these tasks based on their impact on the project's success. Sometimes, this means prioritizing the task with the most visible impact on users, but other times, it means prioritizing the tasks that help your team learn the most. You need to decide which will impact project success more.

Next, select tasks to complete during the first sprint. The sprint planning will happen in a sprint planning meeting (makes sense, right?), run by either the product owner or a scrum master. Working with the development team, select items from the backlog to be completed during the upcoming sprint. This must be a collaborative effort because the development team needs to weigh in on how long tasks will take, which items they can complete more efficiently, and which will require more time.

Using this input, the scrum master creates the plan for the upcoming sprint. Everyone should leave this meeting with a clear understanding of the goal of this sprint, what they need to accomplish, and what others will be doing. It's worth noting that you will have an overall backlog for the product, and each sprint will have its own backlog.

Then, it's time to execute the sprint. The developers write code, the QA team tests, and so on. The planning in the previous step allows everyone to focus on the most critical work. This reduces distractions, produces higher-quality work, and provides more transparency to all stakeholders about what they can expect from each sprint.

It's common for the team to hold a **retrospective** after a sprint. This is another "agile-y" term that sounds fancier than it is. A retrospective is no different than any other lessons learned, after-action, or debriefing meeting you would have for a project. Where agile differs is in the discipline. A retrospective is held after every sprint. This allows the team to review progress, incorporate lessons learned, and adjust their approach for the next sprint.

Two other elements of agile are worth special mention. The **stand-up** is a short, daily meeting designed to keep the team informed and aligned and to ensure everyone works collaboratively to meet the current sprint's goals. There are some best practices to run successful stand-ups:

- Keep it short: Stand-up meetings should last no longer than 15 minutes to ensure the team stays focused and engaged throughout the session. That's why they're called stand-ups. Remove the chairs from the room.
- Stick to the agenda: The agenda typically includes three questions that each team member should answer: "What did you work on yesterday?" "What are you working on today?" and "Are any roadblocks hindering your progress?"
- Have a designated meeting facilitator. The facilitator should lead the meeting, ensure that team members stay on topic, and address any roadblocks or issues that need to be resolved.
- Encourage participation: The daily stand-up meeting is an excellent opportunity for team members to share updates, ask questions, and address concerns. Encourage everyone to participate and contribute to the discussions.
- The second item worth highlighting is the importance of continuous integration and continuous delivery (CI/CD). Agile teams use CI to ensure that code is integrated and tested throughout the project's lifecycle. CD ensures that the code is always in a releasable state. This process allows rapid, automated software delivery from development to production. With CI/CD, developers can quickly test new code and make changes as needed without halting production or compromising the quality of the product. This results in faster deployments that deliver value sooner. Additionally, CI/CD helps ensure that teams build high-quality software by automating tests and providing feedback on features before they are released.

Agile is challenging to implement if your organization is used to waterfall projects, but the benefits can be tremendous when implemented correctly. Agile can help your team improve product quality, speed delivery, increase collaboration, and improve customer satisfaction. Pick a project and give it a try.

TRACKING

Every project requires careful tracking. It doesn't matter if you use agile or waterfall; you must monitor how efficiently a project progresses. In the IT industry, the mechanisms for tracking can vary greatly depending on the scope of the project and its objectives. They can range from simple tracking systems for individual tasks to more complex platforms that track progress at multiple levels. By monitoring your project, you can compare actual to planned performance, identify and solve issues, and keep your team and stakeholders informed and aligned. Project tracking helps you ensure that your project stays on schedule and within budget and that you deliver quality results.

Just about everyone who has managed an IT project knows about Microsoft Project, even if they've never used it. This powerful software allows users to create detailed schedules, assign tasks to team members, track costs and resources, analyze performance data, and generate comprehensive reports. It also offers features like portfolio analysis and resource pooling, which allow managers to quickly allocate resources across multiple projects and ensure they remain within budget. Project has been traditionally used for waterfall projects, but it now includes tools to manage Scrum and Kanban projects. MS Project, when used well, can rigorously track every detail of a project. However, it comes with heaps of overhead. Unless you are already an expert, there are better, easier tools to use with agile projects.

Many of today's cloud-based project management tools make it easy to get started. These platforms make it easy to create task lists, share documents with team members, coordinate stakeholder conversations, keep everyone up-to-date on progress, set deadlines, and identify potential risks. Some popular examples include SmartSheet, Asana, Wrike, and Monday.com. By the time you read this, others will likely have cropped up.

Don't forget about Microsoft Excel. Excel is not a project management tool, but I've used it to manage more projects than all other tools combined. It's easy to use, lends itself naturally to a "task list" approach, and is easily used to track owners, due dates, dependencies, etc. You can also build Gantt charts in Excel, though this is a manual process. With the online version through M365, you can share updates in real time and collaborate with various stakeholders. Excel is best suited to smaller projects—large lists of linked dependencies will cause problems. But many of your projects will work just fine with Excel.

Agile tools like Jira make it easy for managers to break down large projects into smaller sprints, allowing them to be tracked more effectively over time. They also allow teams to estimate the amount of work needed for each task and adjust resources accordingly throughout the process.

Finally, many companies use custom dashboards as part of their project management processes to visualize progress within various metrics like cost or timeline completion rates. These dashboards typically integrate with existing workflow tools so managers can access updated data without constantly switching between different interfaces.

Regardless of your tool, project tracking has certain best practices you should keep in mind:

- Define your project scope and objectives clearly and communicate them to your team and stakeholders.
- Break down your project into manageable tasks and assign them to responsible team members.
- Use a tool that suits your project needs and preferences.
- Update your project status progress regularly and accurately.
- Monitor your project performance using key performance indicators (KPIs) and metrics.
- Celebrate your project achievements and learn from your project challenges.

Project tracking is vital for any manager who wants to deliver successful projects. These best practices will help you to improve your project management effectiveness.

ISSUES AND RISKS

Pay special attention to issues and risks, as they have the potential to derail your project, blow up your budget, and even hurt your career. Diligent, proactive risk and issue management will help keep your projects and career on track. You'll never plan for every contingency—a major storm may knock out power to your data center, a strike by the nation's railway workers may strand equipment across the country, or a pandemic might force everyone to pack up and work remotely. These are just some of the risks that can, and have, impacted projects in the last 30 years. However, putting some time and effort into forecasting your project's risks and the steps you can take to mitigate them will pay off.

Risks and issues are often used interchangeably, but there are important differences. Issue management deals with problems that have already occurred. These require immediate action to resolve. Risk management deals with uncertainties that may or may not happen in the future and requires proactive planning and strategies to prevent or mitigate their impact. If it's happening, it's an issue. If it might happen, it's a risk.

It might be helpful to think of a few examples. If your lead developer resigns from your company, you have an issue. If your code fails User Acceptance Testing (UAT), you have an issue (or many). If you have three tasks on the critical path scheduled for the same week and all rely on the same developer, you likely have a risk. So, how do you manage them? Identification, analysis, prioritization, response planning, and monitoring & control.

The first step is to pull the team together to brainstorm and document all the possible risks that may arise during the project. Some sources of risks include project scope, schedule, budget, quality, resources, stakeholders, environment, and technology. Use various techniques to identify risks, such as interviews, surveys, checklists, Strengths, Weaknesses, Opportunities, and Threats (SWOT) analysis, and lessons learned. This is often called the **identification** stage.

Next, assess the probability and impact of each risk on the project. This is the **analysis** step. Probability is the likelihood of a risk or issue occurring, while impact is the magnitude of its effect on the project. Use qualitative and quantitative methods to analyze risks and issues, such as risk matrices, probability-impact charts, expected monetary value analysis, and decision trees. You'll want to keep this discussion within the realm of the possible and within your ability to control. There's a risk a meteor might strike the earth and extinguish all life, but it's unlikely, and if it happens, there's not much you can do about it. However, even some remote risks are worth considering depending on your project. If you're building a new data center, you'll want to look at flood maps. Be aware that "100-year floods" are increasing in frequency.[2]

Prioritization is the third step. Rank the risks and issues according to their importance and urgency. When prioritizing, you should consider the risk tolerance of the stakeholders and the organization. Focus on the high-priority risks and issues that need immediate attention and action.

Then, develop strategies and actions to deal with each risk and issue. With risks, there are four categories of activities you can take:

- Avoid—eliminate or reduce the probability or impact of the risk
- Transfer—shift the responsibility or impact of the risk to another party
- Mitigate—decrease the probability or impact of the risk
- Accept—do nothing to mitigate and deal with results if a risk materializes

For issues, you can

- Resolve—find a solution to eliminate or reduce the issue
- Escalate—refer the issue to a higher authority for decision or action
- Defer—postpone dealing with the issue until a later time
- Accept—do nothing and live with the issue (Figure 9.2)

This is called **response planning.** Agreeing on how you will handle each risk and issue ensures alignment and clear expectations. No one will be surprised when a risk materializes or an issue delays your project.

Lastly is **monitoring and control**: Track and review the status and performance of each risk and issue throughout the project lifecycle. These are typically tracked in risk registers and issue logs. You need to update artifacts

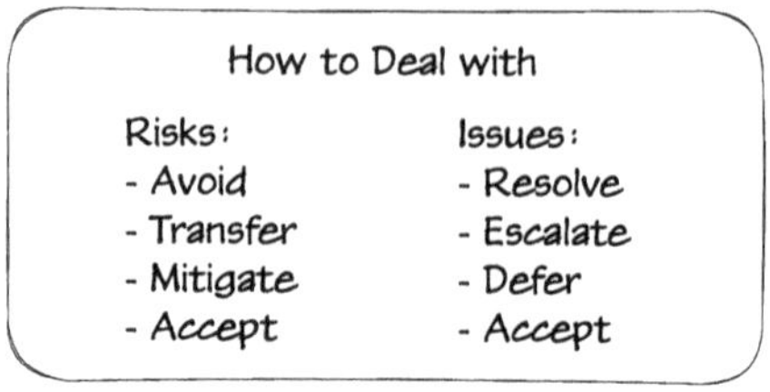

Figure 9.2 Risks and issues.

and communicate the information to relevant stakeholders regularly. We'll talk more about how to do that in the next section.

Issue and risk management is essential to managing any project, but it does not need to be complicated. Think about what could go wrong or what has gone wrong and how to address it. The biggest mistake project managers make, from the most junior, straight-out-of-school project manager (PM) to someone with 25 years of experience, is to cover up, hide, deny, or ignore risks. They rarely resolve themselves. The best thing you can do is raise them early. As a project manager, your job is not to solve every issue and risk but to track them and alert the right stakeholders. You'll do that through reporting.

REPORTING

"Communication is the lifeblood of any organization, the righteous vein that conveys directions with distinction," says Dr. Mark Whitman.[3] Project communication comes in the form of reports. Reporting provides stakeholders with information about the project's progress and allows them to make informed decisions. The reporting requirements vary depending on the scope of the project and its objectives. Your mantra for reporting should be *Accurate, Actionable, and Concise.*

There's no such thing as one-size-fits-all reporting. Determine who will consume your reports and what type of information they need. Different stakeholders have varying interest levels in the project, so it's essential to tailor your reports to each audience. Senior management may require high-level summaries focusing on overall objectives and timelines, whereas more technical audiences might need detailed analyses of specific processes.

It is also essential to consider how the report will be received by different audiences when structuring it. Most executives prefer charts, graphs, and dashboards, while developers might prefer more text with technical details they can study. Additionally, many stakeholders may not have time to read lengthy documents, so ensure that your reports are concise yet comprehensive enough to convey all necessary information. It's a tricky balance you need to find on each project.

When constructing a report for any given audience, there are several critical elements to consider: goals and objectives, scope description, timeline overview, budget status (including variance), resource utilization, risk assessment and response strategies, issues faced (with proposed action plans), highlights/milestones achieved since the last reporting period, and requested changes to scope. Depending on the type of audience receiving the report and their level of involvement in the project management process itself, additional elements such as team performance metrics or customer satisfaction feedback might also be included to provide a more comprehensive picture.

Your goal is to provide all project stakeholders with the information they need to understand the project and make decisions. Your information must be accurate—a loss of confidence in the underlying data will doom your reports—and actionable. Ask yourself, "So what?" when compiling your reports.

Shakespeare famously wrote, "Brevity is the soul of wit." It's also the soul of status reporting. Accurate, actionable, and concise. I've been through some terrible project management meetings where the PM reviewed 75 slides of metrics every week. It was a waste of everyone's time—the PM spent days preparing, the team rushed to provide the PM updates, and we all sat disengaged for 90% of the presentation. Instead, distill the project into 5–7 key metrics that strongly correlate to success or failure. Report regularly on those metrics. You can have others available if asked, but avoid death by PowerPoint.

Project reporting is largely an iterative and evolutionary process. If you join a project partway through, pick up where the last manager left off. If you're starting a new project, start small and seek feedback. You don't need to track every metric right out of the gate. Instead, focus on your mantra—Accurate, Actionable, and Concise.

PRIORITIZING AND ESTIMATING

Projects requiring prioritization of work the same way your day-to-day activities do. Earlier, we discussed the Eisenhower Matrix for prioritization and the Eliminate, Automate, Delegate approach. Those skills are excellent for your personal and team workload. But when it comes to managing projects, other tools will make your life easier and your projects more successful. Each tool starts with a product roadmap or, if using agile, starts with a backlog.

As you prioritize your work, you need to estimate the duration and effort required to deliver each component. Estimation is as much art as science, and you will undoubtedly get better with experience. You should trust the more experienced people on your team and do your best to build estimates from the bottom up. There are a few pitfalls that managers fall into, but you can avoid them simply by knowing about them.

Don't assume that everything will go well throughout the project lifecycle. Leave time for issues that will inevitably crop up. Add some slack in the schedule for when your developer gets stuck, when a unit test fails, or when users report defects during UAT. Murphy's law is very real. Things will go wrong. Building a schedule based on perfect execution is a recipe for failure.

The other mistake managers make is assuming you can compress a timeline by adding resources. Sometimes, this works, but adding people often only worsens the problem. I had a boss who used to say, "Nine women can't make a baby in a month." While not the most polished metaphor, there is a lot of truth to it. Frederick Brooks, a technical leader at IBM's computer division in the 1960s, wrote an entire book called *The Mythical Man-Month*,[4] which, among other things, argues that cost varies directly with the number of people and duration, but progress does not. It's tempting to throw resources at a problem, but you're better off admitting you're behind schedule and replanning.

Three popular prioritization tools to help with your project are The $100 Test, MoSCoW, and Kano. There are many others, but these provide examples for you to consider.

- **The $100 Test** requires you to gather the relevant stakeholders and prioritize a list of items. Each stakeholder is given an imaginary $100. They divide the money among the features they want to prioritize, with the most important receiving extra money. Ultimately, you tally the total "bids" for each item and prioritize them from highest to lowest. This gives all your stakeholders a voice and lets the group collectively set priorities.
- **MoSCoW** is a straightforward tool for identifying your "Must Have," "Should Have," "Could Have," and "Won't Have" features. "Must Have" refers to requirements that must be met for the project to be deemed a success. "Should Have" represents high-priority items that ought to be included if possible, with potential workarounds distinguishing them from "Must Haves." "Could Have" features are desirable but not essential and should be included if time and resources permit. "Won't Have" items are explicitly designated as out of scope but may be revisited in the future.
- **Kano**, developed by Professor Noriaki Kano, classifies items as basic, performance, and excitement. This model takes a customer satisfaction approach. Basic items are the minimum necessary for the product to be useful. Performance items are those that customers value and drive buying decisions (think extra storage in a laptop). Excitement items drive customer delight. These might be items the customer didn't know they wanted but will set your product apart.

Each method creates a prioritized list of project features, but each takes a slightly different approach to get there. You can experiment with multiple systems, but be sure to land on a single prioritized list for your projects.

NOTES

1 Ries, E. (2024, March 8). *What is an MVP?* Lean Startup Co. https://leanstartup.co/what-is-an-mvp/.
2 High Meadows Environmental Institute. (2019, August 27). *'100-year' floods will happen every one to 30 years, according to new coastal flood prediction maps - High Meadows Environmental Institute.* https://environment.princeton.edu/news/100-year-floods-will-happen-every-one-to-30-years-according-to-new-coastal-flood-prediction-maps/.
3 Whitman, M. (n.d.). *Chapter II: Communications is the Life Blood of Any Organization.* Pressbooks. https://milnepublishing.geneseo.edu/drinkswearstealandlieleadershipinfoureasysteps/chapter/chapter-ii-communications-is-the-life-blood-of-any-organization/.
4 Brooks, Frederick P., Jr. (1982). *The Mythical man-month : Essays on software engineering.* Reading, MA: Addison-Wesley Pub. Co.

RECOMMENDED ADDITIONAL READING

Brooks, Frederick P., Jr. (1982). *The Mythical Man-Month: Essays on Software Engineering.* Reading, MA: Addison-Wesley Pub. Co.
Martin, R. C. (2019). *Clean agile: Back to Basics.* Financial Times/Prentice Hall.
McConnell, S. (2006). *Software Estimation: Demystifying the Black Art.* United States: Microsoft Press.
Sutherland, J. (2014) *Scrum: The Art of Doing Twice the Work in Half the Time.* New York: Crown Business.

Chapter 10

Change management

Change is an unavoidable constant in business and one of the principal sources of risk to any game plan. Accounting for that inevitable change and managing the risks associated with that variability often means the difference between success and failure. It requires foresight, nimbleness, structure, and resilience. In an IT setting, this is especially true. Projects lead to changes. Patches lead to changes. Upgrades, tweaks, and scheduled releases lead to changes. Change both drives and bedevils IT organizations. When we speak of change, we mean anything that alters the production (and certain non-production) environment. In most IT shops, change is constant and unavoidable. How well they manage those changes separates good IT organizations from bad.

Change management is risk management. It improves efficiency and reduces the number of late nights you'll need to spend at the office. Good change management practices set successful IT organizations apart from those that struggle. It separates staff who spend their weekends at breweries and ballgames from those who spend their weekends at their desk or locked in a data center.

There are two ways to think about change management and two ways people use the term. Organizational Change Management helps companies adapt to change. It minimizes resistance, enhances employee buy-in, smooths transitions, and helps to ensure that the full value of changes is captured. Organizational change management asks questions like: what's the proper organizational structure, how do we communicate changes to affected audiences, what training do we need to deliver, and do we have the right sponsorship? These are all important considerations. If you are working on a project delivering large-scale change to your organization, make sure someone is focused on organizational change management.

The other type of change management, sometimes called change control, is the step-by-step process of making changes to your organization's production environment—how you launch a new product, patch a server, make network routing changes, etc. What are the processes, documents, and approvals needed? All organizations need a formal change control process

DOI: 10.1201/9781003562160-13

for production to ensure uptime and environmental stability for their customers. Lower environments (Sandbox, Development, Testing, etc.) may be managed more loosely. Higher non-production environments (UAT, Staging) can be a mixed bag depending on your organization.

ORGANIZATIONAL CHANGE MANAGEMENT

Ask anyone how to fix something, and they will give you 15 ways to improve it. We are chock full of good ideas. We all want to make things better. Yet tell those same people that you're going to change how things are done, and they will inevitably dig their heels in. Everyone wants to improve, but no one wants to change. This is the fundamental paradox of organizational change management. Douglas Sherwin captured the sentiment well in 1975 when he wrote, "Change is great when you are its agent; it is only bad when you are its object."[1] The goal of Organizational Change Management is to overcome this resistance to change.

The ADKAR model[2] is a change management framework designed to help organizations adopt and sustain change. The model identifies five key stages employees go through during a change:

- **Awareness:** Understanding the need for change and why it's happening
- **Desire:** Being motivated to support the change
- **Knowledge:** Having the information and training to understand how to change
- **Ability:** Having the skills and behaviors to implement the change
- **Reinforcement:** Sustaining the change over time

This model focuses on guiding individuals through the change process by breaking down resistance and barriers along the way. It takes the approach that organizational change is really the sum of many individuals changing their behaviors and attitudes. The model also focuses on building sustainable change through hands-on practice so people get comfortable with new ways of working, refresher sessions to review processes and answer questions, and peer support to build internal capacity.

One of the most effective ways to bring about organizational change is to involve as many people across the organization as possible. Researchers Michael Norton, Daniel Mochon, and Dan Ariely coined "The Ikea Effect" to describe our bias toward things we helped create. They explained the Ikea Effect like this: "Labor alone can be sufficient to induce greater liking for the fruits of one's labor: even constructing a standardized bureau, an arduous, solitary task, can lead people to overvalue their (often poorly constructed) creations."[3]

The idea applies to more than Swedish furniture. Involve employees in the early stages of planning change initiatives. Use focus groups or surveys to gather input and encourage team members to share their ideas on how to improve current processes. Organize collaborative sessions where employees can work together to design new workflows, processes, or tools. This not only boosts engagement but also results in solutions that have practical buy-in from the team. Finally, Keep all team members informed about how their input shapes the change. Let them see how their wobbly chair begins to take shape.

BLOCKING AND TACKLING: THE FUNDAMENTALS OF CHANGE MANAGEMENT

Change management in IT isn't glamorous. It doesn't attract attention when things go well, but when it fails, it can bring an entire organization to its knees. A single, poorly executed change can lock users out of critical systems, take down revenue-generating platforms, or corrupt production databases. It's often not a cyberattack or a sophisticated external threat that causes the biggest disruptions—it's our own internal mistakes. The companies that get change management right are the ones that have mastered execution—doing the simple things well, over and over again, without shortcuts or surprises.

In football, coaches emphasize that games are won not by gimmicks or elaborate strategies but by executing the fundamentals—blocking, tackling, and disciplined play. IT is no different. The organizations that handle change well don't do anything revolutionary. They plan properly, test thoroughly, document their actions, schedule changes at the right time, and communicate with the right people. They understand that the key to stability is consistency.

The temptation in IT is to chase complexity, to believe that a sophisticated change management system with layers of approvals and automated workflows will prevent failure. But the process alone doesn't guarantee success. In fact, overcomplicating change management can create its own risks—frustrating engineers, slowing down business innovation, and encouraging people to find ways around the system. The best IT teams understand that the process should enable execution, not obstruct it.

Plan first, then move

Every IT leader has seen a change fail because it wasn't properly planned. When a deployment goes wrong, the root cause is rarely some unpredictable technical failure. More often, it's because someone assumed something would work without verifying, skipped over a key dependency, or underestimated the impact of the change.

Good planning doesn't mean excessive documentation or unnecessary approvals. It means knowing exactly what you're changing, why you're changing it, and how you'll know if it worked. It means identifying dependencies before they become problems and ensuring that no one is caught off guard when a critical system behaves differently than expected. The best IT teams don't treat planning as a bureaucratic hurdle—they treat it as an essential part of the job.

Execution without planning is gambling. If you're relying on luck to get a change into production smoothly, you're setting yourself up for failure. A well-planned change considers every angle—how it will be tested, who needs to be involved, what the risks are, and most importantly, what happens if something goes wrong. If there's no clear rollback plan, the change isn't ready. If a critical team hasn't been informed, the change isn't ready. If testing was rushed, the change isn't ready. The IT teams that succeed long-term are the ones that take planning seriously, every single time.

Testing

The fastest way to break production is to deploy a change that hasn't been tested. Yet, IT teams continue to push untested changes into live environments under the pressure of deadlines and executive demands. The justifications are always the same: "We don't have time," "It's a small change," "We'll test in production." None of these excuses matter when a "small" change locks out thousands of users or takes down a critical database.

Testing is nonnegotiable. It starts with verifying the current system state before a change even begins. If you don't know what "normal" looks like, you'll never be able to tell if something is broken after deployment. Testing in a non-production environment is equally critical. Every IT shop has a story about the change that "worked fine in dev" but failed spectacularly in production. If you don't have a true staging environment that mirrors production as closely as possible, you're taking unnecessary risks.

Even after a change is deployed, verification testing ensures that everything is functioning as expected. There should never be a moment of "we think it worked" or "we hope it's fine." A disciplined IT team verifies success with real data before considering a change complete.

Documentation

No one enjoys writing documentation, but it's one of the most important things an IT team can do. Without it, troubleshooting becomes guesswork, onboarding new employees takes longer, and future changes become riskier. Documentation isn't about writing for the sake of writing—it's about creating a clear record of what was changed, why it was changed, and how it was implemented.

Most teams don't struggle with creating documentation; they struggle with keeping it updated. Outdated documentation is often worse than no documentation at all because it provides a false sense of security. An engineer following bad documentation can cause just as much damage as one working with no guidance at all. The best IT teams make documentation a living part of their change process, not an afterthought.

Don't schedule your own disaster

A good change can still become a disaster if it's deployed at the wrong time. Every IT leader has seen it happen—an important update scheduled during peak business hours, a critical system upgrade done just before a major product launch, or a database migration attempted late on a Friday afternoon before a long weekend.

Timing is everything. Changes should be scheduled when business impact is lowest, when the right personnel are available to monitor and troubleshoot, and when conflicting IT projects won't create unnecessary risk. And if you think Friday afternoon is a good time for a change, study "Read Only Fridays."[4]

Communication

One of the biggest failures in change management isn't technical—it's a failure to communicate. IT teams assume that because they understand what's happening, everyone else does too. But for most users, an unexpected change—no matter how small—can be disruptive. A well-executed technical change can still create chaos if users don't know what's coming.

In the absence of information, your audience is stuck with FUD—fear, uncertainty, and doubt.[5] They assume the worst – that you can't do your job. Clear, timely communication ensures that business teams aren't caught off guard and that IT teams are aligned on expectations. Communication should happen before, during, and after a change. Before the change, stakeholders should understand what's happening and why. During the change, real-time updates ensure that if something goes wrong, the right people know immediately. After the change, follow-ups confirm that everything is working as expected and that there are no lingering issues. Silence after a change breeds confusion, which leads to frustration. Frustration leads to escalations that make your life more difficult.

Discipline wins

Change management isn't about complexity—it's about discipline. The best IT organizations don't take shortcuts. They don't skip planning. They don't push untested code into production. They don't make changes in the dark. They follow a repeatable, disciplined process because they know that small mistakes lead to big failures.

Blocking and tackling aren't exciting, but it's what separates high-performing IT teams from the ones that keep making the same mistakes. IT's reputation is built on trust, and nothing erodes trust faster than failed changes and preventable outages. Master the fundamentals, execute with discipline, and change management stops being a constant battle—it becomes a strength.

STANDARD WORK

Standard Work is a core principle of Lean management that plays a crucial role in creating consistency, efficiency, and quality. Put simply, standardizing work means "identifying the best and easiest way to do the job."[6] It involves documenting the best-known methods for completing tasks clearly and step-by-step so that everyone follows the same procedures. By establishing a well-defined process, you can build a reliable baseline from which continuous improvements are made over time. Standard Work also makes change management much easier since you start with a known and well-documented baseline.

Standard Work provides a documented process that outlines each task, the sequence in which tasks should be completed, the timing, and the resources required. It is not merely about recording current practices; it is about establishing a standard that ensures everyone in the department operates from the same playbook. This uniformity is critical in environments where minor inconsistencies can lead to significant issues, such as system downtime or security vulnerabilities.

The documented procedures guide all team members, ensuring that processes are repeatable and predictable. As the organization grows or faces new challenges, Standard Work offers a stable foundation upon which further improvements can be made. While borrowed from manufacturing (specifically and most notably from Toyota),[7] this approach is particularly beneficial in IT, where the complexity of tasks and the fast-paced nature of technological change require attention to detail and a consistent methodology.

By documenting every process—from initiating a change to completing a system update—Standard Work reduces the risk of errors. The standard operating procedures (SOPs) include defined checkpoints and reviews, which help make sure critical steps aren't overlooked. This consistency is essential for maintaining the reliability of systems and reducing the likelihood of mistakes that could compromise security or performance.

With Standard Work, you map out processes in detail, identifying redundant steps and eliminating bottlenecks. This detailed mapping makes it possible to streamline workflows, reducing the time and effort needed to complete a task. As every team member adheres to the same process, tasks are completed more quickly and efficiently, which is particularly important during periods of high demand or when deploying critical updates.

A significant benefit of Standard Work is its role in communication and training. For new hires, a well-documented SOP provides clear guidance on how to perform their tasks, thereby reducing the learning curve. Established team members also benefit, as they have a reference that reinforces best practices and clarifies expectations. This uniform understanding across the team minimizes miscommunication and ensures that everyone is aligned with the department's goals and procedures.

The nature of IT is dynamic, with technologies and processes evolving rapidly. Standard Work is designed to be a living document that is continuously reviewed and updated. Managers can use performance metrics and team feedback to identify areas for improvement and adjust the procedures accordingly. This iterative process fosters a culture of continuous improvement, where every team member contributes to refining the methods and tools used in day-to-day operations.

Standard Work integrates necessary controls, risk assessments, and quality checks into everyday processes. With every change or update being meticulously documented, there is a clear audit trail that simplifies both internal and external reviews. This systematic approach ensures that the department adheres to industry standards and enhances overall security and reliability by reducing potential vulnerabilities.

How can you take advantage of standard work on your team? Begin by mapping out the current workflows for essential IT functions, such as change management, incident response, and system maintenance. It is important to detail every step of the process, including the individuals' roles and the tools or resources used at each stage.

Transform the process maps into written SOPs with detailed, step-by-step instructions. Each SOP should clearly define responsibilities and expected outcomes and include any necessary forms or checklists. Input from those performing these tasks day to day is important to ensure the procedures make sense. These documents need to be straightforward and accessible so that they can be easily understood and followed by every team member.

Standard Work offers a powerful framework for managing IT processes with consistency. By implementing Standard Work, you can ensure that every process—from routine maintenance to major system changes—is executed flawlessly.

NOTES

1 Sherwin, D. (1975). Strategy for Winning Employee Commitment. In *Harvard Business Review on Management*. Harper & Row.
2 *The ProsCi ADKAR® Model | ProsCi.* (n.d.). https://www.prosci.com/methodology/adkar.
3 Norton, M. I., Mochon, D., & Ariely, D. (2011). The IKEA effect: When labor leads to love. *Journal of Consumer Psychology*, 22(3), 453–460. https://doi.org/10.1016/j.jcps.2011.08.002.
4 Larrabee, S. (2024, November 29). *Arguments for a Read-Only Fridays*. FatLab Web Support. https://fatlabwebsupport.com/blog/arguments-for-a-read-only-friday/.

5 Brown, J. (2021). *The security Leader's communication playbook: Bridging the Gap Between Security and the Business*. CRC Press.
6 Dennis, P. (2015). *Lean Production Simplified: A Plain-Language Guide to the World's Most Powerful Production System* (3rd ed.). CRC Press.
7 Ohno, Taiichi (1988). *Toyota Production System: Beyond Large-Scale Production*. CRC Press.

RECOMMENDED ADDITIONAL READING

Brown, Jeffrey W. (2022). *The Security Leader's Communication Playbook: Bridging the Gap between Security and the Business*. CRC Press.
Dennis, P. (2015). *Lean Production Simplified: A Plain-Language Guide to the World's Most Powerful Production System* (3rd ed.). CRC Press.
Kotter, J. (2012). *Leading Change*. Boston, MA: Harvard Business Review Press.
Ohno, Taiichi (1988). *Toyota Production System: Beyond Large-Scale Production*. CRC Press.

Chapter 11

Risk and security

You've read the headlines—WannaCry, NotPetya, SolarWinds, Colonial Pipeline, Sony Pictures, and MOVEit. And on. And on. And On. Former FBI Director Robert Mueller said, "There are only two types of companies: those that have been hacked and those that will be. And even they are converging into one category: companies that have been hacked and will be hacked again."

Cyberattacks are growing in scale and cost. They now look more like weather systems than isolated storms—constantly changing, increasing in intensity, and affecting all industries simultaneously. The average cost of a data breach in 2024 was nearly $5M.[1] What keeps Chief Information Security Officers (CISOs) awake at night isn't the stereotypical teenage hacker but well-funded criminal syndicates leveraging artificial intelligence to automate phishing campaigns and exploit vulnerabilities at scale.

According to McKinsey, organizations spent $150 billion in cybersecurity in 2021, 12% more than the year before.[2] Yet, even this may not be enough. That same McKinsey report estimates cyberattacks are growing 100% annually—12 % growth in security spending against a 100% increase in attacks. The gap is widening (Figure 11.1).

Organizations face a brutal paradox because customers demand seamless digital experiences while expecting ironclad security. A single breach can destroy reputations built over years—78% of consumers say they'll stop engaging with a brand after a data breach.[3]

At the same time, security teams are often seen as the "Department of No," constantly clashing with their colleagues who are seen as more innovative, trying to drive the business forward. Your job as a manager is to reframe this dynamic. You're not there to stop progress; you're there to make sure the company progresses safely. Think of cybersecurity like guardrails on the highway. They don't stop traffic. In fact, because they make driving safer, they actually allow cars to go faster. A good cybersecurity program can do the same thing.

 DOI: 10.1201/9781003562160-14

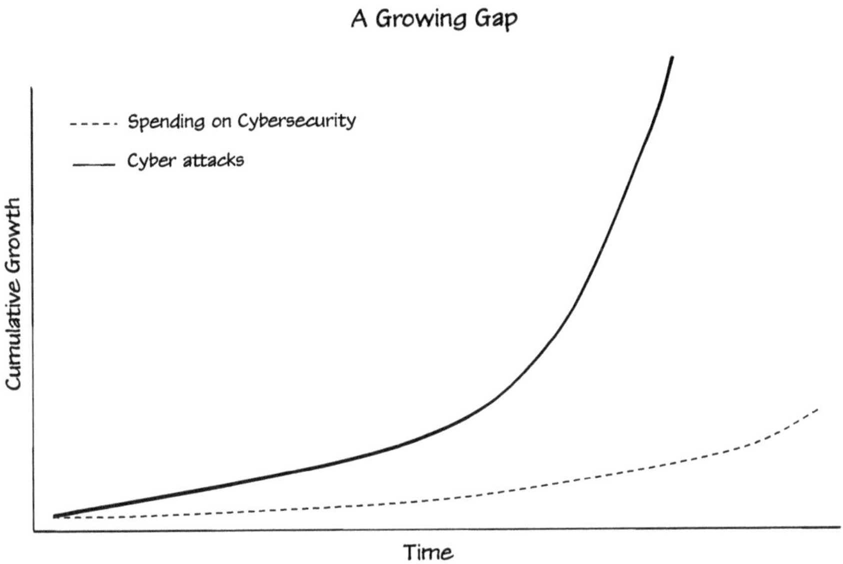

Figure 11.1 Growing cyber gap.

A RISK-BASED APPROACH

Effective cybersecurity programs use a risk-based approach to prioritize threats according to their likelihood and potential impact. They don't rely on rash responses to every new vulnerability or on spending sprees motivated by anxiety. By using this strategy, you can efficiently prioritize important risks, maximize your resources, and avoid wasting time on unimportant problems.

Early in my career, I worked for an organization that identified over 15 million vulnerabilities in its IT systems. The number was staggering. Fixing everything would have been impossible, and chasing every minor flaw would have been a waste of time. Instead, we prioritized those vulnerabilities using a risk-based approach, starting with the ones that presented the biggest and most urgent risks. Without becoming bogged down in a never-ending patching cycle, we gradually strengthened our security posture by chipping away at the list.

Identify your "crown jewels"

A risk-based approach starts with a fundamental question: What are you protecting? This is where a Crown Jewels Assessment comes in. Your organization's "Crown Jewels" are the most sensitive, valuable, and business-critical assets that would cause catastrophic damage if compromised.

To get started, create an inventory of these assets. Then, ask yourself three key questions:

1. What are the potential threats? (Hackers, insiders, or natural disasters?)
2. What security controls are in place? (Firewalls, access controls, or encryption?)
3. How are you monitoring for threats? (Security Information and Event Management (SIEM) tools, alerts, or audits?)

Any high-risk assets without strong controls should be your first priority. A healthcare organization might identify patient medical records as one of their "Crown Jewels." They would then assess potential threats such as hackers attempting to steal this sensitive information, review security controls like encryption in place to protect the data, and monitor for threats using SIEM tools to detect any unauthorized access. If they find that certain records are at high risk with weak controls, they would prioritize implementing stronger security measures to protect these assets.

Prioritize risks

Not all risks are created equal. Let's say your Crown Jewels Assessment identifies a database of critical financial records as a high-value asset. One possible threat is an earthquake that could destroy the building where the server is housed. If your organization operates on a fault line, this is a valid risk that should be mitigated. But if you're in a region with minimal seismic activity, prioritizing this risk would be a mistake.

On the other hand, phishing attacks on company emails might seem minor when viewed individually. But because phishing is a daily occurrence, the cumulative risk of someone eventually falling for one is significant. That means this risk needs to be addressed—even if each individual attack has a low impact. By focusing on likelihood and impact, organizations can reduce overall risk exposure instead of blindly checking vulnerabilities off a list.

Once you've identified and prioritized risks, you need a plan of action. Just like in project management, there are **four ways** to handle cyber risk:

1. Avoid it
2. Mitigate it
3. Transfer it
4. Accept it

Risk avoidance: The best defense is not playing

The simplest way to eliminate risk is to **avoid it altogether**. If a risk is too severe, the best option might be to remove the exposure completely. For example, some organizations limit the types of data they collect to reduce the impact of a potential breach. If a company never stores customer credit card numbers, there's zero risk of exposing them in a hack.

In another case, an organization I worked with had strict IT policies for employees traveling to China, a country known for state-sponsored cyber espionage. Employees were issued temporary, limited-access laptops, and upon return, those devices were destroyed. While it may be extreme, this strategy effectively eliminated the risk of foreign surveillance malware infiltrating corporate networks due to travel.

Risk mitigation: Reduce the blast radius

Since most risks can't be avoided, the next best strategy is **mitigation**—reducing the likelihood or impact of an attack.

Common mitigation tactics include:

- Multi-factor authentication (MFA) makes it harder for hackers to exploit stolen passwords.
- Security awareness training reduces the success rate of phishing attacks.
- Regular software patching eliminates known vulnerabilities before they're exploited.
- Firewalls, antivirus (AV), and intrusion detection stop many attacks before they succeed.

While no security measure is perfect, well-implemented mitigation strategies make cyberattacks significantly harder and less damaging. One company that was breached wrote in its after-action report: "The breach occurred because an access credential to our cloud computing environment was compromised. That cloud computing account had not been protected by multifactor authentication."[4] Similar breaches struck Target, Equifax, and Deloitte. By combining multiple mitigation strategies, you begin to build "defense-in-depth."

Risk transference: Make it someone else's problem

Some risks can't be avoided or mitigated completely, but they can be **transferred** to someone else.

Two of the most common forms of risk transference are:

- Cyber insurance, which transfers financial liability for cyber incidents to an insurance company.
- Third-party payment processors, which transfer credit card security risks to companies like Stripe or PayPal.

For instance, if a small business uses Stripe to process payments, they benefits from Stripe's advanced security measures and expertise in handling sensitive financial data. This reduces the likelihood of data breaches and financial fraud impacting the business directly. However, in the event of a security incident at Stripe, the small business may still face reputational damage and potential loss of customers due to association with the breach.

Risk transference doesn't eliminate risk. It just makes the risk someone else's responsibility. Your business still faces indirect consequences if an insurance policy doesn't cover ransomware payouts or a vendor gets breached. But in many cases, shifting direct responsibility is a smart business move.

Risk acceptance: Live with the threat

Some risks are simply unavoidable. In these cases, organizations must make a conscious decision to accept them.

Risk acceptance should never be taken lightly. It requires:

1. A thorough assessment of the risk.
2. A formal approval process from leadership.
3. Ongoing review to ensure the decision still makes sense.

For instance, a company may decide to continue using outdated software despite knowing its vulnerabilities because the cost of upgrading is too high. In this case, implementing monitoring and other compensating controls can help mitigate the security risks. However, it is important to ensure that company leadership is aware of and approves this decision in writing to avoid potential consequences in the future.

However, as a new manager, you should never accept risk alone. This is where managing up becomes crucial. Make sure leadership understands the consequences and documents their decision in writing. If things go wrong, you don't want to be held responsible for an unofficial risk acceptance.

Cybersecurity teams will never have enough time or resources to fix every vulnerability. That's why a risk-based approach is essential. Start with a Crown Jewels Assessment to focus on the most critical assets. Prioritize risks based on likelihood and impact. Choose the right strategy to avoid, mitigate, transfer, or accept the risk. Monitor and revisit decisions to stay ahead of evolving threats.

By shifting from reactive security to a risk-based approach, you can allocate resources wisely, protect your most valuable assets, and reduce the chaos of chasing every vulnerability. Cyber threats are always evolving, but with the right strategy, so can your defenses.

POLICIES

Cybersecurity policies serve as a foundation for trust. A company that actively enforces robust security policies signals to customers, partners, investors, regulators, and stakeholders that it takes cybersecurity seriously. These policies act as blueprints for managing risk. They ensure that security efforts are aligned with the organization's broader goals rather than being a patchwork of reactive measures.

One of the most common mistakes organizations make when developing cybersecurity policies is starting from scratch. It's tempting to create a list of everything that seems important, but this can lead to disjointed, inconsistent, and overlapping rules. You're better off aligning with an established cybersecurity framework.

Several respected organizations provide frameworks to guide policy development:

- The National Institute of Standards and Technology (NIST) Cybersecurity Framework
- The International Organization for Standardization (ISO 27001, 27002, and 27005)
- The Center for Internet Security (CIS)
- Health Information Trust Alliance (HITRUST) for Healthcare, Payment Card Industry—Data Security Standard (PCI-DSS) for Payments, and Federal Information Security Act (2014) (FISMA) for federal agencies

By selecting a recognized framework, you can make sure your policies are comprehensive, covering key areas like data protection, access management, incident response, and regulatory compliance. More importantly, adhering to a structured framework reduces the risk of conflicting, overlapping, or missing policies.

The importance of cybersecurity policies is highlighted in NIST Special Publication SP 500-169,[5] which states:

> The success of an information resources protection program depends on the policy generated and on the attitude of management toward securing information on automated systems. You, the policy maker, set the tone and the emphasis on how important a role information security will have within your agency.

Security policies are only as strong as the leadership behind them. Leaders set the tone for the organization, define priorities, enforce policies, and ensure security measures align with business objectives. Think of cybersecurity policies like a Commander's Intent. Just as a military commander provides a clear vision of success and guidelines for achieving it, security policies give employees a structured, adaptable framework for protecting critical systems. They need not dictate every action, much like a commander wouldn't prescribe *how* to take an objective.

Crafting policies is a multistep process:

1. Design and Draft: First, the security team drafts a policy based on the selected framework and the organization's risk profile. If an existing policy is outdated, it is revised to address new threats or regulatory requirements.
2. Review and Approve: Once the draft is complete, ikey stakeholders, including legal, HR, and senior leadership are given a chance to review and provide comments. This ensures the policy aligns with regulatory requirements, employment policies, and corporate culture. Buy-in from senior leadership is critical.
3. Implementation and Enforcement: At this stage, the policy is communicated to all employees in a way that is easy to understand and apply. Additionally, technical controls that can help enforce the policy are established, and monitoring adherence to the policy begins.

If you follow those three steps, you'll end up with a set of policies that have broad buy-in. But there's one more framework to keep in mind to ensure your policies are effective and actionable. All of your policies should be subjected to the 5Ps test. Every policy must be

- **Practical**—Can employees and teams follow this policy without crippling productivity?
- **Purposeful**—Does this policy address a specific risk?
- **Plain**—Can nontechnical employees understand what the policy requires of them?
- **Proven**—Do you have evidence this policy reduces risk?
- **Periodic**—Is there a timeframe when the policy will be updated/reviewed?

A cybersecurity policy that employees can't understand is as ineffective as not having one at all. Effective policies require ongoing communication, education, training, and reinforcement. New employees should be required to review and acknowledge cybersecurity policies as part of their onboarding process. Existing employees should go through security awareness training at least every year. And log-in screens should display reminders. Employees should be required to acknowledge receipt and understanding of security policies. This is crucial not just for compliance but also for legal protection. If an employee violates security policies and the organization takes disciplinary action, having documented proof that they were aware of the policy helps protect the organization from legal disputes.

Beyond reducing risk, cybersecurity policies can provide organizations with legal protection. Ohio, Utah, and Connecticut have passed safe harbor laws that shield companies from liability in the event of a cyber breach if they can demonstrate compliance with recognized cybersecurity frameworks.[6]

This means that an organization with well-documented policies and clear enforcement mechanisms can mount a much stronger legal defense against lawsuits related to data breaches. More states are expected to introduce similar laws, making cybersecurity policies a critical legal safeguard.

Organizations that invest in strong cybersecurity policies gain a competitive edge. Customers, investors, and partners increasingly evaluate security practices before doing business with an organization. Demonstrating a commitment to cybersecurity can enhance an organization's reputation, increase customer trust, and even provide a differentiating factor in the marketplace.

A well-designed set of cybersecurity policies is a strategic asset. It empowers employees to take security seriously, builds confidence among customers and partners, and provides the foundation for a resilient organization in the face of growing cyber threats.

By aligning policies with an established framework, securing executive buy-in, ensuring effective implementation, and reinforcing compliance, organizations can turn cybersecurity policies from an obligation into a strength.

AWARENESS TRAINING: THE HUMAN FIREWALL

When we think of cybersecurity, we often think of cutting-edge tools. Strong encryption, NextGen firewalls, AI-enabled SIEMs, Extended Detection and Response (XDR), etc. But, the biggest vulnerability in any company isn't the technology. It's the people. Human error is responsible for the majority of data breaches. According to the 2021 *Verizon Data Breach Investigations Report*, 82% of breaches involved a human element: falling for a phishing email, using weak passwords, or mishandling sensitive information.[7] You can have the best password policies, the most rigorous patching programs, and the strongest firewalls, but if your users are handing out credentials every time they get a shady email, attackers will always find a way in.

The good news is that training works. Organizations that provide well-designed security awareness training can significantly reduce incidents. A study conducted by the Ponemon Institute and published by Proofpoint found that companies investing in security awareness training cut phishing-related costs by 53%.[8] The return on investment is enormous. But for training to be effective, it has to be more than just a check-the-box exercise.

Progress, not perfection

There's no such thing as perfect security training. Humans are unpredictable, and mistakes will always happen. You could buy the most sophisticated training platform, require mandatory courses for every employee, send out simulated phishing tests every week, and someone, somewhere, will still click on a bad link. The goal of awareness training isn't to eliminate all human error; it's to reduce it over time. A well-designed training program should lead to steady improvement. Your goal is progress, not perfection. The key is to design training that is engaging, directly applicable to your users, and up-to-date.

Clear goals and measurable outcomes

Effective training programs start with goals. What specific behaviors are you trying to change? What threats are most relevant to your organization? Without clear objectives, training becomes unfocused, generic, and forgettable. For example, instead of saying, "We need to teach employees about phishing," a well-defined goal would be: "We want to increase the number of employees who can correctly identify a phishing email from 75% to 85% by the end of Q3."

A defined scope is also essential. Will your training be for all employees, or should certain groups get specialized content? While basic security training is necessary for everyone, some teams—system administrators, developers, executives—require more and different training. System admins may need guidance on managing privileged access, developers should understand secure coding practices, and executives, prime targets for spear phishing, should get extra training on social engineering threats.

Know your audience

Before rolling out training, take a moment to assess your audience's current skill level. You don't necessarily need surveys or formal testing. A simple gut check is enough. Are employees generally aware of security best practices, or are they starting from scratch?

Training should start with the basics, ensuring that everyone understands fundamental security principles—choose strong passwords, don't install sketchy software, and beware of suspicious emails. Over time, you can introduce more advanced concepts. However, overwhelming users too soon can lead to frustration and disengagement. People don't need a deep dive into encryption algorithms. Let your security team worry about that. Instead, focus on training they can implement right away.

Choose the right training materials

Training comes in many forms. Some organizations create their own content, while others purchase prepackaged programs from vendors like KnowBe4 or Ninjio. If you choose a vendor, make sure the content aligns with your specific threat landscape. A generic training video won't be as effective as a course tailored to your organization or industry.

Mix up the format. Long, text-heavy slideshows are a great way to lose your audience. Instead, blend short videos, infographics, interactive modules, and real-world phishing simulations to keep employees engaged. A little variety goes a long way in reinforcing key concepts and preventing training fatigue.

Today, most security training is delivered virtually, often through on-demand learning platforms. Ninjio specializes in short, stackable videos that are highly engaging. Live, in-person training can also be a powerful tool, especially in organizations where employees are primarily on-site.

The advantage of live training is that it fosters interaction. Employees can ask real-time questions, discuss concerns, and share their own experiences. Trainers can read the room and adjust their delivery based on engagement levels. In contrast, virtual training often relies on completion rates alone to gauge effectiveness, making it difficult to tell if the message is actually getting through. Consider blending both approaches: virtual modules for foundational learning and periodic live sessions for reinforcement.

Tracking progress and holding employees accountable

After delivering training, it's critical to track effectiveness. At a minimum, monitor completion rates. Some cyber insurance policies now require annual security awareness training for all employees, meaning you'll need proof that everyone has completed the training. For employees who don't, make sure you have a clear escalation process. Some companies rely on HR, while others escalate supervisors, directors, or even directly to divisional VPs. Find an approach that fits your company's culture.

You should also link training outcomes to security metrics since completion rates only tell part of the story. Are fewer employees clicking on phishing emails? Are more people reporting suspicious messages to IT? Are patch cadences increasing? These data points provide tangible evidence that training is working.

Continuous improvement

One-and-done security training is insufficient. Cyber threats evolve constantly, and training should keep pace. Whether your organization delivers training annually, quarterly, or monthly, each iteration should incorporate your most recent knowledge of the threat landscape. Regularly review your program and update materials based on new threats. For instance, if deepfake phishing attacks become more prevalent, incorporate that into future sessions. And, as new security tools are rolled out, like updated MFA solutions, train employees on how and why to use them. Security is not static, so your training must evolve.

The strongest security programs recognize that technology alone is not enough. A well-trained workforce is a company's last line of defense and, often, its most effective one. Invest in your people and educate them well, and your organization will be more resilient against cyber threats. The best firewall isn't made of code; it's made of people who know how to stop a threat before it happens.

TECHNICAL CONTROLS

Unlike policies, which require employee cooperation, or training, which depends on engagement, technical controls are consistent, measurable, and enforceable. That makes them easier to justify to executives and investors. They provide clear metrics that show a return on investment. A well-implemented security control is like a silent watchdog, constantly monitoring and protecting without needing breaks or buy-in.

While these controls may seem straightforward and effective, they only work if they are properly configured and managed. A firewall is only as strong as the rules configured in it. An intrusion detection system (IDS) is only as good as the intelligence feeding it. MFA is only effective when paired with strong access policies. Every technical control must also balance security and usability. Lock things down tightly, and no work gets done. Leave things too open, and you end up breached.

Passwords

Passwords have been a fundamental computer security measure for more than 60 years, dating back to Massachusetts Institute of Technology's (MIT) early computer systems in the 1960s.[9] But even before the digital age, passwords were used to enter prohibition-era speakeasies and, long before that, to grant entry to restricted areas in Ancient Rome.[10] Despite their long history, passwords remain one of the weakest links in cybersecurity. Attackers exploit stolen, weak, or reused passwords in the vast majority of breaches. As the US Army says, "A strong password is difficult for attackers to guess or crack, and its importance cannot be overstated in a time when 80% of data breaches are due to weak or stolen passwords."[11]

Organizations often attempt to mitigate this risk by enforcing longer and more complex passwords, but complexity alone isn't enough. Humans are wired for convenience, which means they reuse passwords across multiple accounts, store them in easily accessible places, or fall victim to phishing attacks that trick them into giving away their credentials. A robust password policy must go beyond complexity requirements and incorporate MFA.

MFA adds an extra layer of security by requiring users to verify their identity through something they know (password), something they have (a phone or security key), or something they are (biometrics). While MFA dramatically reduces the risk of unauthorized access, not all MFA methods are created equal. Short message service (SMS)-based MFA has known weaknesses, including subscriber identification module (SIM)-swapping attacks. A more secure alternative is using authentication apps like Google Authenticator or hardware security keys like YubiKey, which are more resistant to attacks.

Firewalls and intrusion detection

Firewalls remain one of the most widely deployed technical controls. They act as digital gatekeepers that filter network traffic based on predefined rules. Modern Next-Generation Firewalls (NGFWs) go beyond basic filtering, incorporating intrusion prevention, malware detection, and deep packet inspection to identify and block sophisticated threats. These firewalls analyze network traffic for anomalies and suspicious behavior and can respond before potential attacks escalate.

IDS monitor network activity in real-time, scanning for known attack signatures and suspicious behavior. For example, an IDS can detect if a user is logging in from two locations on opposite sides of the world within minutes—an impossibility known as "impossible travel." When properly configured, these systems provide early warnings about attacks that might otherwise go unnoticed. Some also include protection (intrusion protection systems), where the system goes beyond generating alerts and automatically blocks the threat.

Organizations also rely on SIEM systems, which aggregate logs from multiple sources, including firewalls, network devices, endpoints, and cloud services, to detect patterns of compromise. Leading SIEM solutions like Splunk and IBM QRadar use machine learning to identify emerging threats by correlating seemingly unrelated security events.

Antivirus and endpoint protection

Traditional AV software has been a cybersecurity staple for decades, but modern threats have outpaced its capabilities. Traditional AV relies on signature-based detection, meaning it can only identify known malware. However, new malware variants emerge every day, often with no existing signatures to match against. This is why many organizations have moved to Endpoint Detection and Response (EDR) solutions, which offer behavior-based detection. Instead of looking for a known virus, EDR systems analyze how software behaves—flagging activities like unauthorized encryption of files (a hallmark of ransomware) or attempts to disable security tools.

Next-generation endpoint security also includes automated response capabilities, allowing systems to quarantine infected machines, terminate malicious processes, and roll back changes caused by malware. The best security solutions don't just detect threats—they actively contain and neutralize them before they can spread.

Patching

If there's one technical control that has an outsized impact on security yet is often overlooked, it's patching. The vast majority of exploited vulnerabilities are not due to zero-day attacks but rather to unpatched known vulnerabilities. Cybercriminals don't need to invent new exploits when so many organizations fail to apply existing fixes.

A famous example is the Log4Shell vulnerability[12] in the widely used Log4j logging framework. This vulnerability, present in millions of systems worldwide, went undetected for over eight years. When it was finally disclosed in 2021, attackers raced to exploit it, targeting unpatched systems before organizations could respond. Those with mature patch management programs were able to apply fixes immediately, while others struggled to react, exposing themselves to unnecessary risk.

A robust patching strategy includes:

- Automated scanning tools (e.g., Tenable and Qualys) to identify vulnerable systems.
- Configuration management tools (e.g., Microsoft Endpoint Manager and JAMF) to deploy patches efficiently.
- Risk-based prioritization, ensuring the most critical vulnerabilities are addressed first.

Patching is more than just applying updates. It's having a strategy to respond quickly when a critical flaw is discovered.

Final thoughts: A layered approach to security

No single technical control is enough to secure an organization entirely. Attackers constantly adapt their methods to exploit the weakest links. A well-rounded cybersecurity program will combine many technical controls to create layers of security. It will also recognize that technical controls are not set-it-and-forget-it solutions. They require ongoing monitoring and regular updates to stay effective. An endpoint protection system that blocked yesterday's threats might not detect tomorrow's malware. The security landscape is always changing. You must continuously adapt to stay ahead.

BRINGING IT ALL TOGETHER: DEFENSE IN DEPTH

There are no silver bullets in cybersecurity. Humans will inevitably make mistakes. Systems will fail. Attackers will find ways to bypass the most cutting-edge defenses. Working in security is a constant game of cat and mouse where the mouse keeps getting smarter. We need to work hard to keep up.

We've touched on several strategies organizations use to defend themselves. But none of these works alone. This environment demands that you adopt what military strategists call "defense in depth"—overlapping security measures that provide multiple failure points before critical assets are compromised. Much like medieval castles had walls, moats, and archers at the turrets to defend against marauders, you need firewalls, MFA, and well-trained users to protect against cybercriminals. Each tool plays a role, but don't mistake a plethora of tools for a sound security posture. Conduct a thorough risk assessment and choose the right tools for your organization.

Security is a game of trade-offs. The only way to fully secure a system is to take it offline, lock it behind a reinforced door, and post an armed guard. But that doesn't do your users much good. You need to balance the needs of security and usability. It can be tricky since both targets shift as threats and user expectations change. Do your best. And try to find some way to sleep at night.

NOTES

1 *Cost of a data breach 2024 | IBM*. (n.d.). https://www.ibm.com/reports/data-breach.

2 Aiyer, B., Caso, J., Russell, P., & Sorel, M. (2022, October 27). *New survey reveals $2 trillion market opportunity for cybersecurity technology and service providers*. McKinsey & Company. https://www.mckinsey.com/capabilities/risk-and-resilience/our-insights/cybersecurity/new-survey-reveals-2-trillion-dollar-market-opportunity-for-cybersecurity-technology-and-service-providers.

3 *Global Survey from Ping Identity Shows Consumers Are Abandoning Brands After Data Breaches*. (n.d.). News Release Archive. https://press.pingidentity.com/2018-11-7-Global-Survey-from-Ping-Identity-Shows-Consumers-Are-Abandoning-Brands-After-Data-Breaches.

4 *Security — Timehop*. (n.d.). Timehop. https://www.timehop.com/security.

5 Helsing, C., Swanson, M., Todd, M. A. (1989). *Executive Guide to Protection of Information Resources*. NIST Special Publication SP 500-169. Retrieved from https://nvlpubs.nist.gov/nistpubs/Legacy/SP/nistspecialpublication500-169.pdf on 26 March 2023.

6 Locke Lord. (2021) *"Safe Harbor" Ports in a Cybersecurity Litigation Storm*. Retrieved from https://www.lockelord.com/newsandevents/publications/2021/10/safe-harbor-ports on 26 March 2023.

7 *Verizon Business*. (n.d.). Verizon Business. https://www.verizon.com/business/resources/reports/dbir/.

8 *The 2021 Ponemon Cost of Phishing Study | ProofPoint US*. (2023, October 31). Proofpoint. https://www.proofpoint.com/us/resources/analyst-reports/ponemon-cost-of-phishing-study.

9 McMillan, R. (2012, January 27). The world's first computer password? It was useless too. *WIRED*. https://www.wired.com/2012/01/computer-password/.
10 *Polybius on the Roman military*. (n.d.). https://web.archive.org/web/20080207011711/http://ancienthistory.about.com/library/bl/bl_text_polybius6.htm.
11 *Secure our world—CECOM recommends strong passwords and password managers*. (2024, October 14). https://www.army.mil/article/280417/secure_our_world_cecom_recommends_strong_passwords_and_password_managers.
12 Berger, A. (2024, April 25). What is Log4Shell? The Log4j vulnerability explained (and what to do about it). *Dynatrace News*. https://www.dynatrace.com/news/blog/what-is-log4shell/.

RECOMMENDED ADDITIONAL READING

Hubbard, D. W., & Seiersen, R. (2016). *How to Measure Anything in Cybersecurity Risk*. John Wiley & Sons.
Jaquith, A. (2007). *Security Metrics: Replacing Fear, Uncertainty, and Doubt*. Addison-Wesley Professional.
Perlroth, N. (2021). *This Is How They Tell Me the World Ends: Winner of the FT & McKinsey Business Book of the Year Award 2021*. Bloomsbury Publishing.
Stoll, C. (2005). *The Cuckoo's Egg: Tracking a Spy through the Maze of Computer Espionage*. Simon and Schuster.

Chapter 12

Emerging technology

Technology changes constantly. Vendors introduce new products, customer expectations shift, and new technology leads to new fields. The multitude of changes in the field makes it difficult for IT employees to stay up to date. As a manager, this is doubly true. You must keep up with your current systems, fix issues as they arise, progress on product roadmaps, and stay within your budget. But you also need to look over the horizon for new tools and technology that can enhance your offerings or potentially disrupt your business.

All new technologies go through what Gartner has termed a "Hype Cycle."[1] This framework helps organizations understand the potential for new technology and where that technology sits on a maturity curve. It informs the decision to pilot, invest, and take a wait-and-see approach. It can also help companies understand the risks and challenges of investing in new technology. The Hype Cycle has five key phases or milestones:

- Innovation Trigger: This is when a new technology is introduced. People are excited about the potential of the technology, but there is little real-world experience with it.
- Peak of Inflated Expectations: This is when the hype about the technology reaches its peak. There is a lot of investment but also a lot of failures.
- Trough of Disillusionment: This is when the hype about the technology dies down, and people start to realize that it is not as revolutionary as they thought it was. There is a lot of disillusionment and disappointment. Many organizations abandon the technology.
- Slope of Enlightenment: In this phase, organizations start to understand the actual potential of the technology and how it can be used to solve real-world problems. There is a slow but steady increase in adoption of the technology.
- Plateau of Productivity: This is the phase when the technology has matured and is widely adopted. It is used to solve real-world problems and provides a clear business benefit.

DOI: 10.1201/9781003562160-15

Like any framework, the Hype Cycle has its limitations. For one, it assumes that all technology follows the same pattern. This isn't always true. Some technologies will progress through the phases more quickly—some may skip a phase altogether. Second, it's a snapshot in time. Gartner updates their Hype Cycles annually, but innovation and adoption don't follow a prescribed calendar. Finally, the Hype Cycles published by Gartner are based on the well-informed but subjective opinions of Gartner Analysts.

Use the Hype Cycle as a model when you evaluate new technology for yourself. Regardless of where Gartner thinks a particular technology is, it's helpful to think about the overall maturity of that technology and what the future might look like. Learn to recognize when something is at the peak of inflated expectations vs. when it's in the trough of disillusionment. Such a distinction can help you evaluate what you're hearing about emerging technology.

Above all, make sure you have a business case for emerging technology. Don't buy a fancy new toy just because it's popular or you saw it at a conference. Many projects have wasted precious time, talent, and treasure because someone built a solution in search of a problem. You'll see this from vendors all the time. "Buy our new version of XYZ powered by AI!" What's the AI? How does it enhance the product? What about it will make my team or my business more successful? If you can't answer these questions, save your time and money. Stick with the tried and true. Living on the bleeding edge is exciting but can also be bloody.

In this chapter, we'll discuss some key emerging technologies as of this writing. These are intended primarily as examples. Technology changes quickly, and some of these will likely have matured by the time you read this. Others may fall out of favor and become irrelevant. And some will likely require further development—still in the emerging category. Learn about these technologies, but also learn how to assess new technology as a discipline. I can't tell you what will come next, but whatever it is, you'll be asked to figure out how to fit it into your organization.

THE INNOVATOR'S DILEMMA

Harvard Professor and noted business consultant Clay Christensen coined the name "The Innovator's Dilemma" to describe the difficult choice businesses must make when it comes to adopting new technology.[2] Christensen was writing primarily about what markets a company should target and how to rationalize their existing offerings with new offerings from upstart companies. In his classic book on the topic, Christensen provides numerous examples, like Digital Equipment Corporation (DEC) and IBM failing to adapt as the computer industry changed, integrated steel mills refusing to respond to changes brought by mini-mills, and full-service stores like Sears being unable to cope with the rise of discount retailers like Costco.

As a new manager, you're not in a position to direct how your company goes to market. You can't change corporate strategy. But there is an excellent lesson that forms the foundation for *The Innovator's Dilemma*: Emerging technology tends to improve faster than most of us expect and tends to change consumer expectations in unforeseen ways.

When digital cameras were first sold, Kodak had a lion's share of the photography market. They made so much money producing, selling, and developing films that it was impossible for management to change course and adapt to the revolution of digital photography. It's not that Kodak didn't see the change coming. In fact, the first prototype of a digital camera was created by Steve Sasson in 1975.[3] Can you guess where Steve worked? Yup, Kodak.

The camera was huge, slow, complicated, and produced poor-quality images. Kodak, sitting on its massive cash flow and world-class film quality, failed to grasp how this new invention might one day change its business.

That's one of the difficulties of emerging technology. The early iterations are bad. When faced with a camera the size of a mailbox, lacking a screen, and requiring close to 30 seconds to take a picture, Kodak made the "correct" call and dismissed it as a threat to its film business. But, of course, digital cameras improved. Apple released the iPhone, which had a camera built right in. Suddenly, carrying a phone and a camera seemed like too much.

The idea of waiting hours or days for a photo lab to develop images was no longer palatable. Around the same time, social media took off, and people wanted to take photos and share them instantly. Kodak's business model no longer worked. The "new" technology—digital cameras—and the complementary technology—social media—created an ecosystem that demanded new business models.

There are two lessons to take from this:

- Emerging technology will get better. Emerging technology based on processing power, memory, or network effects will improve faster than most expect (I'll explain why in the next section).
- Complementary technology changes will create new uses, new consumer demand, and new business models that are hard to foresee.

As you manage emerging technology, keep these two lessons in mind: the first iteration will be the worst iteration, and complementary technologies will open new possibilities. Find some time and mental space to imagine how the technology might improve and what that would mean for your business.

MOORE'S LAW

Throughout the history of technology, some very smart people have been proved very wrong. In 1943, Thomas Watson, the President of IBM (yes, that IBM), said "I think there is a world market for maybe five computers." A few decades later, in 1977, Ken Olsen, the founder and CEO of Digital Equipment Corporation, said, "There is no reason for any individual to have a computer in his home."[4] These were two giants of the computing industry who badly misjudged the market and the future implications of the very technology they were helping to pioneer.

What happened? The technology improved! And it improved more rapidly than either man could have predicted. How do emerging technologies improve so rapidly? Some of the improvements are surely due to market forces and the natural agility of smaller companies to change more quickly. But much of it also hinges on what's known as Moore's Law.

In 1965, Gordon Moore, then a director at Fairchild Semiconductor and future CEO of Intel, predicted that the density of transistors in an integrated circuit would double approximately every two years. At the time, Moore predicted that this would hold true for the next 10 years. In reality, Moore's Law predicted the rise of the semiconductor industry for more than 55 years (there's some debate as to whether the law holds after 2010).

Double the transistors meant double the raw processing power without a corresponding doubling of costs. This means the price of the same amount of raw computing power roughly halved every two years.

Think about this example: Apollo 11, which took man to the moon for the first time, had roughly 80 KB of memory and could perform approximately 40,000 instructions per second. Apple's iPhone 15 Pro has 8 GB of memory (about 1,000,000 times more than Apollo 11), and the iPhone can perform 35 trillion instructions per second (about 875,000,000 times more than Apollo 11). The computing for Apollo 11 is estimated to have cost around $200,000 at the time (closer to $1.5 million in today's money). The iPhone 15 Pro costs $999 as of this writing. That's Moore's Law at work. In 50 years, we've seen an enormous increase in computing power and a corresponding enormous decrease in cost.

The raw power and ever-decreasing costs opened up possibilities for new products and new use cases. Researchers in the 1950s and 1960s could never have predicted how cheaper, faster computers would change the world. How could they imagine the rise of Snapchat and TikTok? Who would waste such a valuable resource as memory and computing on videos of kids dancing? Back then, every kilobyte of memory was carefully managed. Today, we think nothing of using an extra megabyte or ten. Mobility, networking, cloud computing, and 5G wireless have emerged to complement cheaper computing and open a new world of possibilities.

When looking at today's emerging technology, some of the parallels are easy to see. In 2022, scientists at IBM built a quantum computer with 433 qubits, making it the most powerful quantum computer in the world. How long before we're talking kiloqubits or megaqubits? Artificial intelligence (AI) applications are growing at an astounding rate. When will AI have its iPhone moment?

Futurist and innovation expert Chunka Mui, in his book "A Brief History of a Perfect Future," refers to Moore's Law as one of the "Laws of Zero." He and his coauthors predict that over a long enough time horizon, computing and networking become essentially free. As Mui et al say, "When something is free, you can throw as many of those resources as you want at a problem."[5]

When thinking about emerging technology within your team, where does Moore's Law apply? What does that mean over the short-term and the long-term? There's another famous law used when forecasting innovation and emerging technology. Let's look next at Amara's law to see how to assess innovation over different time horizons.

AMARA'S LAW

Amara's Law, named after the renowned futurist Roy Amara, is a fundamental principle that governs our perception and adoption of new technologies. It states that "we tend to overestimate the effect of a technology in the short run and underestimate the effect in the long run."[6]

This observation is crucial in an era of rapid technological advancement, where the hype and excitement around emerging technologies can often obscure their true long-term impact. Amara's Law reminds us to approach new technologies with a balanced and nuanced perspective, considering both their immediate and long-term implications.

The Gartner Hype Cycle,[7] a widely recognized framework for understanding the maturity and adoption of technologies, aligns closely with Amara's Law. The cycle consists of five stages: the Innovation Trigger, the Peak of Inflated Expectations, the Trough of Disillusionment, the Slope of Enlightenment, and the Plateau of Productivity.

In the early stages of a technology's lifecycle, the hype and enthusiasm often outpace the actual capabilities and practical applications, leading to the Peak of Inflated Expectations. This is where Amara's Law comes into play, as we tend to overestimate the short-term impact of the technology. However, as the technology matures and its true potential becomes clearer, we often underestimate its long-term transformative power, as it moves through the Trough of Disillusionment and the Slope of Enlightenment.

Amara's Law is also closely linked to Moore's Law, which describes the exponential growth in computing power. As technology advances, the pace of change can be difficult to comprehend, leading us to underestimate the long-term implications. For example, the rapid progress in AI and generative AI models has caught many by surprise, with the technology quickly moving from obscurity to the Peak of Inflated Expectations.

To effectively navigate the changing landscape of technology, it is crucial to apply Amara's Law. By recognizing the tendency to overestimate short-term impacts and underestimate long-term effects, we can make more informed decisions and better prepare for the future.

Some practical applications of Amara's Law include:

1. Resist the temptation to get swept up in the hype and instead focus on the technology's long-term potential and practical applications.
2. Stay informed about the latest technological advancements and be ready to adapt as the landscape evolves.
3. Adopt a mindset of continuous learning and be open to the transformative power of emerging technologies, even if the initial impact seems limited.

By understanding and applying Amara's Law, you can navigate the complex world of emerging technology with greater clarity and foresight, making more informed decisions and better preparing for the future.

ARTIFICIAL INTELLIGENCE

AI has been around for decades but has only recently become a mainstream technology. AI has made significant progress in natural language processing, machine learning, and deep learning in the past few years. This progress has led to the development of new AI-powered applications that are changing how we live and work. AI is a branch of computer science that deals with the creation of intelligent agents—systems that can reason, learn, and act autonomously.

AI is already used in various industries, including healthcare, finance, and manufacturing. In healthcare, AI is used to develop new drugs, diagnose diseases, and provide personalized treatment plans.[8] In finance, AI detects fraud, manages risk, and makes investment decisions.[9] In manufacturing, it's used to automate tasks, improve quality control, and optimize production.[10] AI can be a powerful tool for improving efficiency, reducing costs, driving innovation, and promoting revenue growth. However, AI also poses some challenges, such as the potential for job displacement and the need for new skills. The emergence of AI is having a profound impact on the IT industry. You need to understand AI to make informed decisions about how to use it in your organization.

One of the most recent advances in AI is the broad adoption of Generative AI, a type of AI that can create new content. Services like ChatGPT from OpenAI, Bard from Google, and the new Bing from Microsoft can generate new text based on user prompts. Services like MidJourney and DALL-E 2 create entirely new images. And things like Amber Music, JukeBox, and Musify make novel music across various genres. As generative AI matures, new services will crop up, and new use cases will be developed.

It's important to note that generative AI is imperfect. You need to be careful of inaccurate answers provided by AI. This is especially true if you're using AI to write code. You should never put AI-generated code into production until it's carefully tested in a lower environment and reviewed by a knowledgeable developer. AI may be good enough to remove these constraints someday, but we're not there yet.

So, how does this AI work? There are different ways to train a generative AI model. One common approach is to use a technique called deep learning. Deep learning is a type of machine learning that uses artificial neural networks to learn from data. Neural networks are inspired by the human brain, and they can learn complex patterns from large amounts of data. Another common approach is to use a technique called reinforcement learning. Reinforcement learning allows an AI agent to learn how to act in an environment to maximize a reward. The agents learn through trial and error and are rewarded for desired behaviors and punished for undesired ones. In the context of generative AI, reinforcement learning can be used to train an AI agent to generate text, images, or other content likely to be rewarded by a human.

Of course, technology like this has many implications for your role as an IT manager. Some specific implications of generative AI you should consider:

- **Automate tasks:** Generative AI can be used to automate various tasks, such as writing code, generating reports, and creating marketing materials. This can free up IT managers to focus on more strategic tasks. Just remember to review the output—mistakes are common.
- **Drive innovation:** Generative AI can drive innovation by generating new ideas and solutions. This can help IT organizations stay ahead of the competition.
- **Supplement Resource Capacity:** Generative AI can be used to automate tasks that humans currently perform. Viewed in a negative light, this will threaten jobs. But looked at more positively, this could help expand your current team's capacity. Can you offload tasks to AI and free up your team to work on something else?

You also need to be aware of the potential risks associated with generative AI and take steps to mitigate those risks. For example, you can:

- Understand the capabilities and limitations of generative AI so that you can make informed decisions about how to use it.
- Implement security measures to protect your organization from the risks associated with generative AI, such as fake news, disinformation, or faulty code.
- Upskill your employees so that they can adapt to the changes that generative AI will bring to the IT industry and help your organization capture value.

Given the recent media attention AI has received, the speed at which it is developing, and the many potential uses, it's safe to assume AI will not only survive the trough of disillusionment but quickly make its way through the trough. None of us quite knows what the future looks like regarding AI, but the more we can understand its many forms and think creatively about how best to use it, the more likely we are to come out ahead.

5G NETWORKS

5G is the next generation of cellular network technology.[11] It offers rapidly faster speeds and significantly lower latency than previous generations of cellular networks. But it's about more than just loading your TikTok videos faster. 5G is being used to power a variety of new applications, such as self-driving cars, virtual reality, and augmented reality. Plus, it will make your mobile browsing faster, too.

5G has several implications for those of us in IT Management. It will also require us to upgrade our networks. This can be a costly and time-consuming process and will need to be planned well in advance. In some companies, traditional wired and wireless networks have severe limitations. Imagine working for a mining company. You have increasingly more smart devices, autonomous trucks, safety sensors, and equipment diagnostics, but getting WiFi down a mineshaft is tough.[12] The same is true of extensive manufacturing facilities. All those concrete walls and steel beams wreak havoc on wireless signals. But 5G can overcome these challenges. You'll need to build the infrastructure, but it can unlock new possibilities.

5G will create new business opportunities to develop and deploy new applications. You need to be aware of these opportunities and develop strategies to exploit them. 5G will enable massive IoT networks with incredible device density.[13] Those same mines can now take advantage of autonomous mining vehicles, that manufacturing facility can deploy sensors with more agility to capture more data than ever before. Coupled with AI, 5G can enable automation that we've been unable to achieve. It will also enable better mission-critical communications for public safety, transportation, and public health.

While 5G is sure to unlock wonderful new applications, it will also create new challenges for businesses, especially when it comes to security and privacy. Be aware of these challenges so that you can develop strategies to mitigate them. 5G networks will increase the attack surface as they will connect a much larger number of devices to the internet. 5G will also use new technologies and protocols, creating new attack vectors for cybercriminals. Finally, because of the newness, 5G networks are currently deployed in a fragmented manner. Different vendors use different technology and protocols.[14] This increases the complexity of securing everything.

Some specific implications of 5G for IT managers:

- Network upgrades: 5G requires new network infrastructure, which can be costly and time-consuming. IT managers must develop a plan for upgrading their networks to support 5G.
- New applications: 5G will enable new applications, such as virtual reality, augmented reality, and self-driving cars. IT managers must be aware of these opportunities and develop strategies to take advantage of them.
- Security and privacy: 5G creates new security and privacy challenges. IT managers will need to develop strategies to mitigate these risks.
- Skills development: 5G will require new skills from IT professionals. IT managers will need to develop a plan for upskilling their employees.

5G is a complex and rapidly evolving technology. You'll need to stay up-to-date on the latest developments and understand the implications of 5G for your organization. Keep an eye on the market and the evolving technical landscape, but don't rush to dive in unless you have a reasonable business case and a way to pilot the technology safely.

BLOCKCHAIN

I assume everyone has heard about blockchain and cryptocurrency at this point. It'd be hard not to, given the dramatic rise and fall and rise again of Bitcoin. But, while Bitcoin is built on a blockchain, the two are not synonymous. The implications for blockchain technology extend far beyond cryptocurrencies.

The first blockchain was created in 2008 by Satoshi Nakamoto, the pseudonymous creator of Bitcoin. The Bitcoin whitepaper, which described blockchain technology, was published in October 2008.[15] The first Bitcoin block, the genesis block, was mined on January 3, 2009.[16] So blockchain, being more than a decade old, is not necessarily a new technology, but its applications and broader implications are still emerging.

Blockchain is a distributed ledger technology that allows for secure, transparent, and tamper-proof transactions. In a blockchain, data is stored in blocks linked together in a chain, forming a chronological record of all the transactions or data stored in the blockchain. Each block contains a cryptographic hash of the previous block and the data for the current block. The transactions are verified by network nodes and then added to the block. Once a block is added to the chain, it cannot be changed or deleted. This creates a tamper-evident record that is difficult to alter because any changes made to a previous block would be reflected in all subsequent blocks.

Blockchain technology enables various applications, such as cryptocurrency, supply chain management, and identity verification. It can establish decentralized trust and accountability without relying on a central authority or intermediary. Let's look at the example of supply chain management.

Blockchain can help manage supply chains by providing an immutable record of all transactions within the supply chain. This includes the movement of goods, the transfer of ownership, and the completion of required certifications or inspections. All parties involved in the supply chain have access to the same information in real time without the need for intermediaries. Blockchain also improves efficiency by reducing the time and costs associated with manual record-keeping and reconciliation. With a blockchain-based system, many of the tasks related to supply chain management can be automated, such as validating certificates and inspections, tracking inventory levels, and executing smart contracts. These systems have the potential to transform supply chain management by providing greater transparency, traceability, and efficiency while reducing the risk of fraud and errors.

While blockchain technology might revolutionize various industries, it is not a panacea. Blockchain has its own limitations. Scalability and energy consumption are two current challenges facing the industry. It isn't easy to scale blockchains because all the nodes on the network must verify all transactions. The verification takes longer as the network and the number of transactions grows simultaneously. According to a 2020 paper, Bitcoin can only process seven transactions per second, on average.[17] Compare this with Visa. They processed 259.3 Billion transactions in 2022, which works out to more than 8,000 transactions per second.[18]

The second challenge blockchains face is the high energy consumption needed to operate. This is particularly true for blockchains that use a proof-of-work (PoW) consensus algorithm, such as the Bitcoin blockchain. In a PoW blockchain, nodes (i.e., computers) compete to solve complex mathematical problems in order to add new blocks to the blockchain. This process requires a significant amount of computational power and energy, as each node must perform multiple calculations to verify the correctness of the proposed block. As the number of nodes and transactions increases, so does the energy required to maintain the network. This high energy consumption impacts the carbon emissions of blockchain miners, an essential consideration as organizations seek to reduce their carbon footprint as part of their Environment, Social, and Governance (ESG) goals. High energy consumption also makes blockchains more expensive and limits their ability to scale. According to a report from the White House,

> As of August 2022, published estimates of the total global electricity usage for crypto-assets are between 120 and 240 billion kilowatt-hours per year, a range that exceeds the total annual electricity usage of many individual countries, such as Argentina or Australia.[19]

Ongoing research and development are aimed at improving the efficiency and usefulness of blockchain technology. Researchers are studying more efficient hardware and algorithms. Miners are making greater use of renewable energy. Others are investigating solutions to the scaling problem using sharding or splitting the blockchain into smaller pieces and off-chain solutions that process transactions more efficiently outside the blockchain.

Perhaps the biggest question mark around blockchain at the moment is the regulatory environment. Governments have been closely watching early cryptocurrencies and other blockchain implementations. The immutable nature of blockchain creates specific challenges for data privacy, and the anonymous nature of early implementations could run afoul of Know Your Customer and other anti-money laundering requirements. There is a broad range of potential outcomes, but regulators will likely act soon.

The promise and pitfalls of blockchain are complex. While the underlying technology may be over a decade old, most believe we're just scratching the surface of what blockchain can do. Most of the attention has focused on various cryptocurrencies as speculative investments, but plenty of people have begun the hard work to build practical, useable solutions leveraging the blockchain.

QUANTUM COMPUTING

While 5G may be the next frontier in networking and extended reality (XR) might be the next frontier in entertainment, quantum computing offers the same promise in the field of computing. It's not nearly as far along as 5G, but the potential is more dramatic. Quantum computing uses the principles of quantum mechanics to perform calculations. Quantum computers are still in their early stages of development, but they have the potential to be much more powerful than traditional computers. There are no commercially practical applications for computing yet, but it's worth understanding the promise and the widespread ramifications of commercially viable quantum computing.

Today's computers, sometimes called classic computers, use bits to represent data as either a 1 or 0. Quantum computers differ fundamentally. Instead of classic bits, they use quantum bits (qubits), representing both 0 and 1 simultaneously. This allows quantum computers to perform certain computations exponentially faster than traditional computers. There are several ways to implement qubits, including superconducting circuits, trapped ions, and photonics. Regardless of how they are implemented, all methods require careful control and isolation from the environment to prevent them from losing their quantum properties.

Quantum computers also require specialized algorithms. To run a quantum algorithm, qubits are first initialized in a known state, typically a superposition state. The algorithm then applies a series of operations to manipulate the state of the qubits. Finally, the qubits are measured to obtain the output of the computation. Building and operating a quantum computer requires advanced engineering and a deep understanding of quantum mechanics. Today's quantum computers face challenges with qubit stability, decoherence, scalability, and cost. While quantum computers are still in their early stages, researchers are working to overcome these challenges and build larger, more powerful quantum computers that can solve practical problems.

The practical implications, given time, are enormous. One of the most talked about impacts is the obsolescence of current cryptography. Quantum computers can break many cryptographic systems, such as public-key cryptography, used to secure information today. This could significantly impact the security of financial transactions, military communications, and personal data. Even with strong passwords, most currently implemented authentication protocols would fall to brute-force attacks in seconds. Encrypted military communications, including diplomatic cables, battlefield communications, and even the nuclear command and control structure, could be undermined.

Current cryptographic standards rely on math problems like factoring integers and computing discrete algorithms. These problems are computationally difficult for current computers to solve. However, they are trivial for a sufficiently powered quantum computer running Shor's Algorithm.[20] Thankfully, researchers are already at work on post-quantum cryptography.[21] With hard work and luck, we'll have new cryptographic systems when quantum computing is commercially viable.

Not all of the implications are so scary, however. Quantum computing also promises to accelerate scientific research by simulating complex systems and materials more quickly than classic computers can. This same acceleration can be applied to supply chain analysis, logistics, and portfolio management.

While widespread quantum computing may still be a long way off, some companies are investing early. Azure offers Quantum-Computing-as-a-Service.[22] JP Morgan, Volkswagen, and Lockheed Martin are also reportedly investing in their own quantum infrastructure.[23] These are early investments, but you can expect them to ramp up in the next few years. You may not encounter quantum computing in your first role, but given the scale of investment and the disruptive nature of the technology, it's wise to keep an eye on new developments.

FINAL THOUGHTS

These are just a few examples of emerging tech you may encounter in your organization. Your company may kick off a proof-of-concept or small pilot. Maybe you've been asked to evaluate the technology and present a case for investment. Perhaps you're just curious. Spending an hour or two each

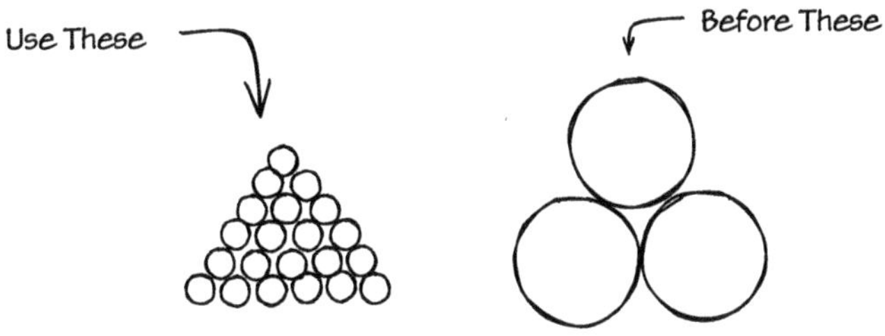

Figure 12.1 Bullets, then cannonballs.

month reading about the latest developments will ensure you're not caught off guard when your boss asks you to investigate something new. Keep the Hype Cycle in mind, and make sure you aren't wowed by slick marketing and overly optimistic projections of future capabilities. Before committing to an investment, confirm that your use case is a good fit for the technology and that you have the skills to implement and support it.

Toys are fun, but toys for their own sake don't have a place in a professional IT organization. Find your use case, experiment in a safe and prudent manner, watch your budget, and track the value you get from small bets. Attaching yourself to a successful pilot can help build your brand within your organization. But a big bet gone wrong can just as quickly derail your career growth. A strong business case should back each step of your foray into emerging technology.

When you invest, remember that one of your primary goals during early pilots is learning. Even failed pilots can be valuable if you learn the right lessons. What can you learn about the resources needed to scale this technology successfully? What can you learn about the costs? Does the technology integrate with your current environment? Does it deliver the promised benefits? When you capture this kind of data, even if the answers aren't what you hoped, you'll move your team and organization forward (Figure 12.1).

In *Great by Choice*,[24] Jim Collins writes about the concept of bullets before cannonballs. First, fire your bullets—low-risk, low-cost experiments that help you learn. Once you're sure that your aim is correct, then you fire your cannonball—your big bet with all the resources you can muster. Use your bullets to obtain validation for an idea with empirical evidence and high conviction before committing all your resources.

NOTES

1 *Gartner Hype Cycle Research Methodology | Gartner*. (n.d.). Gartner. https://web.archive.org/web/20250129105254/https://www.gartner.com/en/research/methodologies/gartner-hype-cycle.
2 Christensen, C. M. (2013). *The innovator's dilemma: When New Technologies Cause Great Firms to Fail*. Harvard Business Review Press.

3 *Steven Sasson | National Inventors Hall of Fame®*. (2025). https://www.invent.org/inductees/steven-sasson.

4 Olsen would later claim his quote was taken out of context and he was referring to centralized computers used to control a home - somewhat like today's smart home devices.

5 Mui, C., Carroll, P., & Andrews, T. (2021). *A brief history of a perfect future: Inventing the World We Can Proudly Leave Our Kids By 2050.*

6 Roller, J. (2024, September 5). *Amara's Law and Its Place in the Future of Tech.* IEEE Computer Society. https://www.computer.org/publications/tech-news/trends/amaras-law-and-tech-future.

7 *Gartner Hype Cycle Research Methodology | Gartner.* (n.d.). Gartner. https://web.archive.org/web/20250129105254/https://www.gartner.com/en/research/methodologies/gartner-hype-cycle.

8 Women's, B. D. N. |. B. A. (2024, December 12). How AI can help diagnose rare diseases. *Harvard Medical School.* https://hms.harvard.edu/news/how-ai-can-help-diagnose-rare-diseases.

9 McKendrick, J. (2023, October 5). Artificial intelligence opens up the world of financial services. *Forbes.* https://www.forbes.com/sites/joemckendrick/2023/02/24/artificial-intelligence-opens-up-the-world-of-financial-services/?sh=414f3c4db0ee.

10 Rapp, K. (2022, January 7). *Artificial intelligence in manufacturing: real world success stories and lessons learned.* NIST. https://www.nist.gov/blogs/manufacturing-innovation-blog/artificial-intelligence-manufacturing-real-world-success-stories.

11 *What is 5G?* (n.d.). Everything You Need to Know | 5G FAQ | Qualcomm. https://www.qualcomm.com/5g/what-is-5g.

12 Iom. (n.d.). *Long-range Wi-Fi to improve mine connectivity.* https://www.iom3.org/resource/long-range-wi-fi-to-improve-mine-connectivity.html.

13 *5G will accelerate a new wave of IoT applications.* (n.d.). IBM Newsroom. https://newsroom.ibm.com/5G-accelerate-IOT.

14 Morris, I. (2023, November 14). *5G on Track but Fragmentation Still a Concern.* https://www.lightreading.com/5g/5g-on-track-but-fragmentation-still-a-concern.

15 Poovski, L., & Soussou, G. (2018, May 14). A brief history of blockchain. *Legal Tech News.* https://pbwt2.gjassets.com/content/uploads/2018/05/010051804-Patterson.pdf.

16 CoinDesk. (n.d.). The Genesis Block: the first Bitcoin block. *Nasdaq.* https://www.nasdaq.com/articles/the-genesis-block:-the-first-bitcoin-block.

17 Yang, D., Long, C., Xu, H., & Peng, S. (2020). A Review on Scalability of Blockchain. *ICBCT '20: Proceedings of the 2020 2nd International Conference on Blockchain Technology.* https://doi.org/10.1145/3390566.3391665.

18 *Visa Fact Sheet.*
A global payments technology company at a glance retrieved from https://usa.visa.com/dam/VCOM/global/about-visa/documents/aboutvisafactsheet.pdf on 2 April 2023.

19 House, W. (2022, September 8). *FACT SHEET: Climate and Energy implications of Crypto-Assets in the United States.* The White House. https://web.archive.org/web/20250107091206/https://www.whitehouse.gov/ostp/news-updates/2022/09/08/fact-sheet-climate-and-energy-implications-of-crypto-assets-in-the-united-states/.

20 *Explore gates and circuits with IBM Quantum Composer | IBM Quantum Learning.* (n.d.). https://quantum-computing.ibm.com/composer/docs/iqx/guide/shors-algorithm.
21 Computer Security Division, Information Technology Laboratory, National Institute of Standards and Technology, U.S. Department of Commerce. (n.d.). *Post-Quantum Cryptography | CSRC | CSRC.* https://csrc.nist.gov/projects/post-quantum-cryptography.
22 *Azure Quantum - Quantum Cloud Computing Service | Microsoft Azure.* (n.d.). https://azure.microsoft.com/en-us/products/quantum.
23 Intelligence, S. (2022, December 15). The state of quantum computing in 2023. *Verdict.* https://www.verdict.co.uk/quantum-computing-predictions/.
24 Collins, J., & Hansen, M. T. (2011). *Great by choice: Uncertainty, Chaos and Luck - Why Some Thrive Despite Them All.* Random House.

RECOMMENDED ADDITIONAL READING

Christensen, C. (2013). *The Innovator's Dilemma: When New Technologies Cause Great Firms to Fail.* Harvard Business Review Press.
Mui, C., Carroll, P. B., & Andrews, T. (2021). *A Brief History of a Perfect Future: Inventing the World We Can Proudly Leave to Our Kids.* Future Histories Press.
Suleyman, M., & Bhaskar, M. (2023). *The Coming Wave: Technology, Power and the Twenty-First Century's Greatest Dilemma.* Jonathan Cape.

Part Three

Measures

You've mastered managing your team, and you've put the right methods in place to ensure work flows smoothly. Now comes the final piece—telling your team's story.

In IT, that story is told through the measures we track and report. Every organization relies on metrics, but IT is uniquely obsessed with them. Whether it's server uptime, API response times, defect resolution rates, or employee turnover, we measure everything—and for good reason. Data is what separates gut feelings from informed decisions.

But measurement is a double-edged sword. If done well, it provides clarity and accountability, helping teams improve performance, justify investments, and communicate value. But if done poorly, it becomes a bureaucratic mess—a never-ending flood of dashboards, spreadsheets, and meaningless KPIs that obscure more than they reveal. Anyone who has sat through a 120-slide project review meeting knows that not all data is valuable.

As a new manager, you may find yourself inheriting a set of existing metrics—some useful, some outdated, and some outright misleading. Or you might be building your measurement framework from scratch. Either way, your job isn't just to track numbers; it's to select, refine, and interpret the right measures to guide your team's success.

The old management adage says, "What gets measured gets managed." This is true—but it's only half the story. The real truth is that what gets measured also gets manipulated. If you tie bonuses to incident resolution times, your team may start closing tickets prematurely just to hit the target. If you reward engineers for writing more code, they might start writing bloated, inefficient software.

The key to effective measurement isn't tracking everything—it's tracking the right things. The measures that drive improvement, that align with business goals, and that give you a clear, honest picture of what's working and what's not (Figure P3).

DOI: 10.1201/9781003562160-16

Figure P3 Financial, technical, and operating measures.

In the chapters ahead, we'll break this down into three core categories of measures:

- Financial Measures—How do you track IT spending, cost efficiency, and return on investment?
- Technical Measures—What performance metrics truly indicate the health and reliability of your IT systems?
- Operational Measures—How do you measure the productivity, effectiveness, and engagement of your team?

Managing measures effectively means more than tracking performance—it means using data to tell the right story, make better decisions, and advocate for your team's needs. When done right, it can help you secure funding, influence leadership, and drive long-term success.

Let's dive in.

* * *

Chapter 13

Measuring the value of IT

IT is a force multiplier. It helps open new markets, release new and better products, and improve internal operations. Every modern business relies on technology to deliver products, engage customers, or enhance efficiency. Yet, despite this reliance on IT, many organizations struggle to quantify its true value. As IT leaders, we are constantly competing for resources. Our teams are composed of some of the highest-paid professionals in the company. Infrastructure, software, security, and cloud services all come with ever-increasing price tags. Emerging technologies like AI, automation, and advanced analytics introduce new capabilities but also drive up costs. The demand for IT services will always grow faster than the budgets that support them. This creates an ongoing tension: How do we justify IT spending? How do we prove that our investments are delivering real impact? More importantly, how do we help executives, especially Chief Financial Officer (CFO)s, see IT as an asset rather than a cost center?

The harsh reality is that many IT leaders struggle to make this case effectively. In a recent KPMG survey, 51% of technology executives admitted they had seen no measurable improvement in performance or profitability from digital transformation efforts over the past two years.[1] These are the very people championing technology initiatives, yet the majority can't demonstrate clear business value.

It's no wonder IT organizations are constantly asked to do more with less, to find efficiencies, and to cut expenses. Most Business leaders intuitively understand that technology is vital to their company's success. At the same time, they struggle to balance the scales between a need for IT and a need to contain costs. If we don't take control of the narrative, the conversation will always be framed in terms of cost reduction rather than value creation.

This is why measurement matters. If you can't measure the impact of IT, you can't defend its role in the business. And if you can't defend its role, you can't secure the funding, support, and influence your team needs to thrive.

DOI: 10.1201/9781003562160-17

MEASURING WHAT MATTERS

It's important to remember that IT has no inherent value on its own unless your company sells IT products or services. Instead, IT creates value by making other functions more efficient, more effective, or easier to operate. Business context matters. A faster server, a more secure network, or a perfectly optimized database means nothing unless it delivers measurable business benefits. The latest, most expensive, fastest server from HP is not worth the box it ships in if it doesn't enable the business to operate better, faster, or more cost-effectively.

Yet, many IT teams fall into the trap of only measuring technical performance instead of business impact. They proudly report on uptime percentages, transaction speeds, or storage capacity, but fail to connect these numbers to growth, efficiency, revenue, or profitability.

Consider two ways of reporting the outcome of a storage upgrade project:

1. "We upgraded our storage infrastructure, reducing query response time by 40%."
2. "The improved storage infrastructure reduces our power costs by $150,000 per year and improves the performance of our key applications."

The second statement frames IT's impact in business terms, and that's what senior leaders care about. Your job as an IT leader is to frame the value of IT solutions in a way that resonates with business stakeholders.

One of the biggest responsibilities of an IT leader is securing resources, not just funding for projects but also headcount, infrastructure, and executive support. Every budget cycle is a battle. If you can't quantify the impact of your team's work, you'll always be vulnerable to budget cuts and resource constraints. This is where objective measurements become your best weapon. Instead of relying on anecdotes and gut feelings, well-defined metrics allow you to:

- Demonstrate return on investment (ROI) on IT initiatives.
- Showcase efficiency gains that reduce costs.
- Justify new investments by proving past successes.

Imagine you need funding for a cybersecurity initiative. Instead of saying, "We need $2M to upgrade our security stack," you make the case with data:

- "We have seen a 300% increase in phishing attacks over the past year."
- "Industry benchmarks show that a single data breach costs companies an average of $4.5M."

- "Investing in this security upgrade will reduce our risk exposure by 70% and prevent potential losses far greater than the investment cost."
- The conversation shifts from cost to value.

IT AS A STRATEGIC ENABLER

Great IT leaders position IT as a strategic enabler of business success. The best way to do this is by aligning IT measures with business outcomes. Instead of reporting on network uptime, report on how improved reliability increases order fulfillment efficiency. Instead of tracking help desk resolution times, highlight how faster support leads to higher employee productivity.

Executives don't want or need raw technical data. They need insights that drive business decisions. This means choosing the right measures, framing them effectively, and communicating them in a way that resonates with senior leadership. IT leaders who fail to measure value will always struggle to defend their budgets, secure resources, and influence strategic decisions. Those who embrace measurement gain the power to shape the narrative, justify investments, and position IT as a key driver of business success. IT is not just a cost center. It can be an opportunity generator. But proving value requires clear, compelling, and data-driven storytelling.

In the next chapters, we'll dive deeper into how to select the right measures, avoid common pitfalls, and use data to build a compelling case for IT investment.

ENTERPRISE ARCHITECTURE

Enterprise Architecture is a term that often invokes confusion or indifference. It's frequently misunderstood, sometimes dismissed as a bureaucratic exercise, and—more often than not—poorly applied. Yet, when done well, enterprise architecture is a powerful tool that connects an organization's strategy to its daily operations. It creates a clear blueprint, ensuring that every project, system, and investment serves a larger business goal rather than existing in isolation.

Think about all the work happening in your IT organization at any given moment. Some of it aligns neatly with the company's priorities. Some of it is legacy work—tasks that were once important but persist solely due to inertia. And some of it happens simply because no one else is available to do it. Without a structured approach, IT teams can end up spread too thin, working on initiatives that have little impact on the company's success. Enterprise architecture helps avoid this fate.

At its core, enterprise architecture is about alignment. It starts with a high-level corporate strategy, and then breaks that strategy down into supporting initiatives, projects, and specific actions. When properly implemented, this process ensures that every effort contributes to the company's broader goals. But alignment isn't just about ensuring teams work on the right projects—it's also about tracking, measuring, and demonstrating progress in a meaningful way. That's where enterprise architecture and measures intersect.

A strategy is only as good as its execution, and execution is only as good as the ability to track whether it's working. Without clear measures, IT risks becoming a black box—an area where money is spent but the impact is unclear. If enterprise architecture defines what to do, measurement ensures we can answer the question: "Is it working?" One company that mastered this approach was Southwest Airlines.

The southwest airlines example

Earlier in my career, I had the opportunity to consult for Southwest Airlines, a company that applied enterprise architecture better than any other I've encountered. Their approach was both structured and intentional, ensuring that every business decision tied directly to their core strategic objectives. But what made their model even more powerful was their ability to measure execution.

At the time, Southwest was at a pivotal moment. They had just acquired AirTran Airways, a move that posed both opportunities and challenges. They also operated a single aircraft type—the Boeing 737—and only flew domestic routes within the lower 48 states. Their corporate strategy could be imagined as being structured around three major themes[2]:

1. Expand the Network—Opening international destinations to drive growth.
2. Conquer the Cost Mountain—Maintaining leadership as a low-cost carrier in the face of increasing competition from new and legacy airlines.
3. Integrate with Excellence—Seamlessly merging AirTran into the Southwest model while dealing with the challenge of new aircraft types and new routes.

Rather than treating these as vague aspirations, Southwest used enterprise architecture to decompose these strategic themes into high-level initiatives. Each initiative was further broken down into discrete projects, and each project had a clear mandate: specific resources, assigned funding, and measurable outcomes.

But what made Southwest's approach different was that they didn't stop at simply identifying these strategic initiatives. They made sure every project was tied to a meaningful measure of success. Every budget request, every new system implementation, and every operational change had to

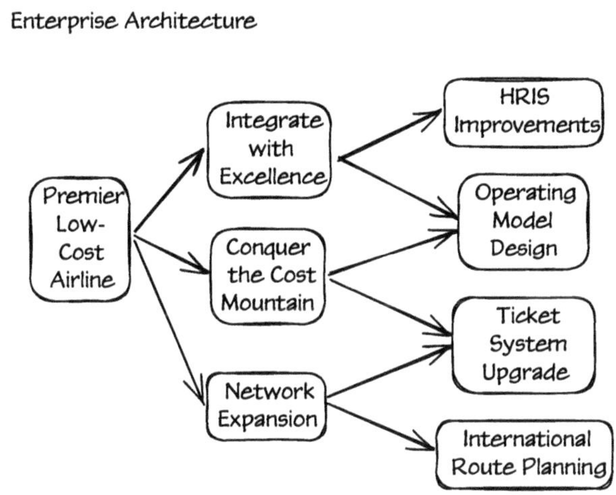

Figure 13.1 Enterprise architecture.

demonstrate a clear, quantifiable impact on one of their strategic themes. If a project couldn't show how it contributed to reducing costs, expanding the network, or improving operational efficiency, it didn't get funded.

Viewed from above, the structure resembled a pyramid:

- At the top sat the company's strategic vision.
- Below it were a few broad themes, each representing a major business objective.
- These themes funneled down into carefully structured initiatives and projects, all designed to deliver on those objectives.
- At the base of the pyramid, specific measures tracked progress, ensuring leadership had visibility into execution.

For example, to expand their network, Southwest needed to introduce new aircraft types, upgrade their ticketing and reservation systems, and reconfigure their route planning models. Every one of these initiatives had associated key performance indicator (KPI)s that tracked whether the changes were delivering on the intended strategy (
Figure 13.1).

Enterprise architecture in action

I was part of the team responsible for implementing the new ticketing system to support Southwest's international expansion. The project was incredibly complex, touching nearly every part of the business. We had to determine which aircraft would fly which routes, how many seats were available, which regulatory requirements apply, and how to integrate these changes without disrupting Southwest's famously efficient operations.

But, because everyone involved understood the bigger picture, decision-making became far easier. When we faced difficult trade-offs, we had a common heuristic: maintain low ticket prices while growing the network. This clarity of purpose allowed us to navigate thousands of decisions without getting lost in the weeds. The measures we used, tracking cost per available seat mile, turnaround time efficiency, and revenue per passenger, ensured that our execution aligned with the strategy.

This level of discipline and structure is rare. Many organizations struggle to connect their high-level strategy to execution, and most IT teams don't think about their work in these terms. Instead, managers look around at the work their teams are doing and try to retroactively piece together a justification. This approach is flawed. It treats strategy as an afterthought rather than a guiding principle.

Enterprise architecture as a measurement framework

Enterprise architecture is only as effective as its ability to provide visibility into execution. Without clear measures tied to strategic initiatives, IT becomes just another cost center, with leadership questioning whether investments are delivering results. This is why measurement is so critical. If Southwest had simply announced its growth plans without defining how success would be measured, it would have been flying blind. Instead, it built a system that tied every initiative to clear, quantifiable outcomes—a practice IT leaders should adopt.

For your team, this means tracking more than just uptime and ticket resolution times. It means aligning operational and financial metrics with business outcomes, ensuring that every investment in technology has a direct impact on the company's broader objectives.

Southwest Airlines succeeded because they used enterprise architecture as a leadership tool, not just a technical exercise. Their approach ensured that every project, investment, and decision aligned with their broader goals—and that progress was measurable at every stage.

As an IT leader, you have a unique opportunity to drive this kind of clarity within your organization. By applying the principles of enterprise architecture and ensuring that your team's efforts are both strategically aligned and rigorously measured, you can elevate IT from a reactive function to a proactive business enabler.

INVESTMENT OR EXPENSE

Is IT an investment or an expense? For those of us working in IT, the answer seems obvious. IT investment is critical for the long-term success of any company. Many of us demonstrated that clearly when, overnight, we pivoted entire organizations to remote work in response to the COVID-19 pandemic. Without prior investments in cloud services, VPNs, mobile workstations, virtual desktops, teleconferencing software, and security tools, remote work would have been impossible.

However, we also have to recognize that we have a biased view. We live and breathe IT every day. The rest of the organization doesn't. Most executives don't spend their time thinking about network latency, system uptime, or software deployment cycles. Their focus is elsewhere: on market expansion, revenue growth, operational efficiency, and cost control. How they perceive IT depends largely on how well IT supports these business priorities.

Answering the investment vs. expense question honestly and objectively is critical to understanding how your company views IT. It determines how budgets are allocated, how projects are prioritized, and what measures matter most to leadership. If IT is seen as an investment, the company is more likely to spend on redundant systems, disaster recovery, and automation. If IT is seen as an expense, leadership will focus on cost minimization, vendor negotiations, and reducing headcount wherever possible.

The distinction is also somewhat industry-specific. Financial services, healthcare, and e-commerce companies rely heavily on IT as a strategic enabler and tend to invest more aggressively. In contrast, construction firms, manufacturing plants, and traditional retail chains often view IT as an overhead cost, aiming to spend as little as possible while maintaining basic functionality.

So how do you determine where your company falls on this spectrum?

The investment perspective

If IT is treated as an investment, the company recognizes that technology drives competitive advantage. This means the business is willing to spend more, take more risks, and experiment with new technologies, even if some of those experiments fail.

Organizations that invest in IT:

- Maintain higher staffing levels with more specialized expertise.
- Have redundant systems and robust security measures to ensure resilience.
- Fund pilot projects and innovation initiatives to explore emerging technologies.
- Accept that some investments will fail but are willing to take calculated risks.

Companies in this category don't just ask, "How much does IT cost?" They ask, "What value does IT create?" They recognize that short-term spending leads to long-term gains and actively seek ways to leverage IT for business transformation and growth.

For example, Amazon and Tesla invest heavily in IT because technology underpins their business models. Amazon's entire supply chain is optimized through AI-driven forecasting, robotic automation, and cloud computing, while Tesla's vehicles rely on continuous software updates and over-the-air enhancements. In these cases, IT is a core differentiator.

The expense perspective

On the other hand, if IT is viewed as an expense, leadership focuses on reducing costs, minimizing risk, and maintaining basic operations. You're unlikely to pilot emerging technology or make big bets on the next big thing. Technology spending is viewed in some businesses as a "necessary evil." The goal for managers at companies in this category is to spend as little as possible to deliver satisfactory results. Satisfactory. In my experience, this can be a frustrating environment to work in. You'll see problems that you know how to solve but that the company prefers to live with.

Signs that your company views IT as an expense:

- IT budgets are shrinking or flat despite increased demand.
- Most spending goes toward maintenance rather than innovation.
- There is hesitation to adopt new technology unless it directly reduces costs.
- IT leaders struggle to secure funding for anything beyond critical fixes.

If you work in an organization like this, don't fight city hall. You're not in a position to convince your company its approach to innovation is wrong. Instead, spend your time and effort focused on operational excellence. Learn how to manage the best-performing department in the organization. Do more with less. Reduce waste.

IT leaders don't get to decide whether their organization treats IT as an investment or an expense—but they can influence the conversation. By aligning IT initiatives with business goals and tracking measurable outcomes, IT leaders can prove their department's value. If IT is currently seen as an expense in your company, focus on efficiency and cost control. If IT is seen as an investment, lean into innovation and long-term transformation. Either way, the goal is to position IT as an indispensable driver of business success.

RUN, GROW, TRANSFORM

The Run, Grow, Transform model[3] provides a structured way to assess where IT efforts are focused and how resources are allocated. While most IT teams intuitively understand this framework, many don't use it to influence decision-making and drive strategic alignment. Applying this model will give you an idea of where your team spends its time and how your budget is allocated across each category. But, the real value in this model comes from using it to drive forward-looking investment decisions. Compare your current spending across these three categories with how innovative your company says it wants to be. Are you over or underinvesting in the grow and transform buckets?

The best way to illustrate this is through a real-world example. Let's look at Home Depot and how this model might be applied to a complex retail business.

Run: Keep the lights on

"Run" covers everything necessary to keep the lights on—help desk operations, cybersecurity, compliance, infrastructure maintenance, and basic software licensing. Without these essential services, business operations grind to a halt. For a company like Home Depot, this means ensuring their point-of-sale systems function reliably, warehouses process shipments efficiently, and their e-commerce site remains operational 24/7. Imagine if Home Depot experienced frequent outages in its store inventory management system. If this system fails, employees can't check stock levels, customers leave frustrated, and revenue is lost. Fixing these issues doesn't generate new revenue or drive innovation. It won't make for fancy spreads in *CIO Magazine*. But, it's essential work. Without it, Home Depot wouldn't stay in business very long.

For IT leaders, the challenge with Run investments is that they are non-negotiable yet often undervalued by the business. Because they don't directly contribute to new growth, they're at constant risk of budget cuts or underfunding. The key is to measure and communicate the impact of operational stability. How much is it worth to your company that your core systems are stable?

Grow: Expand capabilities

"Grow" investments focus on expanding capabilities and enhancing customer experience. These initiatives don't keep the business running; they make it run better.

For Home Depot, a Grow initiative could involve enhancing their mobile app to provide customers with better product recommendations, live inventory updates, and a streamlined checkout process. This might also include improving supply chain analytics to reduce stockouts and enhance forecasting, reducing waste while ensuring high-demand products remain available. Unlike Run investments, Grow projects have a direct financial impact either by increasing revenue, reducing costs, or improving customer satisfaction.

IT leaders can use this model to argue for projects that demonstrate clear ROI, such as:

- Automating manual processes to reduce labor costs.
- Implementing better analytics to optimize purchasing and inventory.
- Enhancing security measures to reduce fraud and data breaches.

While "Run" is about keeping the business operational, "Grow" is about making the business more efficient and competitive. It's an area where IT can prove its value beyond mere cost control, positioning itself as a strategic enabler of business success.

Transform: Drive market disruption

"Transform" is the highest-risk, highest-reward category. It's where IT is tasked with helping the company reinvent itself. Transform initiatives involve significant technological shifts, such as launching new products, expanding into new markets, or embracing disruptive innovations.

For Home Depot, an example of a Transform investment could be a fully autonomous store experience, where customers can use mobile devices and AI-powered kiosks to navigate the store, find the right products, and check out without ever interacting with an employee. These types of initiatives require business buy-in, executive support, and a willingness to take calculated risks. Not every Transform initiative will succeed, but those that do can position a company to launch new products, enter new markets, and adopt new business models. The challenge IT leaders face is ensuring that these high-risk projects are executed strategically. Not unfocused experiments. Well-planned initiatives with clear business objectives and measurable outcomes. Beware that Transform investments are the first to be cut in downturns.

Most IT teams spend the majority of their budget in the Run category, with limited funds allocated for Grow and Transform initiatives. This is particularly true in industries where IT is viewed more as an operational function (expense) than a driver of change (investment). However, you can use this model to shape conversations with leadership.

One of the most valuable exercises is to map out your IT spending across these three categories and present it to your CFO, CIO, or business leaders. If Run activities consume 85% of your budget, are you underinvesting in growth and transformation? Can you set targets to gradually move more into the grow and transform buckets? This forces a discussion about how to free up resources for innovation. But keep in mind that there's no "correct" mix of these categories. Some companies may need to double down on Run investments to ensure operational stability, while others might be at a stage where Grow and Transform projects are critical for competitive advantage. Each company needs to find its own optimal distribution. IT leaders who can proactively guide these discussions become trusted advisors and can help shape investment strategies rather than merely executing decisions made by others.

NOTES

1 *KPMG Survey: Majority of US businesses say they have not seen an increase in performance or profitability from digital transformation investments.* (n.d.). KPMG. https://kpmg.com/us/en/media/news/kpmg-us-tech-survey-report-findings.html.
2 GMR Group. (2014, March 15). *Southwest Airlines Way* [Slide show]. SlideShare. https://www.slideshare.net/slideshow/southwest-airlines-way/32338295.
3 George, S. (2017, December 8). *Align IT functions with business strategy using the Run-Grow-Transform model.* Gartner.com. Retrieved June 9, 2024, from https://www.gartner.com/smarterwithgartner/align-it-functions-with-business-strategy-using-the-run-grow-transform-model.

RECOMMENDED ADDITIONAL READING

Bell, S. C. (2012). *Run Grow Transform: Integrating Business and Lean IT.* Routledge.
Harris, M.D.S., Herron, D., & Iwanicki, S. (2008). *The Business Value of IT: Managing Risks, Optimizing Performance and Measuring Results.*
Kotusev, S. (2018). *The Practice of Enterprise Architecture: A Modern Approach to Business and IT Alignment* (2nd ed.). SK Publishing.

Chapter 14

What gets measured

Measurement is one of the most powerful tools an IT leader has. It tells you what's working, what's not, and where you need to focus. Without it, you're guessing—flying blind in a world where gut instinct isn't enough. IT is complex. Systems interact in ways that even the smartest engineers can't always predict. If you don't have clear ways to measure what's happening, you can't fix problems, improve processes, or prove the value of what your team is doing.

Measurement is also about learning. The right measures reveal patterns, highlight inefficiencies, and give you leverage in budget discussions. They help IT move from a reactive firefighting role to a strategic business function. When done right, measurement makes it clear how IT contributes to the company's success. And when you can prove your impact with data, people tend to listen.

That's why getting measurements right is so important. Too often, organizations go to one extreme or the other. Some track everything—dozens of dashboards, hundreds of KPIs, so much data that no one knows what actually matters. Others track almost nothing, relying on gut feelings and anecdotes to make multi-million-dollar decisions. Neither approach works. The goal isn't to collect as much data as possible; it's to collect the right data and use it well.

I once worked with a team that spent more time building PowerPoint reports than doing actual work. Every week, they assembled a 120-slide deck for a three-hour executive review. The slides were meticulously updated, polished to perfection, and mostly ignored. Eight highly paid consultants spent entire days tweaking alignment, rewording bullet points, and formatting charts. Meanwhile, the actual project—the thing that was supposed to matter—was slipping behind schedule. Measurement should drive action, not create busy work.

On the flip side, I've also worked with teams that had no real metrics at all. Everything was anecdotal. They thought they were performing well, but there was no way to prove it. When budget season came around, they had no data to back up their funding requests, and no way to show leadership why they needed more staff or better tools. They knew their systems were

DOI: 10.1201/9781003562160-18

stable, their security posture was solid, and their project delivery was on track, but without numbers, none of that mattered. Leadership wanted evidence, and they didn't have it. That's the risk of not measuring: you might be doing a great job, but no one will believe it.

So, what should you measure? The right answer depends on your business, but in IT, most useful metrics fall into three broad categories: technical, operational, and financial.

Technical measures tell you how well your systems are performing, things like uptime, latency, and incident response times. These numbers are your early warning system. If your infrastructure is starting to buckle under the load, you want to see it coming before customers start complaining.

Operational measures focus on how well your team is working, service desk response times, project delivery speed, and system deployments. They highlight efficiency and help you spot process bottlenecks before they become major problems.

Financial measures are all about the money, budgets, ROI, cost savings, and total IT spend. These numbers matter because they're the ones executives care about most. If you can tie IT investments to business outcomes—lower costs, higher revenue, and better margins—you'll have a much easier time getting the budget and resources you need.

But measurement isn't just about tracking numbers—it's about using them to make decisions. Data should tell a story. If an important system is going down too often, do you need better infrastructure, better monitoring, or better processes? If ticket resolution times are creeping up, is it because of staffing issues, bad documentation, or something else? The numbers help you ask the right questions, but it's up to you to interpret what they actually mean.

The best IT leaders translate numbers into insights. If you're talking to engineers, sure, you might dive into latency graphs and API response times. But if you're talking to the CEO, you'd better be able to explain how IT improvements are driving customer satisfaction, reducing costs, or opening up new revenue streams. The audience matters. Numbers alone don't persuade people; stories do.

Measurement also has a way of shaping behavior, for better or worse. Ever heard the phrase, "What gets measured gets managed?" It's true, but there's a catch. What gets measured also gets manipulated. If you measure engineers by the number of tickets they close, don't be surprised if they start closing tickets faster, even if the fixes are rushed or incomplete. If you measure a team's productivity by lines of code written, you might end up with bloated, inefficient software. That's why choosing the right metrics is so important. Bad metrics create bad incentives.

It's also why measurement has to evolve over time. IT isn't static. The metrics that matter today might be irrelevant a year from now. Smart IT leaders review their measurement frameworks regularly, keeping what works and ditching what doesn't. If a metric isn't driving decisions, helping secure funding, or making the team better, it's just noise.

In the next chapters, we'll break down technical, operational, and financial measures in more detail, how to pick the right metrics, avoid common mistakes, and make sure your data actually drives action. But the big takeaway is this: measurement isn't about hitting a number. It's about creating clarity. It helps you understand what's working, fix what's broken, and prove IT's value to the business.

And if you do it right, it gives you something even more important than data. It gives you influence.

PURPOSE OF MEASURES

There's an old saying in business: if you can't measure it, you can't manage it. While not entirely true—some of the most important things in leadership and IT aren't easily measurable—it's still a guiding principle for decision-making. Good measures reduce uncertainty, clarify priorities, and help leaders make smarter choices.

Douglas W. Hubbard, in his book *How to Measure Anything: Finding the Value of Intangibles in Business*, lays out four reasons why measurement matters:

1. Decision-makers usually have imperfect information about a decision.
2. Quantitative models are more accurate than expert judgment alone.
3. Measurements inform uncertain decisions.
4. There are many ways to measure many things, but perfect information is rarely possible.

As Hubbard explains, "Management needs a method to analyze options for reducing uncertainty about decisions."[1] The purpose of each of your measures should be to reduce uncertainty about some decision. Do you need more staff? Should an extra item be added to a project's scope? Is your budget sufficient? The right measure can help you answer each of these.

Take a simple example like hiring. If an IT leader suspects their team is short-staffed, they might *feel* like they need to hire two more engineers. But without measuring backlog growth, ticket resolution times, and productivity trends, that decision is just a guess. A strong set of measures would either validate the need for additional resources or reveal alternative solutions. Maybe process inefficiencies or outdated tools are the bigger issue. Measurement provides a reality check.

Clarifying the role of measurement

Different measures serve different purposes, and you must be deliberate about how you choose and use them. Some measures are meant to track ongoing performance, ensuring that key systems and processes remain stable. Others help in forecasting trends, allowing organizations to be proactive rather than reactive. Some measures are essential for compliance and risk management, while others exist primarily to justify budgets and investment decisions.

Imagine a CIO presenting to the executive team. If they walk into the boardroom and rattle off technical uptime percentages, database query speeds, and firewall log events, they've already lost their audience. But if they can say, "Due to our security investments, we've reduced downtime by 23%, saving $2 million in lost productivity," then the conversation shifts. The right measure, framed the right way, turns IT from a cost center into a strategic enabler.

Many IT teams fall into the trap of either tracking too much or too little. Some managers try to measure everything, drowning in reports and spreadsheets that don't actually drive decisions. Others take the opposite approach, relying on gut instinct and anecdotal evidence, making it difficult to secure funding or justify priorities. You should strike a balance, focusing on a handful of key measures that provide meaningful insight. Instead of tracking dozens of KPIs, zero in on the 5-7 metrics that truly matter for your team's objectives.

For example, let's say an IT team is responsible for internal support. They might start by tracking first-call resolution rates, average ticket closure times, and user satisfaction scores. If those three metrics remain strong, they know their service quality is high. If one starts to slip, they investigate further. But if that same team starts tracking 20+ different KPIs, including granular statistics on every aspect of the service desk, they risk losing sight of what's truly important. A bloated measurement system creates noise, not clarity. If a metric isn't driving a decision, it's probably not worth tracking.

Before adopting any new measure, ask:

- What decision will this data inform?
- Who is the audience for this measure?
- Are we incentivizing the right behaviors?

Practical uses of measurement in IT

So, what kinds of decisions can measurement support? There are many, but some of the most common purposes include the following:

- Performance Monitoring: Keeping an eye on system uptime, response times, and issue resolution speeds to ensure smooth IT operations.
- Efficiency Improvement: Identifying bottlenecks in workflows, outdated processes, or inefficient resource allocation.
- Proactive Issue Detection: Spotting patterns that indicate emerging problems before they turn into crises.
- Resource Allocation: Ensuring that people, time, and budget are being distributed where they deliver the most value.

Each of these categories ties back to one core function: enabling IT leaders to make informed, strategic decisions. The best organizations aren't just good at collecting data; they're good at using it. At its core, measurement is about creating clarity in decision-making. It helps you prove your value, advocate for the resources you need, and ensure your team stays focused on what truly matters.

WHAT GETS MEASURED GETS MANAGED

There's an old adage in management: "What gets measured gets managed." When something is measured, it becomes a focus, and when something is a focus, it is far more likely to improve. At its core, this principle reflects how human attention works. We prioritize what we track, whether it's sales performance, personal fitness, or system uptime.

Take, for instance, fitness trackers. The concept of walking 10,000 steps per day originated in 1965,[2] but it wasn't until devices like Fitbit and Apple Watch gained widespread adoption that step counts became a mainstream obsession. Suddenly, people had daily, real-time feedback on their movement patterns, and their behavior changed. A study from Brigham Young University[3] found that people who wore pedometers walked significantly more than those who didn't, even when controlling for other factors. They didn't necessarily even set out to exercise more. Just knowing their step count made them more aware of their activity level, which in turn influenced their choices.

This same principle applies in business. A company that starts tracking customer satisfaction scores will inevitably begin looking for ways to improve them. A software engineering team that monitors bug resolution times will naturally work toward quicker fixes. Measurement directs attention and drives action.

The Toyota example: measuring for impact

A classic example of effective measurement comes from Toyota's Production System,[4] a methodology that transformed modern manufacturing. Toyota revolutionized automobile production by focusing on eliminating waste (*muda*), inconsistency, and inefficiency. They measured precise operational inefficiencies, idle time between steps in the production line, materials wasted due to defects, and even the exact number of seconds it took for a worker to retrieve a tool. These weren't vague performance goals, but discrete, quantifiable items that could be measured precisely.

Toyota dramatically improved efficiency, reduced costs, and set the standard for quality in the automotive industry. More importantly, their approach to measurement was balanced. They focused on eliminating waste, but not at the expense of innovation or flexibility. If they had obsessed solely with reducing costs, they might have cut corners on quality or overlooked customer satisfaction. Instead, they created a system that measured what mattered. They aligned their metrics with their larger business goals. That balance is critical. If you measure the wrong thing or focus too narrowly on a single metric, you can create unintended consequences (more in the next section).

The danger of oversimplified metrics

The biggest risk in measurement is measuring the wrong things in the wrong way. If an organization focuses too much on one measure, they can develop a myopic, counterproductive focus that distorts behavior.

Imagine you manage a customer service call center. It makes sense to measure average call time and try to keep the number low. Shorter calls meant greater efficiency. But what happens if that's all you measure? Agents begin rushing customers off the phone, often without fully resolving their problems. Customer satisfaction drops, call volumes increase because customers have to call back multiple times, etc. The metric designed to improve efficiency ends up making the system worse. You simplified too much. If you couple average call time with customer satisfaction and first call resolution, you have a workable, simple set of measures.

This same phenomenon happens in IT. If a help desk team is evaluated solely on how quickly they close tickets, they will prioritize speed over solving the root cause of a problem. If software engineers are measured on lines of code, they will produce bloated, inefficient software. Measurement shapes behavior. Make sure you're shaping the behavior you want.

What's your 10,000 steps?

The goal is to measure what matters: the numbers that drive the right decisions, align teams, and provide visibility into actual performance. What's your equivalent of 10,000 steps? What metrics are you tracking simply because they are easy to measure rather than because they actually indicate success?

It's tempting to default to simple, easily quantifiable numbers, but those numbers aren't always the ones that matter most. Instead of focusing only on ticket closure times, IT leaders should ask: are we measuring how many issues reoccur? Are we measuring the impact of issues on productivity? Are we identifying patterns that allow us to prevent future incidents? Instead of tracking how many projects are completed, we should be asking: Did those projects actually deliver value? Did they improve efficiency, profitability, or customer experience? The right measurements tell you not only what's happening, but why it's happening and how you can improve it.

The real value of measurement isn't in the numbers themselves. It's in how they shape behavior and influence strategic decisions. The right metrics tracked the right way, can transform performance and create accountability. The wrong metrics, blindly followed, can do the opposite.

So yes, what gets measured gets managed. But only if you're measuring the right things.

WHAT GETS MEASURED GETS MANIPULATED

For the cynics among us, there's a fine line between managing to a set of measures and manipulating those measures. The moment a metric is tied to performance evaluations, bonuses, or promotions, the risk of gaming the system increases. When numbers drive decisions, people naturally find ways to make those numbers look better—even if it comes at the cost of actual performance.

The phenomenon isn't new. In 1956, social scientist V.F. Ridgway warned about the dangers of over-reliance on measurement, stating, "Judicious use of a tool requires awareness of possible side effects and reactions. Otherwise, indiscriminate use may result in side effects and reactions outweighing the benefits."[5] His words still hold true today.

Perhaps the most famous example of measurement manipulation is the Cobra Effect, a cautionary tale about how well-intentioned incentives can backfire spectacularly. When the British government sought to reduce the number of deadly cobras in Delhi, they implemented a bounty system: bring in a dead cobra and get paid. At first, the program seemed to work. More cobras were turned in, and deaths decreased. But then, people started breeding cobras to collect more bounties. When the government caught on and scrapped the program, the breeders released their now-worthless snakes into the wild, increasing the cobra population rather than reducing it.[6]

This same perverse incentive dynamic plays out in modern organizations all the time. When the wrong measures are tied to rewards, people optimize for the metric, not the outcome.

The survey that lied

I once worked with a client that sent out an annual employee engagement survey. Morale at the company was terrible. They had just been acquired, layoffs were looming, and IT work was being outsourced. Given the mood in the office, I expected engagement scores to be abysmal. But, when the results came out, they showed high engagement and exceptional satisfaction. Something didn't add up.

It turned out that IT staff had figured out how to game the system. If a department's scores were too low, management responded with listening sessions, team-building exercises, additional training, and frequent check-ins. While this may have sounded good on paper, employees found the interventions tedious and disruptive. So, they manipulated the survey results to ensure they wouldn't have to endure another year of forced "engagement initiatives."

This is the dark side of measurement. If a number becomes a target, it ceases to be a useful measure. Instead of revealing the truth, it becomes a performance theater, distorting reality rather than reflecting it.

The many ways people game metrics

Metric manipulation can take many forms. Some of the most common include:

- Gaming the System: Employees inflate or skew numbers to hit performance targets without actually improving anything.
- Cherry-Picking Data: Organizations only report numbers that support a positive narrative while burying negative insights.
- Shifting the Goalposts: When teams realize they can't hit a metric, they redefine success to match their performance.
- Optimizing for the Wrong Things: Employees focus on what is measured rather than what matters, often to the detriment of broader goals.

Take cloud cost optimization, for example. Many organizations track and reward IT teams for reducing cloud spend, encouraging engineers to find ways to cut costs on infrastructure. But if cost reduction becomes the primary metric, teams may shut down redundant backups, downsize instances beyond acceptable performance thresholds, or eliminate proactive monitoring tools—all in the name of making the budget look better. On paper, cloud costs go down, but in reality, the organization is becoming more vulnerable to downtime, degraded performance, and undetected security incidents. A cloud system that's cheap but prone to failure or blind to emerging risks isn't a success—it's a ticking time bomb.

Similarly, consider patch compliance rates—a common metric in security and IT operations. If teams are expected to hit near-perfect compliance numbers within a strict timeframe, they might start rushing patches through without proper testing or marking systems as "patched" before full deployment is confirmed. The result? The numbers look great, but the organization is potentially exposed to untested software bugs, system crashes, or incomplete security fixes. The illusion of success replaces actual risk mitigation, leaving the company in a worse position than before.

How to prevent metric manipulation

The key to preventing measurement distortion isn't to stop measuring but to measure wisely. Here are a few ways to keep your metrics honest:

- Use Multiple Measures—A single metric rarely tells the full story. If you're measuring code quality, don't just look at lines of code—track defect rates, performance benchmarks, and user impact as well.
- Watch for Unintended Consequences—Ask yourself: "What's the worst way someone could manipulate this metric?" If it's easy to game, rethink how you track success.
- Encourage Transparency—Foster a culture where employees can discuss challenges openly rather than feeling pressured to inflate numbers.
- Check for Gut Instinct Mismatches—If the numbers say one thing, but your real-world observations tell a different story, investigate further.
- Incentivize Outcomes, Not Just Metrics—Structure rewards based on overall business impact rather than just hitting a number.
- Look for Patterns, Not Just Snapshots—A single month of perfect numbers might mean the system is working—or it might mean someone found a loophole. Trends over time are more valuable than isolated points of data.

Measurement is a powerful tool—but only when used wisely. You should understand that metrics are a means to an end, not an end in themselves. Use data to inform decisions, not dictate them, and know that context matters just as much as the numbers themselves. The right measures shine a light on performance, helping organizations improve and make smarter decisions. The wrong measures distort reality, leading to manipulation, perverse incentives, and missed opportunities for genuine improvement.

So, as you establish measures for your team, ask yourself: Are we tracking what truly matters? Or are we just tracking what's easy? The difference could determine whether your organization is actually improving or just playing the numbers game.

NOTES

1 Hubbard, D. W. (2007). *How to measure anything: Finding the Value of "Intangibles" in Business*. John Wiley & Sons.
2 Calechman, S. (2019, July 11). *10,000 steps a day — or fewer?* Harvard Health. https://www.health.harvard.edu/blog/10000-steps-a-day-or-fewer-2019071117305.
3 Allen, C. (2022, September 20). *BYU study: Wearing a pedometer — even if you don't look at it — may boost step counts*. News. https://news.byu.edu/intellect/byu-study-wearing-a-pedometer-even-if-you-dont-look-at-it-may-boost-step-counts.
4 Ohno, T. (1988). *Toyota Production System: Beyond Large-Scale Production*. Productivity Press.
5 Ridgway, V. F. (1956). Dysfunctional consequences of performance measurements. *Administrative Science Quarterly*, *1*(2), 240–247. https://doi.org/10.2307/2390989, https://www.jstor.org/stable/2390989.

6 This story has been referenced in multiple sources, but verifying it's authenticity has proven impossible. It may well be apocryphal.

RECOMMENDED ADDITIONAL READING

Hubbard, D. W. (2007). *How to measure anything: Finding the Value of "Intangibles" in Business.* John Wiley & Sons.
Huff, D. (2023). *How to Lie with Statistics.* Penguin UK.
Muller, J. Z. (2019). *The tyranny of metrics.* Princeton University Press.
Rosling, H., Rosling, O., & Rönnlund, A. R. (2018). *Factfulness: Ten Reasons We're Wrong About The World - And Why Things Are Better Than You Think.* Hachette UK.

Chapter 15

Financial measures

If you're leading an IT team, you know the drill—there's never quite enough money to do everything you want, and leadership always seems to wonder why IT costs so much. You're stuck between making do with limited resources and justifying every dollar you spend. Managing an IT budget is about selling the vision of what technology can do for the business. The best IT leaders don't just crunch numbers; they tell a story that makes executives see IT as an investment, not a bottomless pit of expenses.

There's more than one way to put together a budget. Some companies use zero-based budgeting (ZBB), which basically means you have to justify every single dollar from scratch each year. It's great for cutting out waste but can be a nightmare in terms of effort. You start every year with zero and then build a ground-up model of how much your team needs for the coming year. Most organizations use a traditional budget. This year's numbers, with a few tweaks based on performance and priorities, become next year's numbers. Traditional budgeting tends to be easier. Take last year's budget add 3% (or 5% or -8%) and you've got your new budget. There's the hybrid approach, where ongoing expenses roll over, but new projects require extra justification. No matter what system your company uses, your best move is to stay ahead of the game. If you wait until the last minute to fight for funding, you've already lost.

Now, here's where a lot of IT leaders trip up: talking about budgets in a way that nontechnical executives actually care about. If you walk into a meeting and say, "We need more money for cloud services," you'll probably get a polite nod and a firm no. But if you frame it as, "Investing in cloud infrastructure will improve reliability, cut downtime, and save us money in the long run," now you've got their attention. Executives want to see clear business outcomes—cost savings, efficiency gains, and competitive advantages. If you can connect IT spending to measurable business success, you'll have a much better shot at getting the resources you need.

Another big piece of the puzzle is understanding the difference between capital expenditures (CapEx) and operating expenses (OpEx). CapEx is for big one-time investments—think servers, data centers, or software development. OpEx covers the ongoing stuff like cloud subscriptions, maintenance,

DOI: 10.1201/9781003562160-19

and salaries. The rise of Software as s Service (SaaS) and cloud computing has shifted a lot of IT costs from CapEx to OpEx, which can create challenges because OpEx hits the company's bottom line more immediately. If you want to avoid a battle with finance, be ready to explain why a more flexible, OpEx-heavy model makes sense, whether it's scalability, predictability, or better flexibility.

Of course, getting the budget approved is just step one. Spending it wisely is just as important. IT leaders need to be ruthless about evaluating whether they're getting the most value for their money. That means regularly reviewing vendor contracts, optimizing cloud usage, consolidating software licenses, and making sure your spending aligns with business priorities. It's also about building a culture where your team thinks critically about costs. If everyone understands the budget isn't just "free money" but a strategic tool, you'll have a lot less waste and a lot more efficiency.

Beyond just managing the current budget, great IT leaders always have an eye on the future. Technology is moving fast, and if you're not thinking ahead, you're falling behind. AI, automation, and data analytics aren't just buzzwords. They're reshaping industries. Innovation takes investment, and if you want leadership to greenlight new technology, you need a strong business case. A good strategy is to start small: run pilot programs, gather accurate data, and show measurable results before asking for full-scale funding. Once you can prove the value, getting buy-in is much easier.

If you can frame IT spending as a driver of business success, you'll stop having to fight for every dollar and start shaping the company's strategy. IT leaders who master this aren't just managing costs. They're leading innovation, shaping the business, and making an impact where it really counts.

BUDGET GROWTH

Over time, IT budgets tend to grow. Companies rely on more and more technology to drive efficiency, improve security, and support innovation, which means they need to spend more and more on technology. As an IT manager, this probably sounds great—more money, right? But budget growth comes with higher expectations, more scrutiny, and the constant need to demonstrate value. The key is to approach it strategically, ensuring that increased funding leads to increased results.

IT budgets grow for a few key reasons. If the business is expanding, IT spending often increases to support a larger workforce, more customers, or new services. Even in stable organizations, IT costs can rise due to ongoing maintenance, security demands, and the adoption of new technologies. Cloud services, software licenses, and infrastructure upgrades all contribute to cost increases. Beyond that, cybersecurity threats continue to evolve, requiring constant investment to mitigate risk. Simply put, IT's role keeps growing, and the budget follows suit, at least when properly justified. Digital transformation, automation, and data analytics are no longer optional. They are core business functions. Leadership expects IT to deliver not just operational stability but also strategic value.

But no one is going to simply hand you more money. Growing your budget requires a clear, well-documented plan that outlines how additional funding will drive improvements. This should be an ongoing conversation with your boss and leadership team. IT leaders who wait until the budget season to make their case are already behind. The best approach is to continuously track IT costs, measure their impact, and link spending to business objectives.

A good practice is to maintain a rolling list of priorities. What would you do if the budget increased by 10%? What would you cut if you had to reduce spending by 5%? By preparing for different scenarios, you can adapt to shifting financial conditions and make a stronger case for funding when the opportunity arises.

As IT budgets grow, staffing costs often represent the largest expense. Salaries for technical roles continue to rise, and competition for skilled employees remains high. When planning for budget growth, you need to consider not just salary but also recruiting, training, and retention costs. High turnover can be expensive, both in terms of direct hiring costs and lost productivity. Budgeting for professional development, certifications, and career growth opportunities can help retain talent and reduce long-term staffing costs.

You also need to account for cost increases for all of your existing contracts. Depending on the contract, your costs may increase as usage increases. Your cloud costs will increase as you add storage and computing resources. Your SaaS costs may increase as you add users or new products. Multi-year SaaS contracts, hardware and software maintenance, system integrators, and other contracts also include "escalators" after the first year. Even if you don't add products or use more of a service, you can expect the pricing to increase by 2–15% every year (or sometimes more). It's important to reach out to your vendors and suppliers early to understand those increases before you lock in a budget that's too small to accommodate them.

Lastly, your budget needs to account for technology change. The servers and switches you buy today will be obsolete in just a few years. The replacements will be more expensive. The software you run will need to be replaced. Your team will eventually need new computers. Technology changes quickly. These changes always come with costs. Don't forget them in your budget.

Modern, flexible IT systems can reduce costs for your organization, but the cost savings rarely show up in the IT budget. You must continue to advocate for the funds you need, even when those conversations are uncomfortable. Even when your organization decides to cut overall expenses by 10%, you still have to make the case for a proper budget. You won't win all of these negotiations, but you owe it to your team to try.

CapEx VS. OpEx

A budget usually consists of two separate categories: Operating Expenses (OpEx) and Capital Expenditures (CapEx). These items are treated differently under accounting rules, and thus, are tracked differently in budgeting. Understanding the difference between these categories is critical so you don't end a fiscal year unspent money you can't access because it's in the wrong bucket.

Whenever you spend money on something, you'll need to determine if it's an operating expense or a capital expenditure. There are formal accounting rules that will help your finance or accounting team make this determination, but the easiest way to think about it is to ask yourself: "Does this create an asset?" If it creates an asset, it's likely to be a capital expenditure. If it doesn't create an asset, it's likely to be categorized as an operating expense. Another way to think about this is "will this have a useful life of multiple years?" Think about more traditional capital expenditures. When your company buys or builds a new office, they will amortize the cost of that purchase over many years. Under current Generally Accepted Accounting Principles (GAAP), office buildings are depreciated over 39 years. So, if your company spent $100M on a new building today, you will likely be retired before that asset is fully depreciated.

In IT, we sometimes buy whole buildings, but more often, we buy servers, build software systems, pay employee salaries, etc. Each of these items gets a separate accounting treatment (servers are generally depreciated over 5 years, software is usually 3–5 years, and employee salaries are usually an operating expense). The rules can be complex (capital leases, anyone?), so it's best to work with your accounting team to make sure you are budgeting for the right items.

Software-as-a-service and the growing frequency of subscription-based license models can present a particularly difficult challenge to IT managers. Historically, a company would buy some hardware, buy a software license, install that software on said hardware, and use it for as long as they wanted. They might pay maintenance fees to the vendor, but in general, they owned the software forever. Today, we more commonly license software for a specific period of time and pay each and every year. Under accounting rules, this software generally must be treated as OpEx. This can strain budgets that are used to treating such systems as capital expenses. Get ahead of these situations early by working closely with your finance and accounting teams (Figure 15.1).

Depending on your organization, you may have an easier time getting capital money than operating or vice versa. In general, OpEx is included in the key financial metric called EBITDA (Earnings Before Interest Taxes, Depreciation, and Amortization). By reducing the costs counted against EBITDA, a company's financial performance looks better to investors. For this reason, it is sometimes easier to approve a capital project than an

CapEx	OpEx
Purchasing New Servers	Salaries and Wages for IT Staff
Building a New Data Center	Software Maintenance and Support
Upgrading Network Infrastructure	IT Consulting Services
Buying Company Laptops and Desktops	Internet and Connectivity Costs
One-Time Software Licenses	Regular Software Updates and Patches
Storage Hardware Acquisition	IT Training Programs
Enterprise Software Development	Data Backup and Recovery Services
Virtualization Infrastructure	Security Monitoring Services
IT Facility Construction	IT Helpdesk Support
Purchasing Furniture and Office Equipment	Cloud Service Subscriptions

Figure 15.1 CapEx vs. OpEx.

increase in operating expenses. This is part of the reason it's so important to categorize your budget items properly.

Proper budget categorization can be a game-changer. Consider the case of an organization that wanted to install wireless projectors in each of its 200 conference rooms. The IT team initially assumed they would need to find an extra $100,000 in the operating budget to move forward. However, a discussion with the finance team revealed a more efficient solution. By packaging the projectors, installation costs, and the first year of the service contract into a single capital project, the IT manager not only found a way to fund her project but also had the resources to hire contractors for the installation. This not only removed a significant burden from her small team but also empowered them to tackle their backlog of work.

RECOMMENDED ADDITIONAL READING

Fields, E. (2011). *The essentials of finance and accounting for nonfinancial managers*. AMACOM/American Management Association.

Gentle, M. (2010). *An introduction to IT Project Financials - budgeting, cost management and chargebacks*. Lulu.com.

Kemp, S. (2002). *Budgeting for managers*. McGraw Hill Professional.

Lee, R. D., Jr, Johnson, R. W., & Joyce, P. G. (2020). *Public budgeting systems*. Jones & Bartlett Learning.

Chapter 16

Technical measures

As an IT leader, part of your job is to make sure the systems under your responsibility function as expected. That means knowing what's happening within your technical environment, and for that, you need reliable measures. Whether you manage networks, applications, infrastructure, or end-user devices, you have specific performance indicators that show whether things are running smoothly or headed for trouble.

Fortunately, today's IT systems generate more data than ever before. Nearly everything is logged, monitored, and reported. The challenge isn't collecting data. It's figuring out which data actually matters. Drowning in dashboards, logs, and alerts doesn't make you a better IT leader. What does is the ability to separate useful signals from the overwhelming noise and ensure your measures provide meaningful insights.

RULES OF EFFECTIVE MEASURES

To make technical measurement effective, you need to follow five basic rules: data must be accurate, meaningful, shared, up-to-date, and understood. These might seem obvious, but time and again, I've seen IT managers make poor decisions or waste hours in unproductive meetings simply because one or more of these principles were ignored.

Accurate data

Accurate data is the cornerstone of effective decision-making. If you base your analysis on flawed information, you're worse off than if you had no data at all. Inaccurate technical measures can lead to bad decisions, wasted resources, and avoidable outages. Imagine a network team using faulty bandwidth utilization data to make upgrade decisions. If the numbers overestimate demand, the company will spend money on unnecessary infrastructure. If the data underestimates actual usage and they don't invest, performance will suffer.

DOI: 10.1201/9781003562160-20

The same applies across IT. If storage teams rely on inaccurate disk utilization metrics, they may fail to expand capacity in time, leading to critical failures. If security teams misinterpret threat detection logs, they might chase false positives while missing real attacks. Precision matters. Ensuring accuracy requires verifying data sources, automating collection processes to minimize errors, and regularly auditing metrics for inconsistencies.

Meaningful data: avoiding vanity metrics

Not all data is useful. IT teams often track numbers because they're easy to measure, not because they provide real insight. Metrics should tie directly to business objectives or operational success. If a measure doesn't help you make decisions or improve outcomes, it's just noise.

For example, tracking server uptime might seem essential, but if your team never experiences unexpected outages, is that really the most useful measure? A more meaningful metric might be "time to recover from failure"—because no system is perfect, and how quickly you can respond when something goes wrong is what really matters.

Similarly, some organizations track the number of tickets closed in IT support. While this might seem like a productivity metric, it can incentivize technicians to rush through tickets without solving problems properly. A more valuable measure might be the first-call resolution rate, which tracks how often an issue is truly resolved without needing follow-ups. Every technical measure should be examined through the lens of "Does this number help us make better decisions?"

Up-to-date data

Technical measures need to reflect current reality, not outdated conditions. IT landscapes change quickly, and old data can lead to disastrous decisions. A cybersecurity team that relies on week-old vulnerability scans may think their systems are secure while attackers exploit new weaknesses. A cloud operations team that bases scaling decisions on last quarter's traffic trends could find itself overwhelmed when demand spikes unexpectedly.

Timely data allows you to be proactive instead of reactive. That means using real-time monitoring, automated alerts, and frequent reporting cycles. It's not enough to measure things once a month—your data should be fresh enough that decisions made today won't be obsolete by tomorrow.

Shared data

Technical measures lose value if they remain locked inside IT. A network engineer might care about latency spikes, but if those spikes impact customer transactions, the business needs to know. An application team might track API response times, but if poor performance leads to lost sales, that information is critical for leadership.

Sharing key measures across departments ensures alignment between IT and the rest of the business. Security teams need to communicate risks to leadership, support teams need to share incident trends with product managers, and infrastructure teams need to keep finance informed about capacity planning needs. Transparency leads to better decisions and stronger collaboration.

That doesn't mean dumping raw technical data on nontechnical audiences. The key is translating technical measures into meaningful business insights. If a CIO asks about system availability, don't respond with raw server uptime percentages. Instead, say something like: "We've improved reliability by 20%, reducing unplanned downtime from six hours last quarter to less than one hour this quarter. That saved the company an estimated $250,000 in lost productivity." Data should support the story you're telling, not require executives to decode technical jargon.

Understood data

Just because a measure is accurate and timely doesn't mean it will be understood by the people who need to act on it. I've seen IT teams present security reports loaded with security incident and event management (SIEM) log entries and expect executives to grasp the importance. That's not how communication works.

Different stakeholders require different levels of detail. Engineers need deep diagnostics, managers need trend analysis, and executives need impact summaries. If you're presenting to senior leadership, your metrics should focus on business outcomes, financial impact, and risk mitigation. If you're working with technical teams, you can dive into logs, latency, and error rates.

> Think of it like this: you wouldn't present CPU utilization statistics to a sales VP—but you might show how slow system performance is impacting order processing times. Tailoring measures to your audience ensures they drive action instead of confusion.

Good IT managers don't track everything—they focus on the right things. The best measures are accurate, meaningful, current, shared, and understood. They provide clarity, not clutter.

If you take nothing else from this section, remember this: Technical measurement is all about using data to make better decisions. Whether that means preventing downtime, improving security, optimizing performance, or proving IT's value to the business, your success depends on choosing the right numbers and presenting them in the right way.

FINDING THE RIGHT TECHNICAL MEASURES

When it comes to tracking technical measures, you have an overwhelming number of options. Every system, application, and infrastructure component generates data, and modern IT environments provide more performance metrics than ever before. That's both a blessing and a curse. The challenge is deciding which data actually matters. Your job as a manager isn't to track every available metric but to identify the ones that provide real insights into your team's performance and impact. The right measures tell a clear, accurate, and actionable story about what's happening in your environment. They help you detect problems before they escalate, justify investments, and improve decision-making at every level of the organization.

But choosing the right measures requires more than just technical know-how. You need to consider who will use the data, what decisions it will inform, and how it aligns with your goals. A well-chosen set of metrics can elevate IT's role in the organization, while a poorly chosen set can create confusion, waste time, and undermine credibility.

Clarity and specificity matter

Good measures are clear and specific, allowing for accurate tracking over time. Ambiguous or vaguely defined metrics can lead to misinterpretation, misaligned priorities, and poor decision-making.[1]

I once worked with a company that had recurring network outages. Employees frequently complained, "The internet isn't working." In response, the network manager, like a broken record, would say, "The internet is fine. Our WiFi is down, but the internet works." Technically, he was correct. But to employees, that distinction was meaningless. If they couldn't access their email or SaaS applications, the internet may as well have been down. Instead of splitting hairs over terminology, a better measure would have focused on real user impact, such as network availability from an end-user perspective rather than raw infrastructure uptime.

This is a good reminder that your technical measures must align with how people actually experience your systems. It's not enough for the network to be up if employees can't access critical applications or for a server to be "running" if it's running too slow to be useful. The right measures tell the whole story, not just the technical details.

Avoid vanity metrics

Some numbers look good on a dashboard but provide little real value. These are called vanity metrics, statistics that might make a team feel productive but don't actually reflect meaningful outcomes.

I've worked in organizations that proudly reported the number of IT tickets closed per week as a success metric. Meanwhile, users regularly complained about the poor quality of IT support. A high ticket closure rate doesn't mean much if employees are reopening tickets for the same issue because it wasn't resolved the first time.

I've also seen development teams measure success by lines of code written. That might sound productive, but in reality, more code isn't necessarily better. An efficient developer writes clean, concise, and maintainable code, not the most lines. If the goal is to improve product quality and speed to market, a better measure would be something like defect rates in production, cycle time for new features, or customer-reported issues.

Vanity metrics erode credibility. No one is fooled by numbers that don't reflect real value. Focus on measures that actually matter to your customers and users.

Choosing the right categories of measures

A useful framework for selecting measures is to organize them into three categories based on who they serve:

1. **Internal Measures for Your Team**—These are the operational numbers that help your team monitor and improve performance. If you're leading a development team, you might track sprint velocity or defect density. If you're managing infrastructure, you might focus on CPU utilization, storage capacity, or incident response times. These are metrics that your team needs to run effectively, but they may not be relevant outside your group.
2. **Measures for Management Reporting**—These are the numbers that help you communicate IT's impact to leadership. Your management team doesn't need a deep dive into server uptime logs or code review scores. They care about things like how long it takes to deliver new features, how IT is reducing costs, or whether incidents are being resolved efficiently. These measures should provide insights that help justify decisions about staffing, budgeting, and process changes.
3. **Business-Relevant Measures for External Reporting**—Finally, some measures are shared with other departments, executives, and even customers. These should be directly tied to business goals. For example, a SaaS company might track customer churn rates tied to application performance, or an e-commerce platform might measure cart abandonment rates due to site speed issues. The key is to ensure these numbers make IT's contribution to the business crystal clear.

The biggest mistake IT managers make with measurement usually isn't tracking too little. It's tracking too much. The more metrics you monitor, the harder it is to separate signal from noise. A handful of well-chosen metrics, consistently tracked and acted upon, will always be more valuable than dozens of numbers no one actually uses.

Start small. Choose five to seven key measures that align with your team's objectives. Track them rigorously for a few months and assess whether they provide useful insights. If they don't, adjust. Drop the ones that aren't adding value and experiment with others. Your goal isn't to measure everything. It's to measure the right things well.

SECURITY MEASURES

Security measures are a subset of technical measures, but they are worth mentioning separately, given the critical nature of cybersecurity. While many of us think security is the job of the chief information security officer (CISO) and her team, the truth is that security is everyone's job. An organization's security depends on the collective efforts of everyone who works there. Application teams need to write secure code, server teams need to keep the environment patched, network teams need to configure proper segmentation, and the desktop support team needs to deploy and maintain security tools and PC patches.

If you lead an IT team, you must understand how your work contributes to security and what measures you need to track to ensure your team is supporting the broader security strategy. While dedicated security teams will monitor and report on dozens, if not hundreds, of security-related metrics, every IT team has a role to play. To manage security effectively, you need the right mix of measures that reflect both proactive efforts and actual, observed outcomes. To do this, we use both leading indicators and lagging indicators.[2] Understanding the difference between them is important to develop a well-rounded approach to security management.

Leading indicators

Leading indicators predict future security performance. They highlight preventive measures that reduce risk before an incident occurs. These indicators are forward-looking, meaning they help identify gaps, measure preparedness, and ensure security controls are working as intended. Strong leading measures provide an early warning system for potential security weaknesses.

One example is training completion rates. Human error remains the biggest security risk in most organizations, and phishing attacks alone account for a significant percentage of breaches. If your training completion rates are low, it's a strong signal that your employees may be vulnerable to social engineering attacks. High completion rates, on the other hand, suggest that employees are more aware of potential threats and better equipped to recognize and report suspicious activity.

Another crucial leading indicator is patching cadence—the speed and consistency with which security patches are applied. Attackers routinely exploit unpatched systems, and delaying updates significantly increases the risk of a breach. Tracking patching performance across applications, servers, and endpoints allows IT leaders to ensure that vulnerabilities are addressed promptly.

The number of active security projects is another useful measure. If security initiatives, such as penetration testing, endpoint hardening, or network segmentation, are consistently in progress, it signals a proactive approach to reducing risk. On the other hand, a lack of ongoing projects may suggest complacency, leaving security gaps unaddressed.

These leading measures focus on security processes and behaviors. They provide insight into whether teams are taking security seriously, adhering to best practices, and putting safeguards in place before an attack happens.

Lagging indicators

While leading indicators measure prevention efforts, lagging indicators reflect what has already happened. These measures provide a retrospective look at security performance by tracking incidents, breaches, and the financial and operational impacts of security failures.

One of the most telling lagging indicators is the number of security breaches. This metric is a direct measure of how well an organization's security defenses are holding up. A high number of breaches suggests underlying weaknesses, while a declining number could indicate that security investments are paying off. However, it's important to interpret this metric in context. A low breach count doesn't necessarily mean that security is strong. It could simply mean that threats haven't materialized yet.

Another valuable lagging indicator is downtime caused by security incidents. Security is all about maintaining business continuity. If security breaches or attacks are frequently causing system outages, preventing employees from accessing critical applications, or slowing down operations, it's a sign that security vulnerabilities are having a tangible impact.

Financial loss is another key measure. The cost of security incidents quantifies the financial impact of breaches, including recovery expenses, legal fees, regulatory fines, and reputational damage. While security professionals are often focused on technical defenses, executives and board members tend to be more concerned with the bottom line. Showing how security incidents translate into financial loss can be an effective way to secure funding for future security initiatives.

Lagging indicators serve as a scorecard for security performance. They tell you how well security measures have worked in practice and highlight areas that need improvement. However, by the time the lagging indicators reveal a problem, the damage has already been done. That's why a balanced approach, using both leading and lagging measures, is critical.

Balancing leading and lagging measures

A good security strategy works to prevent incidents from happening. Relying solely on lagging measures would be like driving a car while only looking in the rearview mirror. You might learn from past mistakes, but you won't see what's coming next.

At the same time, an overemphasis on leading indicators can create a false sense of security. You may feel confident that training programs are working and patches are being applied, but if you never check actual performance, you won't know for sure. The most effective IT teams use a mix of leading and lagging measures to get a complete picture of their security posture. Leading measures help guide preventive efforts while lagging measures validate whether those efforts are making a real difference.

For example, if patching cadence is improving but attacks are increasing, it may indicate that attackers are shifting tactics or that other vulnerabilities are being overlooked. If employee training rates are high but phishing-related incidents are still occurring, it may signal that the training material isn't effective or that additional controls, such as email filtering, are needed.

Finding the right balance between predictive security measures and historical performance indicators allows you to refine your security strategies, invest in the right areas, and continuously improve your organization's resilience against cyber threats.

TECHNICAL VS. OPERATIONAL MEASURES

Understanding the difference between technical and operational measures is essential for any IT leader. Both categories serve distinct purposes, and getting them right will help you effectively manage systems, services, and teams. If you only focus on one and ignore the other, you'll struggle to see the full picture.

Technical measures focus on system performance, efficiency, and capacity. These are the numbers that tell you how well your infrastructure is running—things like uptime, response times, network latency, and CPU utilization. These measures provide a real-time pulse on IT systems, alerting you when something isn't functioning as expected. If an application is sluggish, or a database is maxed out, technical measures help pinpoint the issue before it escalates into a crisis.

Operational measures, on the other hand, are all about how IT functions as a business service. These track efficiency, effectiveness, and alignment with business goals. They include things like incident resolution time, project delivery success, vendor performance, and budget adherence. Unlike technical measures, which focus on what the technology is doing, operational measures focus on what IT is delivering to the business.

New managers often struggle with operational measures because they aren't always straightforward. Most IT professionals are comfortable tracking CPU load or disk space. But what about team productivity? What about employee engagement? How do you measure whether IT is providing value to the organization? These questions require a different mindset—one that looks beyond infrastructure health and into the broader impact of IT on business outcomes.

For instance, if a cloud-based application has 99.99% uptime, that's a strong technical measure. But if the IT support team is taking an average of ten days to resolve user issues with that application, then there's an operational failure—one that no amount of system uptime will fix. You need both perspectives to ensure IT is truly serving the business.

To make these measures more actionable, it helps to break them down into four core categories: people, services, vendors, and project delivery.

- **People measures** focus on your team's performance and well-being. Are you staffed appropriately for the work required? Is employee turnover too high? Are workloads distributed fairly? Do team members have the right mix of skills? A team that is burned out or under-resourced will struggle, no matter how efficient the infrastructure is.
- **Service measures** assess the quality of the services IT provides. How quickly does your team respond to incidents? Are SLAs being met? Are IT costs aligned with budgets? If a system is always available but too slow for users to complete their work efficiently, uptime alone isn't enough—it needs to be paired with an operational measure that reflects actual usability and responsiveness.
- **Vendor measures** track how well third-party providers meet expectations. Are they delivering what they promised, when they promised? Are their costs and service levels aligned with the contract? A vendor may boast high availability, but if their product updates introduce instability, you have an operational problem that needs to be addressed.
- **Project delivery measures** keep large IT initiatives on track. Is the project scope creeping out of control? Are deadlines slipping? Is there a pattern of launching new systems that end up being underutilized? These measures help ensure IT investments lead to meaningful business outcomes rather than just ticking off technical checkboxes.

The best IT managers find a balance between technical and operational measures. Too often, teams lean heavily toward one and neglect the other. If you're only focused on technical data, you might miss the fact that IT processes are inefficient or the business isn't seeing value from your work. On the flip side, if you focus only on operational metrics, you might end up making business-friendly decisions that put too much strain on technical resources, leading to outages or degraded performance. Keep both perspectives in view. Use technical measures to keep systems running smoothly and operational measures to ensure you are actually delivering what the business needs.

NOTES

1 Lewis, B. (2023, May 19). Bad metrics are worse than no metrics. *CIO*. https://www.cio.com/article/408921/bad-metrics-are-worse-than-no-metrics.html.
2 Watts, S. (n.d.-b). *Leading vs Lagging Indicators: What's The Difference?* BMC Blogs. https://www.bmc.com/blogs/leading-vs-lagging-indicators/.

RECOMMENDED ADDITIONAL READING

Fenton, N., & Bieman, J. (2014). *Software Metrics: A Rigorous and Practical Approach*, Third Edition. CRC Press.
Hayden, L. (2010). *IT Security Metrics: A practical framework for measuring security & protecting data*. McGraw Hill Professional.
Stewart, J. (2012). *Measuring your IT: Identifying the Metrics That Matter*. IT Governance Limited.

Chapter 17

Improving measures

CONTINUOUS IMPROVEMENT

In technology, standing still is falling behind. The IT landscape is constantly shifting, with new technologies, methodologies, and threats emerging every day. The only way to stay relevant and keep your team and organization competitive is by making incremental changes that add up over time. The way to ensure the next seismic shift in technology doesn't leave you behind is through continuous improvement.

Leading IT organizations build a culture where learning, optimizing, and refining are baked into daily operations. They don't wait for problems to become crises before they act. Whether it's fine-tuning a process, adopting a better tool, or strengthening security measures, small, consistent improvements compound over time into meaningful progress.

Many organizations have formal continuous improvement programs, but you don't need an executive mandate or a dedicated task force. Continuous improvement really starts with a shift in mindset. You need to believe that every process can be a little better, that every tool can be improved, and that every person can grow. If you get your team to think this way, they will start identifying opportunities for improvement, often in ways you never considered.

I worked with one organization that referred to this as "cleaning out the corners." Once a quarter, we would set aside part of a day to brainstorm small, cheap improvements that could be quickly implemented. Dusting the corners of a room doesn't take much time, but it prevents dirt from spreading. These were small tweaks that eliminated friction, reduced waste, and improved efficiency. We didn't need extra funding or more people. We worked with what we had, and, because they happened regularly, they built momentum over time.

DOI: 10.1201/9781003562160-21

Principles of continuous improvement

Continuous improvement is about habits, not heroics. It doesn't require massive projects or sweeping changes. Instead, it follows a few core principles that make progress consistent, sustainable, and measurable.

First, focus on processes, not people. When something goes wrong, it's easy to blame an individual. But in most cases, the real issue lies in the process. Was there a gap in the documentation? Did an unnecessary approval step slow things down? Were teams operating with outdated assumptions? By analyzing processes instead of assigning blame, you create an environment where people feel safe suggesting improvements rather than covering their tracks.[1]

Second, embrace incremental change. There's a temptation to swing for the fences—to roll out a massive new system or completely overhaul a workflow. However, large-scale change is expensive and disruptive and often fails due to unforeseen consequences.[2] Small, iterative improvements are easier to test, adjust, and integrate. One percent better every week beats a giant leap that never lands.

Next, use data to drive your decisions. The best way to identify what needs improvement isn't guesswork; it's data. Are certain incidents taking longer to resolve than expected? Are projects consistently missing deadlines? Are customers or internal teams expressing frustration about the same issues? Let the numbers tell the story. Once you've made an improvement, use the same data to measure whether it's working.

Engaging your team in the process is also key. The people closest to the work usually have the best insights into what's slowing them down. When teams feel like they have a voice, they're more likely to suggest and embrace improvements. If leadership dictates every change from above, it's met with skepticism. But when employees are part of the process, they take ownership of the outcome.

Finally, celebrate progress, no matter how small. Recognizing and rewarding improvements—whether through a simple shoutout in a meeting or a more formal recognition program—creates momentum. If people feel like their ideas are valued and their contributions make a difference, they're far more likely to keep looking for ways to improve.

Improve yourself

Continuous improvement isn't just for teams. It's for you, too. The best IT leaders are always learning. The tools for growth are more accessible than ever. What did you learn this quarter, and how did you apply it? What skills do you want to develop in the next three months? If you dedicate just two hours a month to focused learning, whether through industry reading, online courses, or networking with peers, you'll put yourself ahead of 99% of your colleagues.

Imagine if you read just one textbook in your field every year. It wouldn't take much time—just a few pages each week—but over the course of a decade, that knowledge would compound into an enormous advantage. Most people don't put in the time to continue learning. If you're the one who does, you'll stand out. The IT world is too fast-moving for complacency. If you're not actively improving, you're falling behind. But by fostering a culture of learning, experimentation, and small, consistent improvements, you'll set yourself and your team up for long-term success.

START, STOP, CONTINUE

One of the most valuable exercises you can do with your team is Start, Stop, Continue. It's a simple but powerful framework that helps teams take a step back from their daily grind and reflect on their work. When you're deep in the day-to-day demands of IT, it's easy to focus on the next sprint, the next release, or the next incident. But without pausing to reflect, opportunities for improvement can slip by unnoticed. Just because it worked last year doesn't mean it's still working now.

This exercise forces a deliberate pause to ask three fundamental questions:

- What should we start doing that we aren't doing today?
- What should we stop doing because it's no longer effective or valuable?
- What should we continue doing because it's working well?

When used consistently, Start, Stop, Continue help build a culture of continuous improvement without requiring massive overhauls or disruptive shifts. It provides a structured way to fine-tune team operations, trim inefficiencies, and double down on what's working.

To get the most out of this exercise, set aside dedicated time for the discussion. This isn't something you squeeze into the last five minutes of a meeting. Block off a couple of hours every six months and make it a formal event on the calendar. A few weeks before the session, let your team know what to expect so they can come prepared with ideas.

Providing a simple template for them to jot down thoughts in advance prevents the loudest voices from dominating the conversation. When people show up with ideas already written down, there's a better chance that quieter team members will contribute rather than being drowned out by those who are more vocal in meetings. You can also collect ideas ahead of time if you find you aren't hearing from everyone in the meetings.

Once the session starts, spend the first hour brainstorming freely. The key is to capture everything without debating feasibility. Let people call out inefficiencies, highlight blind spots, and suggest improvements. If you get stuck, ask some guiding questions:

- What slows us down?
- What do we always complain about?
- What's missing that would make our jobs easier?
- What are we doing well that we should protect?

This open-ended discussion creates engagement. The goal is to get people talking without immediately filtering ideas.

After an hour of brainstorming, refine the list into realistic actions. Not everything can be implemented, so you'll need to prioritize based on impact, feasibility, and alignment with your goals. Oddly enough, you should start with the "Stop" list. This is often the easiest to tackle. Many inefficiencies persist simply because no one has questioned them. Maybe it's an outdated process, unnecessary reporting, or a legacy tool no one really uses. Eliminating low-value work frees up resources for more critical priorities.

Next, move to the "Start" list. These are new practices, tools, or initiatives the team believes will improve performance. You need to carefully manage prioritization at this stage. You can't roll out ten new processes at once without overwhelming the team. Choose one or two high-impact initiatives to focus on. Finally, reinforce the "Continue" list. Acknowledging what's working well is just as important as fixing problems. If a particular practice, habit, or tool has made life easier, recognizing it ensures it stays part of the culture.

By the end of the session, distill everything down into a simple action plan. What will you start, stop, and continue in the next six months? Assign owners to each action item so that accountability is built in.

Let's say you're leading a software development team. After a Start, Stop, Continue session, your team might land on the following action plan:

- **Start:** Introduce pair programming as a practice to improve code quality and knowledge sharing.
- **Stop:** The weekly status report. It takes hours to compile, but no one reads it.
- **Continue:** Daily standups because they help with alignment and issue resolution.

This may seem simple, but small changes add up. When done regularly, these sessions refine how your team works, making sure energy is spent on what truly drives results.

Start, Stop, Continue is effective because it empowers your team to take ownership of its improvement. Too often, teams wait for leadership to dictate change. This process flips the script, giving your team a voice in shaping how they work. (See Ikea Effect in Chapter 10 for more.)

It also helps cut through noise. In IT, there's always a new tool, a new methodology, or a new "best practice" being promoted. But not everything needs to be adopted. This framework helps the team focus on what's relevant and valuable rather than chasing trends.

And finally, it's a low-effort, high-impact exercise. It doesn't require executive buy-in, big budgets, or massive process overhauls. It's just a few hours of structured reflection that leads to meaningful improvements. If you want to build a culture of continuous improvement without overwhelming your team, Start, Stop, Continue is one of the easiest and most effective tools you can use. It's not about sweeping transformations—it's about small, incremental changes that compound over time.

If you haven't done this exercise with your team before, block time on the calendar now. You might be surprised by what you learn and by how much smoother your team's day-to-day operations become as a result.

NOTES

1 Fishman, C. (1996, December 31). They write the right stuff. *Fast Company*, 6, 28121. https://www.fastcompany.com/28121/they-write-right-stuff.
2 Standish Group. (2020). *Chaos Report 2020*. Standish Group.

RECOMMENDED ADDITIONAL READING

Anderson, L., Fleming, D., Hamilton, B., & Wardwell, P. (2021). *Continuous improvement: Seek Perfection, Embrace Scientific Thinking, Focus on Process, Assure Quality at the Source, and Improve Flow & Pull*. CRC Press.

Bell, S. (2005). *Lean Enterprise systems: Using IT for Continuous Improvement*. John Wiley & Sons.

Liker, J. K., & Franz, J. K. (2011). *The Toyota Way to Continuous Improvement: linking strategy and operational excellence to achieve superior performance*. McGraw Hill Professional.

Epilogue

The fourth M: Mastery

As we reach the end of this book, we need to pivot our focus. We've explored how to lead teams, align our work with business goals, and measure the things that matter. But as you continue your journey, there's something just as important as members, methods, and measures. You! Being an effective IT manager is more than running staff meetings, reviewing project budgets, and generating performance metrics. It's about how you show up every day. It's about the decisions you make, the resilience you develop, and the reputation you build. That's why the epilogue shifts focus from leading teams to leading yourself.

Success in IT leadership requires a bias for action—the ability to make decisions confidently and move forward, even when you're unsure. It requires a strong personal brand. The way you are perceived by peers, executives, and outsiders will shape the opportunities available for career growth. And it demands resilience—the ability to navigate setbacks and stay effective under pressure. This job is hard. Mistakes are inevitable. How you respond to those mistakes will determine your career trajectory.

The tools and models in this book will help you lead IT teams, but these final lessons will help you thrive as a leader. As we close, let's explore what it takes to build a career that is not only successful but meaningful and lasting.

BIAS FOR ACTION

Leaders who succeed don't ponder decisions indefinitely. They gather enough information to make an informed choice, and they act. Afterward, they evaluate the outcome and then adjust. That's how progress happens—by moving forward, learning, and adapting. Colonel John Boyd coined the term "OODA Loop" to describe how to make better decisions—Observe, Orient, Decide, Act.[1] Once you make a decision or take a step, observe the results and start the loop again (Figure 18.1).

The best decision you can make is often the one you can act on right now. Waiting for a perfect plan usually means waiting too long. You've likely seen

DOI: 10.1201/9781003562160-22

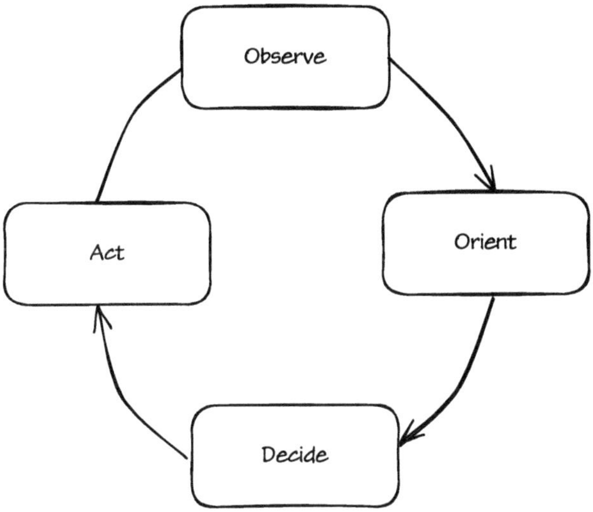

Figure 18.1 OODA loop.

Facebook's famous motto, "Move Fast and Break Things." If you wait until you have perfect clarity, the opportunity will pass you by. Action beats inaction every time.

Leading is like learning to swim. You can read all the books, watch all the videos, and memorize all the techniques, but at some point, you have to get in the water. Leadership works the same way. You can't become an effective manager by analyzing every possible scenario and waiting for the perfect conditions before you act. You have to start making decisions and leading your team today.

The United States Marine Corps teaches officer candidates something called the 70% Rule—take action when you are 70% confident in your decision. "As leaders, we must guard against waiting for a perfect sight picture, which may never come, leading to inaction."[2] A well-thought-out plan, executed with confidence, is more likely to succeed than waiting for perfect information. You can debate the Marine Corps if you like, but good luck.

Of course, this doesn't mean you should make reckless decisions. Do your due diligence. Think through the consequences. But once you have enough information, act. Hesitation kills momentum and it creates confusion and frustration for your team. No one likes working for a leader who can't make a decision. That's not to say all decisions should be rushed. Some choices, like major architectural changes, security decisions, or hiring for a critical role, deserve careful consideration. But most decisions don't fall into that category. For most, you need to be comfortable moving forward with incomplete information.

General George S. Patton once said, "A good plan, violently executed now, is better than a perfect plan executed at some indefinite time in the future."[3] In IT, it's probably best to skip the violence, but the idea holds: speed and decisiveness win.

Building a bias for action in your daily work

A bias for action is also how you should approach every single day. If you consistently get things done, that momentum builds. Good days turn into good weeks, good weeks into good months, and good months into a successful career. If, instead, you put things off, wait for the "right time," or get lost in the analysis, the opposite happens. Procrastination compounds just like productivity does. If you start delaying small tasks, putting off writing a report until tomorrow, rescheduling that difficult conversation, or waiting until Monday to check on a project, you'll soon find yourself overwhelmed. In manufacturing, managers know that too much Work-in-Process causes delays, inefficiencies, and increased costs. The same is true in your work. Stack too many unfinished tasks and you'll never get out from under the load.

The best way to avoid that cycle is to get things done today. Hold yourself to a high standard. Set expectations for your team. Focus on results and you'll start meeting deadlines and exceeding expectations.

Avoiding burnout

Interestingly, this approach also helps prevent burnout. People assume that working harder leads to exhaustion, but often, it's the undone work that drains us. Psychologists have found that unfinished tasks linger in your subconscious. Psychologists call this the Zeigarnik Effect.[4] If you leave work on Friday knowing you have unresolved problems, they will follow you into the weekend. You won't fully relax because, in the back of your mind, you know what's waiting for you in the office on Monday.[5] The weight of unfinished tasks accumulates over time, leading to more burnout.

When you commit to action, you create a sense of closure at the end of each day. If something needs doing, do it. If a decision needs to be made, make it. You won't carry that weight around, which means you can actually turn off and recharge when the workday ends. The best way to sustain high performance isn't to grind endlessly. It's to be fully engaged when you're working and fully disconnected when you're not.

You've probably met people who brag about never taking a vacation or working 80-hour weeks for months on end. That's not impressive. It's a failure of leadership. If you can't step away without things falling apart, you haven't built a strong enough or self-sufficient enough team. Taking breaks isn't a sign of weakness. Use your vacation time. Disconnect on weekends. Don't fall into the trap of equating busyness with productivity. The people who work the longest hours are not the most effective. They're the ones spinning their wheels instead of making decisions and moving forward.

The best leaders act. They make decisions, take ownership, and drive momentum forward. Ask yourself, "What decisions have I been putting off? What tasks am I overanalyzing instead of just doing? Where can I push myself to move faster?" Make a call. Take the next step. Get moving.

PERSONAL BRAND

Most of this book has focused on how to get the best from your team. After all, leadership is primarily about getting results through others. Their success is your success. But if you only focus on managing your team and ignore managing your own career, you're only solving half of the equation. Taking on a management role can be the first step toward a long and fulfilling career in leadership, but it's also a step fraught with risk. Some people crumble under the pressure. Others stagnate, letting opportunities pass them by. The difference between those who rise and those who stall often comes down to personal brand. Your personal brand is how *others* define the value you deliver.[6]

Some IT leaders are known as security experts. Others for delivering complex projects on time and within budget. Some are recognized for driving innovation, cutting costs or disciplined execution. There's no single "correct" way to build a brand. It should develop over time as you shape your skills, hone your interests, and capitalize on the opportunities that come your way. Just as you must actively manage your team for success, you must actively manage your brand to achieve career success.

Define your brand

Before you can build your brand, you need to be clear about what you want it to be. Think about the career you want. The more specific you are, the easier it is to build a reputation around it. If your ambition is to become a CIO, what skills and experiences will make you stand out? What roles should you pursue to open new doors? If you want to be a recognized expert in cybersecurity, what steps will position you as a trusted security authority?

Just as important, consider the kind of work you enjoy. I've seen people chase titles or prestige without really liking the work required to get there. If you think you want to be a CFO but hate analyzing spreadsheets, you might need to rethink your goals. Every career has unpleasant tasks, but if you don't enjoy the day-to-day reality of the role you're working toward, you won't thrive in it.

Establish expertise and authority

To build your brand, you need to establish expertise and authority. Expertise is about what you know. Authority is being recognized for your expertise.

Start by identifying the skills that set you apart. What do you know that others find valuable? Think about past projects, industry trends, or emerging technologies where you have insight. Then, find ways to share that knowledge. Host a lunch and learn for your team. Write an article for your company blog. Post insights on LinkedIn. Even something as simple as mentoring a junior colleague helps build your reputation as an expert. The more you share your knowledge, the more people associate you with that expertise.

Authority comes from recognition. Seek opportunities to be seen and heard. Participate in industry panels, speak at department meetings, or contribute to community events. Every time you do, you reinforce your brand. Early in your career, take every opportunity to speak in front of relevant audiences. It builds credibility and helps sharpen your public speaking skills—critical for any executive.

Grow your brand

Your brand is shaped by who you know and who knows you. Be intentional about building relationships. I don't mean blindly adding LinkedIn connections. Meaningless connections are rarely valuable in building a brand. A strong network is built through genuine relationships, not superficial transactions. Get to know people in your industry. Attend conferences, join professional groups, and engage with thought leaders.

One of the most effective ways to expand your network is to connect others. A former colleague of mine swears by the mantra "ABCD: Always Be Connecting Dots." If you know two people with shared interests, introduce them. If a peer is looking for a job, connect them with someone hiring. These small favors create long-term goodwill and reinforce your reputation as someone who adds value to others.

It may seem counterintuitive, but asking for help can strengthen your personal brand. No one succeeds alone. The best leaders are those who actively seek out knowledge and build relationships along the way. When you seek advice, you're acknowledging someone else's expertise. This makes them feel valued, and, as a result, they become invested in your success.[7] They are more likely to help you again. The key is to follow up. When someone helps you, thank them and let them know how it turned out. People appreciate knowing their advice had an impact.

One of the best ways to build credibility is to take on new challenges. Look for assignments that fill in your experience gaps. Not every move has to be a promotion. Strategic lateral moves can expand your skill set, increase your visibility, and set you up for bigger roles in the future. If you want to be seen as a strong leader, look for high-impact projects where you can make a difference. If you want to build a reputation for innovation, seek out roles that put you at the forefront of emerging technology.

Your personal brand is an ongoing investment, not a one-time project. It evolves with every project you complete, every relationship you build, and every opportunity you take. You don't need to rush it. If you do good work, meet the right people, and share what you learn, your brand will grow. The key is to be intentional. Define what you want to be known for, take steps to reinforce that identity, and remember that reputation isn't built overnight, but it can be destroyed in an instant. Manage it wisely.

FALLING DOWN AND GETTING BACK UP

Learning to manage is a little like learning to walk. You're going to fall down a lot before you figure it out. You'll make mistakes that feel impossible to recover from. You'll hire the wrong person, make the wrong call on a big decision, and handle a tough conversation poorly. You'll second-guess yourself, replaying scenarios in your head, wondering what you should have done differently.

I look back and cringe at some of my early decisions. I've made choices that cost my company tens of thousands of dollars. I've hired people who turned out to be terrible fits. I've probably driven employees to start looking for new jobs. At the time, these felt like mortal failures. Looking back, with the benefit of hindsight, I realize these were skinned knees on the way to my unique gait. Those mistakes didn't define me. They helped shape me. The truth is, if I couldn't look back and see where I went wrong, it would mean I hadn't grown at all.

The beauty of this journey is that we get to learn from those mistakes and do it better the next time because the journey is never finished. Someone once told me, "You aren't defined by the times you fail, but by how you bounce back when you fall short."

You'll make mistakes, too. There are things you don't know today, skills you're not good at, habits you haven't built. That's okay. Pick a few lessons from this book and put them to work today. Maybe you'll spend the next three months focused on holding constructive one-on-ones and learning to delegate effectively. Those two skills alone will drastically improve your effectiveness as a manager. Once you've got those arrows in your quiver, pick a few more. Focus on your staff meetings and setting the right priorities. Start with the basics. A solid foundation is critical.

The path to effective management is not easy, nor is it a straight line. As soon as you master walking on flat ground, you'll find yourself on an uneven mountain trail. You'll realize the hill you just climbed isn't the top of the mountain but another stop along the way. Systems will crash, key employees will quit, and projects will get canceled. It's all part of the climb. If you build a good team, treat them well, and set high standards, you'll be amazed at how far you can go.

In 1917, Cyrus McCormick spoke before the Harvester Club and said, "Scaling the mountain or breasting the stream, he travels farthest who pulls with his team."[8] This poem perfectly sums up the joy I find in managing IT teams. It never ceases to amaze me how a dedicated team, unified around a single mission, utilizing shared methods, and led ably, can accomplish more than even they think is possible. If your success to date has come from individual effort, you're in for a treat. The collective brain power, creativity, ingenuity, and sheer grit of a cohesive team are going to blow you away.

Leading a team is a privilege, a burden, and an honor. You'll make mistakes as you go. We all do. But, the journey is never finished. Do your best. Take it all in. Act with integrity. Continue to grow, but continue to live in the moment. You're embarking on the greatest career adventure I can imagine, and I'll be rooting hard for you.

* * *

NOTES

1 *The OODA loop - the decision lab.* (n.d.). The Decision Lab. https://thedecisionlab.com/reference-guide/computer-science/the-ooda-loop.

2 United States Marine Corps. (n.d.). *Decision making student handout B2B 0237XQ* [Handout]. Marines.mil. https://www.trngcmd.marines.mil/Portals/207/Site%20Images/TBS/B2B0237XQ%20Decision%20Making.pdf.

3 Patton, G. S. (1995). *War as I Knew it.* Houghton Mifflin Harcourt.

4 Savitsky, K., Medvec, V. H., & Gilovich, T. (1997). Remembering and regretting: the Zeigarnik effect and the cognitive availability of regrettable actions and inactions. *Personality and Social Psychology Bulletin*, *23*(3), 248–257. https://doi.org/10.1177/0146167297233004.

5 Syrek, C. J., & Antoni, C. H. (2014). Unfinished tasks foster rumination and impair sleeping—Particularly if leaders have high performance expectations. *Journal of Occupational Health Psychology*, *19*(4), 490–499. https://doi.org/10.1037/a0037127.

6 Avery, J., & Greenwald, R. (2023, July 6). *A new approach to building your personal brand.* Harvard Business Review. https://hbr.org/2023/05/a-new-approach-to-building-your-personal-brand.

7 *Why asking for help is hard, but people want to help more than we realize.* (n.d.). Stanford University. https://news.stanford.edu/stories/2022/09/asking-help-hard-people-want-help-realize.

8 Men and Teamwork: Extract from a speech by Cyrus H. McCromick before the Harvester Club. (1917). *The Harvester World*, *8*(6). https://content.wisconsinhistory.org/digital/api/collection/ihc/id/9289/download.

Acknowledgments

I set out to write a book, expecting a solitary experience. Man alone with his thoughts. I could not have been more wrong. Bringing a book from a half-formed idea to the final product in your hands is the work of many people.

To the team at CRC Press, Gabriella Williams, Dan Swanson, Kshitij Jha, and everyone working behind the scenes, thank you for helping this first-time author through an unfamiliar process. Thanks for answering my endless questions, providing sound guidance, and for key support at critical moments.

Jeffrey Brown, Kevin Lawlor, and Brigitte Rouleau, among others, aided in varying forms throughout the proposal and writing process. For your help, I am deeply grateful.

Chris Caterine was my first sounding board and the first person to read a draft of this book. His feedback was invaluable—even when it annoyed me. Beyond providing insightful criticism of the text, Chris kept me sane throughout the writing process—no small feat.

I've been blessed throughout my career with a string of great leaders who taught me many of the lessons in this book. I thank Mark Raymond, Jon Carroll, Sean Bufano, Tim Peterson, Ahmad Khurshid, Gaurang Patel, Andrew Linn, Michael Cuneo, and Kirk Davis for providing coaching, mentorship, and excellent examples to follow.

Finally, I owe an unpayable debt to the teams I've been lucky enough to manage over the years. Despite the long hours, tight budgets, shifting priorities, and sometimes ambiguous direction from me, you've achieved incredible things. Thanks for having my back.

Index

For Product Safety Concerns and Information please contact our EU representative GPSR@taylorandfrancis.com
Taylor & Francis Verlag GmbH, Kaufingerstraße 24, 80331 München, Germany

www.ingramcontent.com/pod-product-compliance
Ingram Content Group UK Ltd.
Pitfield, Milton Keynes, MK11 3LW, UK
UKHW020201200926
475702UK00004B/565
* 9 7 8 1 0 3 2 9 1 0 5 4 3 *